Walter Gropius Buildings and Projects

Walter Gropius

Birkhäuser
Basel

Layout, cover design and typesetting
Annette Kern, Berlin

Editorial supervision and project management
Henriette Mueller-Stahl, Berlin

Translation from German
Julian Reisenberger, Weimar

Production
Heike Strempel, Berlin

Lithography
bildpunkt Druckvorstufen GmbH, Berlin

Paper
135 g/m^2 Condat Matt Perigord

Printing
Grafisches Centrum Cuno GmbH & Co. KG, Calbe

Library of Congress Control Number: 2019937720

Bibliografische Information der Deutschen Nationalbibliothek

Bibliographic information published by the German National Library
The German National Library lists this publication in the Deutsche Nationalbibliografie; detailed bibliographic data are available on the Internet at http://dnb.dnb.de.

ISBN 978-3-0356-1728-3
e-ISBN (PDF) 978-3-0356-1743-6
German Print-ISBN 978-3-0356-1727-6

P.O. Box 44, 4009 Basel, Switzerland
Part of Walter de Gruyter GmbH, Berlin/Boston

9 8 7 6 5 4 3 2 1 www.birkhauser.com

Table of Contents

Introduction

Walter Gropius is better known as the founder of the Bauhaus than he is for the buildings he designed. He had the vision to see that a new kind of education system could have a greater impact on the built environment than individual buildings. During his lifetime, he was considered one of the greatest architects of the century, along with Ludwig Mies van der Rohe, Le Corbusier and Frank Lloyd Wright, but he could not draw. Partnerships with other architects were therefore essential to his work, and this book, which presents his complete built oeuvre, also documents buildings that he did not design himself.[1]

Walter Gropius was born in Berlin in 1883. Of his father, who was also an architect, he wrote: "He was a rather withdrawn and timid man without sufficient self-reliance, so therefore he never penetrated to the first rank. [...] He designed and built some buildings only in the first part of his career, before he became a municipal employee, [...] In thinking about the tradition of our family and its moral temperature in comparison to the more conservative uncles, our parents came off well in their liberal breadth and in their indestructible kindness and tolerance. [...] I feel that my liberal inheritance has given me a cosmopolitan attitude and breadth of thinking."[2]

However, Gropius abandoned his architectural studies in Munich and Berlin. "My total inability to draw the simplest thing on paper [...] often makes me look with sorrow on my future profession," he wrote to his mother. "It seems almost to be a physical disability, because I immediately get a cramp in my hand."[3] Even as a student he employed a draughtsman, and during his subsequent work in Peter Behrens' studio he was entrusted predominantly with site management. Sigfried Giedion's seminal monograph from 1953 describes Gropius' position at Behrens' studio as "Chief Assistant", an exaggeration that went unnoticed for a long time.[4]

"For years, I spent my evenings at Behrens' and identified with all his work,"[5] Gropius explained. "His wide-ranging and profound interest in the design of the entire environment, which encompassed not only architecture, but also painting, theatre, industrial products, and typography, impressed me greatly. [...] I owe him much, particularly the habit of thinking in principles."[6] Gropius later opened an office together with Adolf Meyer, another of Behrens' employees, but the partnership between the two was not equal, despite their work being presented as joint designs. Gropius would acquire the commissions, or received them through family connections, and was able to pay Meyer. Their early buildings and projects resembled in many respects the work of Behrens, which at that time was in turn influenced by the architectural language of Karl Friedrich Schinkel. Gropius himself stressed that he belonged "to a Prussian family of architects in which the tradition of Schinkel [...] was part of our heritage."[7]

One of their first works was a commission for a shoe last factory with which Gropius shot to fame almost overnight. Reyner Banham wrote of the design of the Fagus factory in 1960: "There can be little doubt that it owes this high esteem in part to Gropius' personal relationship to the historians of the Modern Movement, and also, in part, to the

accidents of photography – it is possible, by a hostile selection of photographs, to make it appear no more 'Modern' than" buildings by Behrens. "The modernity of this group of buildings is visible, indeed, only on parts of two sides,"[8] Banham explained, referring to the glazed corners of the buildings. Nevertheless, Gropius and Meyer's comparative insecurity in this early period can be seen in their project for a hospital (Fig. 1) that was designed after the Fagus Factory. Its strictly neoclassical formal language owes much to Behrens' work, and Gropius evidently found it hard to imagine applying radical industrial building solutions to representative building tasks.

Gropius would later look back on his early work as "youthful sins"[9] and had no interest in publishing them. In omitting such works, complaisant architectural historians and indeed Gropius himself have constructed the impression of a straight path to the development of his work. This book instead traces this development building by building, including his changes in direction. Where photographs reveal discontinuities to his work, this is due not to the selection but rather the fact that the evolution of modern architecture has always been ambivalent and inconsistent. As with other protagonists of the modern movement, his process of development is more akin to a meandering path: a process of searching.

The political upheavals of 1918 in Germany heralded a new spirit and Gropius and Meyer, putting their classicist work behind them, began experimenting with the expressionist architectural language of the zeitgeist, as reflected in their design for the Sommerfeld administration building (Fig. 2). However, this too would soon prove to be a dead end. In 1919 Gropius had still demanded: "Architects, sculptors, painters – we all must return to craftsmanship!"[10] The administration building was consequently to be built of wood with roofs of oriental appearance. While the romantic spirit of this early design gave way to more sober architecture in their later work, they did not discard all its architectural devices. The Bauhaus building in Dessau exhibits a similar arrangement with two buildings connected by a bridging structure that extends over the public street.

As with other architects of his generation, the traumatic experiences of war caused Gropius to reconsider his political views. In a utopian sense, he believed that by fundamentally changing the profession, he could help build a new society. "Capitalism and power politics have made our generation creatively sluggish," declared Gropius, who, like Behrens, called for the unity of the arts under the direction of architecture. "For only through the intimate cooperation and interplay of all artistic disciplines can an age bring forth the polyphonic orchestra that alone deserves the name of art. Since time immemorial, the appointed conductor of this orchestra has been the architect. That means: the architect is the leader of the arts."[11]

With this concept of a comprehensive approach to design, Gropius founded the Staatliche Bauhaus in Weimar in 1919, although architecture was not yet part of the curriculum. The students were trained in the various crafts by both technicians and artists in a combination of what

1 Walter Gropius with Adolf Meyer, project for a hospital, Alfeld 1912

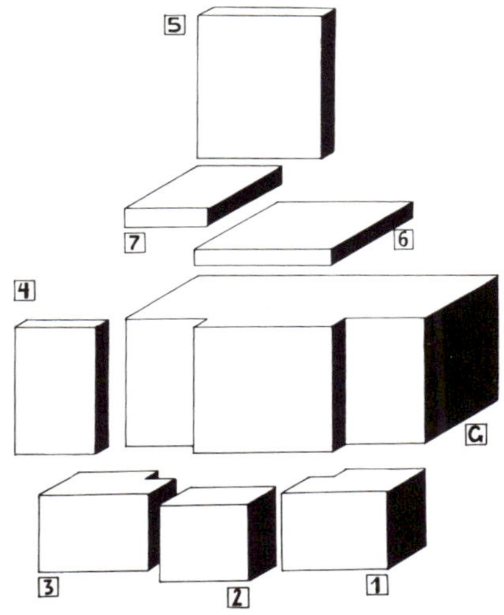

2 Walter Gropius with Adolf Meyer, project for an administration building for Adolf Sommerfeld, Berlin 1920
3 Walter Gropius with Adolf Meyer, "large-scale building kit", house types for a Bauhaus settlement in Weimar, 1922

was called "Werklehre" (technical instruction) and "Formlehre" (artistic instruction). Even though Gropius proclaimed the aims of the Bauhaus in an opening manifesto, those aims changed. In the nine years in which he was director of the Bauhaus, the ideologies of the teaching staff spanned a broad spectrum – from Johannes Itten's mystical convictions to Hannes Meyer's collectivist position – and this can be seen too in Gropius' own architectural work. Even before the introduction of architecture as a course subject, he planned a Bauhaus housing estate that the students would be involved in building. Together with Adolf Meyer, he developed a modular construction system known as "honeycomb construction" in which a basic type (G in Fig. 3) could be varied through the addition of connected cellular rooms. Gropius called the additive design principle a "large-scale building kit". This idea of combining industrially prefabricated building elements to achieve variable configurations built on the principles he had already set out at the age of 26 in his "Programme for the Establishment of a General Housing Construction Society on a Unified Artistic Basis".

While the private houses that Gropius built at the beginning of the 1920s had symmetrical facades and conventional roofs, the models of the Bauhaus settlement were now pure abstract cubes with asymmetrical compositional tendencies as expounded by the Dutch De Stijl movement. A more monumental expression of this tendency can be seen in their design for the Chicago Tribune Tower (Fig. 4). As with their industrial constructions, and in contrast to the winners of the competition, Gropius and Meyer left the skeleton frame of the building unclad, emphasising the building's tectonic expression. Nevertheless, it was not entirely free of decorative aspects: the asymmetrical placement of the balconies follows no functional logic and is motivated purely by artistic considerations.

The Dessau Bauhaus building was likewise an asymmetrical composition, with which Gropius not only demonstrated a new spatial concept but also incorporated the five points of a new architecture – pilotis, roof gardens, free floor plan, ribbon window and free facade design – which Le Corbusier had declared "leaves nothing to us of the architecture of past".[12] Before increasing pressure from conservative political factions caused the Bauhaus to move from Weimar to Dessau in 1925/26, Adolf Meyer had already begun to work independently of Gropius in his own right.[13] Gropius' architecture thereafter took on a more constructivist character. While the architectural dynamism of the Bauhaus building is visually expressed by its asymmetrical composition, a later project posited an architecture able to change constantly like a mechanical apparatus: Gropius' theatre project for Erwin Piscator, which he called "Totaltheater", is based on a system of revolving stages in the centre of the building, around which the auditorium is arranged (Fig. 5). The design allows different types of stages to be set up and combined during a performance and aimed to immerse the audience in the action on stage to the maximum degree. The traditional division between stage and auditorium was to be overcome by using sound and light installations as well as film projections, for which screens were planned that would span between the twelve supports around the perimeter.

4 Walter Gropius with Adolf Meyer, competition design for the Chicago Tribune Tower, 1922

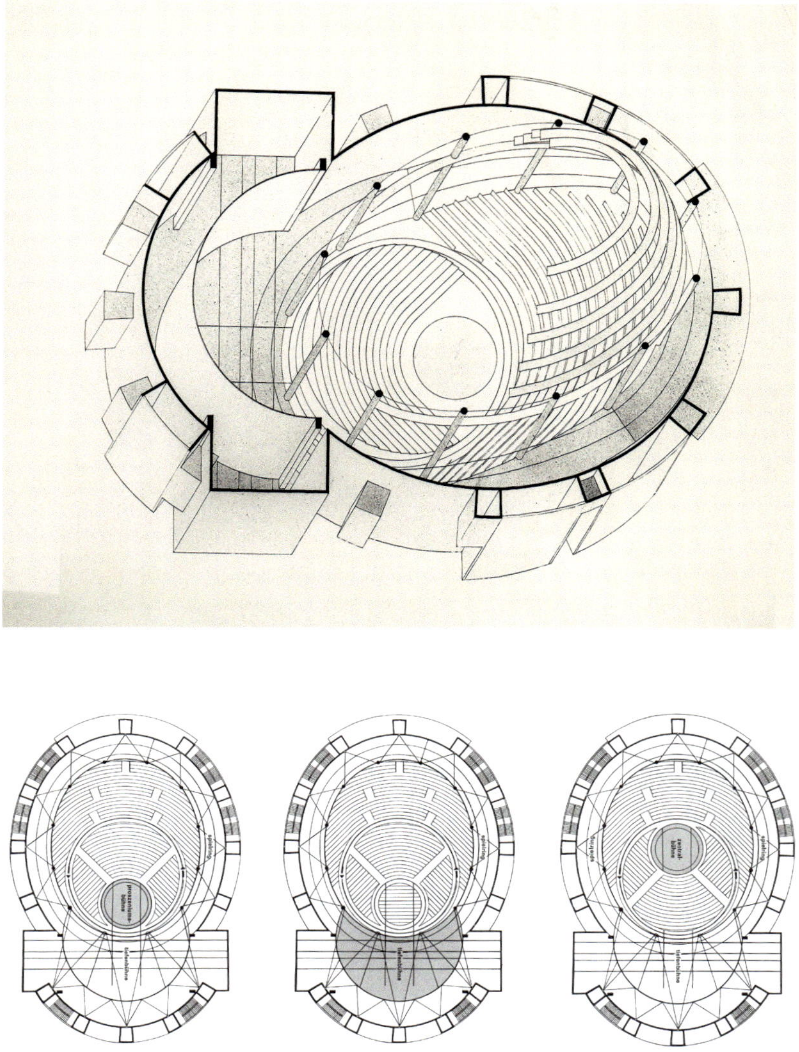

While involved in designing the total theatre project, he invited the Swiss architect Hannes Meyer to the Bauhaus to run the new architectural training programme. The architecture he designed at this time exhibited an increasing tendency towards rational reduction, towards *Sachlichkeit*, as seen in his design for a building complex consisting of city hall, museum and sports forum in Halle (Fig. 6), and shared ideological traits with the work of Hannes Meyer. The shape of the auditorium was determined by acoustic calculations and was to be suspended from a megastructure of iron and glass. Even though Hannes Meyer had confessed to being critical of much of the Bauhaus, with the exception of the stage experiments, Gropius still proposed him as his successor.[14]

Although Gropius made several attempts to realise his patented avant-garde concept of total theatre in various competition entries, the designs were compromises of conventional spatial types. For the two Soviet competitions, the Ukrainian State Theatre (Fig. 7) and the Palace of the Soviets (Fig. 9), Gropius likewise planned changeable stage systems with film projection surfaces on the walls and ceilings, but instead of fusing stage and auditorium, the designs did not depart from the classical opposition of the two realms. Meanwhile Gropius had moved on from De Stijl-inspired asymmetrical compositions to propose clearly arranged, strictly symmetrical floor plans that recalled the principles of the École des Beaux-Arts. His design for the State Theatre exhibited constructivist elements, most notably the membrane-like glass facade that treated the forecourt and entrance foyer as a single unified space and the arcing ramps that seem to draw inspiration from the likes of Le Corbusier. The facades of the Palace of the Soviets were to be clad in natural stone, with bronze window profiles, while the squares in front of the buildings were designed for holding large-scale rallies, complete with grandstand towers for the speakers.

In 1929, Gropius shared the socialist critique of private real estate, declaring at the CIAM Congress (Congrès Internationaux d'Architecture Moderne) in Frankfurt am Main that: "if the minimum dwelling is to be realized at rent levels which the population can afford, the government must therefore be requested to [...] provide the building sites and remove them from the hands of speculators."[15] In this respect, he regarded Russia as a role model: "The most restrictive shackle remains the immoral right to land as private property. Without liberating land from this private enslavement, healthy, viable and economical urban development for the common good can never emerge. The USSR is the only state to have achieved this most important basic requirement without restriction, thus paving the way for modern urban development."[16] Gropius saw the path to "modern urban development" in residential high-rise building and lectured on its benefits, presenting diagrams and calculations detailing the advantages for the illumination and ventilation of dwellings. He proposed minimising the size of dwellings and in turn providing extensive communal facilities, which he presented in exhibitions as installations together with furnished show apartments in order to publicise the project. As the prospect of state subsidies all but vanished with the global economic crisis, Gropius adjusted the project to attract private investors, proposing a chain of high-rise slabs along

5 Walter Gropius, project for a Total Theatre, Berlin 1927, isometric drawing and stage rotation variants

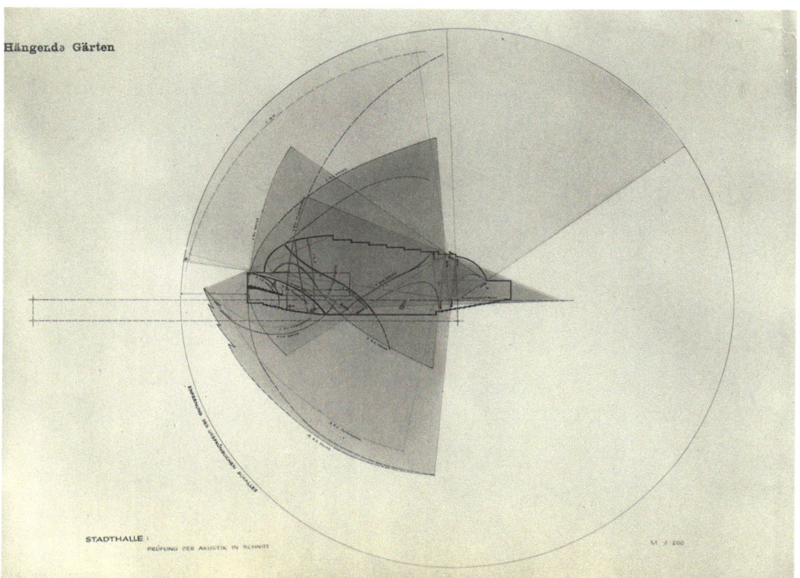

6 Walter Gropius, competition for a building complex comprising a city hall, museum and sports forum, 1927–28, perspective and diagram for appraising the acoustics

the shores of Lake Wannsee (Fig. 8). However, rather than addressing minimum housing needs for all, the project now proposed large, luxury apartments with club rooms, restaurant levels and roof terraces with sports facilities and sun decks. Winfried Nerdinger commented on this remarkable "arbitrary interchangeability of concepts"[17] but also offered an explanation: "Gropius had already written to Giedion from England in 1935, explaining that in Germany he had tried first to win over the workers for new architecture, but that was the wrong way. Now he wanted to begin with houses for the rich and work, as it were, from top to bottom."[18]

Before Gropius emigrated first to England in 1934 and then to the USA to take up a chair at Harvard University, he took part in a last competition for a "House of Labour" (Fig. 10) celebrating the German work ethic. His design for the building complex in the middle of Berlin's Tiergarten continued the architectural and urban planning principles of the Weimar Republic era, this time however with a monumental parading ground lined with swastika flags. Lamenting the changes afoot in Germany, he wrote in 1934 to the President of the Reich Committee for the Fine Arts: "Is it now really true that this strong, new architectural movement of German origin shall be lost for Germany?"[19] And: "You demand the German man. I feel very German in my ideas and the ideas of my spiritual brothers of German origin – and who can make himself a judge over what is German and what is not?"[20] Almost three years later he wrote to him again, now from exile, that his mission was still to "serve German culture", after all "I decisively opposed [...] the fact that a newspaper tried to associate my name with a critique of German conditions."[21]

Gropius remained diplomatic in his role as a missionary of "objective design", which he was convinced would improve the living conditions of the people – even after the residents of the Törten estate he had planned took it into their own hands to adapt the houses to their respective needs. His inability to draw meant that he communicated his design ideas verbally and delegated the necessary revision work to others. In this respect, he saw "the conception which the new kind of architect has of his calling [as] that of a co-ordinating organizer,"[22] and he granted his partners considerable design freedom. Prior to becoming an American citizen in 1944 and founding TAC – The Architects Collaborative the following year as a collective office with seven younger partners, he had already worked in office partnerships with Maxwell Fry, Marcel Breuer and Konrad Wachsmann. Breuer, however, later claimed design authorship of the majority of the joint buildings and projects, including that of the art school at Black Mountain College (Fig. 11).[23] Gropius had received the design commission from the former Bauhaus members Josef and Anni Albers, who taught there and were introducing Bauhaus teaching methods to the USA. The winding shape of the building traces the course of the shoreline, with a section of the building extending out over the water on pillars. The intention was to establish a direct and strong connection with nature. In adapting the buildings to the topography, Gropius and Breuer saw an urban potential that they would later explore in the Aluminium City Terrace settlement.

7 Walter Gropius, Ukrainian State Theatre competition, Kharkov 1930–31
8 Walter Gropius, project for high-rise housing blocks at Wannsee, Berlin 1930–31

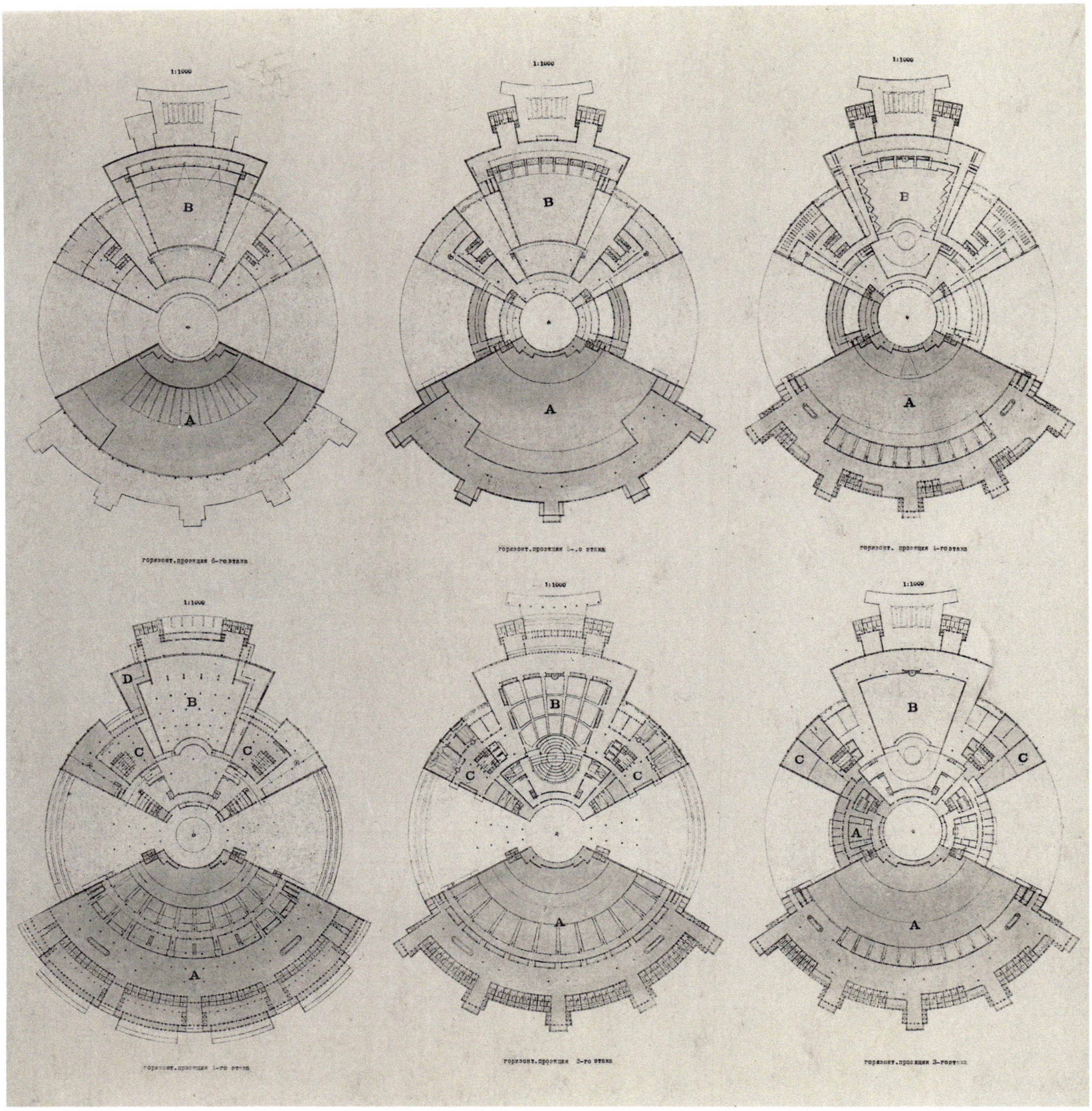

9 Walter Gropius, Palace of the Soviets competition, Moscow 1931 – floor plans and model

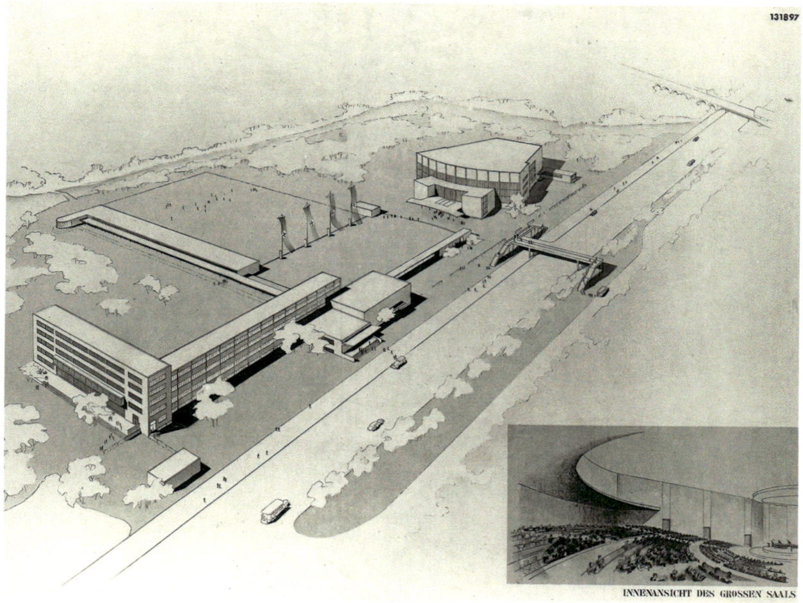

Two other university projects reveal how much Gropius tried to resist and distance himself from the label International Style. The design for the campus of the University of Hua Tung in China (Fig. 12) also relates to the landscape and comprised separate groups of pavilions connected by covered corridors, which together formed an orthogonal building structure that entered into a dialogue with an artificial lake landscape. Its design demonstrated the ability of architecture to adapt to the respective conditions of other countries, explained Gropius while recommending himself for the design of the University of Baghdad, declaring that one must first understand the conditions of a region in order to design for it.[24] The project for the Black Mountain College did not come to pass due to insufficient funding and the Chinese project was stopped by the Maoist revolution. In Baghdad, the project proceeded but political upheavals also led to a temporary halt to the plans of the university (Fig. 13, site plan on p. 172). Planned "as a small town"[25] of almost 300 buildings, only a fragment was actually built so that the compact, labyrinthine character of the master plan, which emulated the characteristics of traditional Arab settlements with their networks of narrow open spaces, was lost. The central auditorium – originally designed for another subtropical city in Florida – was never built.

Despite Gropius' claim to a regionalist approach, the numerous buildings built by The Architects Collaborative around the world seem from today's standpoint all very similar. Gropius was, however, able to make a specifically South American architectural gesture in one of his later works in collaboration with the Argentine architect Amancio Williams: their design for the representative rooms and private living quarters of an embassy in a park landscape (Fig. 15) was elevated seven metres above ground and followed the principle of a megastructure. Like the house Williams had built in 1945 in Mar del Plata, Argentina, as a concrete bridge over a river, the embassy residence also featured wide cantilevers.[26]

Although this book aims to show the complete oeuvre of Gropius' built works, it does not show all the buildings recorded in the "list of works" published in Sigfried Giedion's monograph, as that also includes numerous TAC buildings and projects in which Gropius was not involved. Based on the catalogue of works drawn up by Hartmut Probst and Christian Schädlich and by Winfried Nerdinger in 1985, this book shows only those TAC buildings in which Gropius played a leading role or was jointly responsible together with other partners.[27]

All the colour photographs in this book were taken by the author over the last ten years, and the floor plans have also been completely drawn by the author at a scale of 1:300 and 1:500, and in the case of the site plans at 1:4000.[28] Most of the black-and-white photographs are from the collection of the Bauhaus-Archiv in Berlin. This book focuses predominantly on buildings, with only selected notable examples of exhibition designs and interiors. Furniture and product designs are not included. Gropius' conception of the total scope of architecture and design meant that he also designed door handles and crockery, as well as railway carriages and cars, which were realised as prototypes.

10 Walter Gropius with Rudolf Hillebrecht, competition, Haus der Arbeit (House of Labour), Berlin 1934
11 Walter Gropius with Marcel Breuer, project for Black Mountain College, Lake Eden, North Carolina, 1938–39

He also played a significant role in communicating modern architecture in the media. He published numerous works and found new ways to convey buildings and production methods in print, depicting processes as photographic storyboards. He also photographed and curated exhibitions.

Of all his urban development projects, he attached most value to the large Britz-Buckow-Rudow housing development in Berlin. The Architects Collaborative developed a master plan (Fig. 14) that received only little attention during construction. Gropius regarded his life's work to repair the lost uniformity of the city, however this development seems from today's standpoint much less consistent than the city of the Wilhelmine era. Ruefully acknowledging his waning influence on the project, he concluded: "I must confess that this undertaking is the most disappointing I have ever had to deal with."[29] Ironically, it was this project that was later renamed to bear his name: Gropiusstadt.

"To realise the goal of a 'total' architecture that encompasses the entire visual environment, from the simplest household appliance to the complexities of the city, constant experimentation and searching is required,"[30] explained Walter Gropius while relating the idea of the Bauhaus. Mies on the other hand argued: "We do not like the word 'design'. It means everything and nothing. Many believe they can do everything, from designing a comb to planning a railway station – the result is that nothing is good. We are only interested in building."[31] Even though Mies later managed the Bauhaus himself, his claim to design was less comprehensive than that of Gropius. Mies described Walter Gropius as "one of the greatest architects of our age," and "simultaneously [...] the greatest educator in our field. [...] The influence the Bauhaus had in the world was due to the fact that it was an idea. Such a resonance one cannot obtain with organization alone nor with propaganda. Only an idea has the forcefulness to spread to such an extent."[32]

12 Walter Gropius with TAC and I. M. Pei, project for the Christian Hua Tung University, Shanghai 1948
13 Walter Gropius with TAC, University of Baghdad 1957–83, model of the second master plan from 1960 including the auditorium which was never built

1 Marcel Breuer's own home, for example, was designed by Breuer while working in partnership with Gropius, but the building is listed as a joint work in Gropius' oeuvre of works.
2 Walter Gropius in letters to Klaus Karbe dated 5 May 1967 and to his sister Manon Burchard dated 16 February 1967, cited in: Reginald R. Isaacs, *Gropius: An Illustrated Biography of the Creator of the Bauhaus*, Boston 1991, p. 3–4.
3 Walter Gropius in a letter to his mother dated 21 October 1907, cited in: ibid., p. 23.
4 Jean Krämer was head of the studio. Cf. Stanford Anderson, Karen Grunow and Carsten Krohn, *Jean Krämer – Architect and the Atelier of Peter Behrens*, Weimar 2015.
5 Walter Gropius in a letter to Georg Hoeltje dated 5 June 1958, published in: Helmut Weber, *Walter Gropius und das Faguswerk*, Munich 1961,p. 23.
6 Walter Gropius, "Foreword to the Exhibition", in: *Peter Behrens*, exhibition catalogue, Pfalzgalerie Kaiserslautern 1966, p. 5.
7 Walter Gropius, *The New Architecture and the Bauhaus*, Cambridge, MA 1965, pp. 111–112, originally London 1935.
8 Reyner Banham, *Theory and Design in the First Machine Age*, London 1960, p. 79.
9 See p. 20 of this book.
10 Walter Gropius in: Hartmut Probst and Christian Schädlich, *Walter Gropius – Band 3: Ausgewählte Schriften*, Berlin 1987, p. 72.
11 Walter Gropius in: *Deutscher Revolutionsalmanach für das Jahr 1919*, Berlin 1919, in: ibid., p. 65.
12 Le Corbusier and Pierre Jeanneret, "Five Points of a New Architecture", in: *Le Corbusier und Pierre Jeanneret – Ihr gesamtes Werk von 1910–1929*, Zurich 1930, p. 126.
13 Adolf Meyer's (1881–1929) essential contribution to the partnership is detailed in Annemarie Jaeggi: *Adolf Meyer – Der zweite Mann – Ein Architekt im Schatten von Walter Gropius*, Berlin 1994.
14 Gropius would later distance himself from Hannes Meyer, especially due to his left-wing political activities at the Bauhaus.
15 Walter Gropius, "Sociological Premises for the Minimum Dwelling of Urban Industrial Populations", in: Walter Gropius, *The Scope of Total Architecture*, New York 1962, p. 110, originally published in: *Die Justiz*, 8, 1930.
16 Walter Gropius, "Was erhoffen wir vom russischen Städtebau?" in Hartmut Probst and Christian Schädlich, *Walter Gropius – Band 3: Ausgewählte Schriften*, Berlin 1987, p. 144, originally published in: *Das Neue Russland*, 6/7, 1931.
17 Winfried Nerdinger, *The Architect Walter Gropius*, Berlin 1985, p. 156.
18 Winfried Nerdinger, "Walter Gropius' Beitrag zur Architektur", in: Hartmut Probst and Christian Schädlich, *Walter Gropius – Band 1: Der Architekt und Theoretiker*, Berlin 1985, p. 53.
19 Walter Gropius in a letter to Eugen Hönig dated 27 March 1934, in: Reginald R. Isaacs, *Walter Gropius – Der Mensch und sein Werk*, Berlin 1984, p. 180.
20 In: ibid., p. 180.
21 Walter Gropius in a letter to Eugen Hönig from London dated 31 December 1936, in: Reginald R. Isaacs, *Walter Gropius – Der Mensch und sein Werk*, Berlin 1984, p. 803. In the same letter Gropius wrote: "I am convinced that the development of modern architecture has nothing whatsoever to do with any political system."
22 Walter Gropius, *Bauhausbauten Dessau*, Munich 1930, p. 216 (also published in: *The Scope of Total Architecture*, New York 1962, p. 65).
23 Cf. Joachim Driller, *Breuer Houses*, London 2000, p. 102.
24 Cf. Eduard Kögel, "Nützliche Tradition? Walter Gropius trifft auf China (oder I. M. Pei)", in: Marion von Osten and Grant Watson (Eds.), *bauhaus imaginista – Die globale Rezeption bis heute*, Zurich 2019, pp. 206–211.
25 Walter Gropius et al. (Ed.), *The Architects Collaborative TAC 1945–1965*, Teufen 1966, p. 124.
26 For more information on Gropius' activities in Argentina that first began in the 1930s. See Joaquín Medina Warmburg (Ed.), *Walter Gropius proclamas de modernidad – Escritos y conferencias, 1908–1934*, Barcelona 2018.
27 As described in the book *The Architects Collaborative TAC 1945–1965*. Cf. ibid.
28 The plans on pages 30, 42, 43, 70, 71, 126, 155, 170, 173, 174, 176 and 192 are drawn at a scale of 1:500.
29 Walter Gropius in a letter to Rolf Schwedler dated 19 April 1966, in: Hans Bandel and Dittmar Machule, *Die Gropiusstadt – Der städtebauliche Planungs- und Entscheidungsvorgang*, Berlin 1974, p. 112.
30 Walter Gropius in a lecture given in Hamburg in 1956, in: *Apollo in der Demokratie*, Mainz 1967, p. 15.
31 Ludwig Mies van der Rohe in: *Baukunst und Werkform*, Vol. 6, 1958, cited in: Fritz Neumeyer, *The Artless Word. Mies van der Rohe on the Building Art*, 1991, Cambridge, MA, p. 338.
32 Mies van der Rohe in a speech given on 18 May 1953 on the occasion of the 70th birthday of Walter Gropius in Chicago, cited in: ibid., p. 329.

14 Walter Gropius with TAC, Berlin-Gropiusstadt 1959–72, model of the first master plan from 1960
15 Walter Gropius with TAC and Amancio Williams, German Embassy in Buenos Aires, project for the embassy residence, 1968–69

Metzler House

Dramburg/Pomerania, now Poland
1905–06

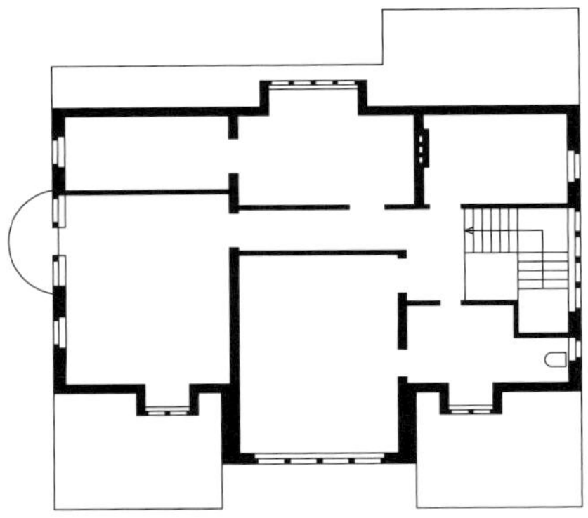

The "country house"[1] with a hipped roof, splayed side mansards, rough-hewn stone base and tapered quoins is situated near the mouth of a small river at the edge of a park. Gropius was recommended to the clients, Otto Metzler,[2] a retired lieutenant, and his wife Elisabeth, by his uncle, whose manor house a few kilometres away served as a model for the house. Erich Gropius' villa was designed by the architecture office Solf & Wichards where Gropius spent a year's internship in 1903–1904. Gropius was still a student when he designed the Metzler House and replicated the romantic half-timbered style of his uncle's house. His placement of the entrance at one corner resulted in a non-systematic floor plan and the spacing of the half-timbered facades was also irregular. In later years, Gropius obviously felt the building lacked clarity, referring to the building and to a granary built around the same time for his uncle as "my youthful sins".[3]

1 "Landhaus" was the term Gropius wrote on the floor plans shown in Małgorzata Omilanowska, "Das Frühwerk von Walter Gropius in Hinterpommern" (Walter Gropius' early works in Farther Pomerania), in: Birte Pusback (Ed.), *Landgüter in den Regionen des gemeinsamen Kulturerbes von Deutschen und Polen*, Warsaw 2007, p. 151.
2 Ibid., p. 131. In earlier publications, it was erroneously called the Metzner Villa.
3 Cited in Reginald R. Isaacs, *Gropius: An Illustrated Biography of the Creator of the Bauhaus*, Boston 1991, p. 14.

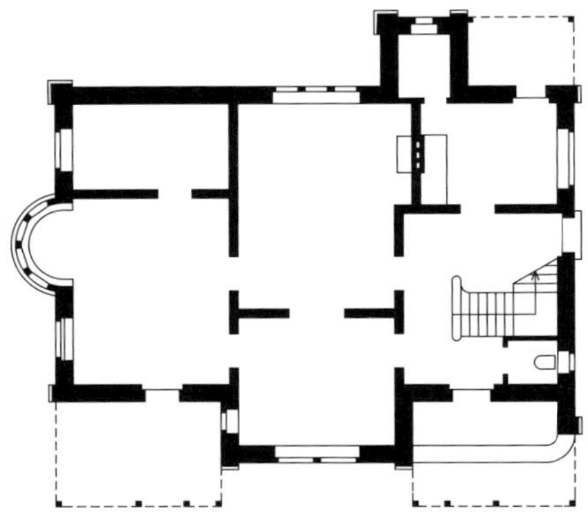

Upper floor plan
Ground floor plan

View from the river
Garden elevation

Janikow Estate

near Dramburg/Pomerania, now Poland
1906–09

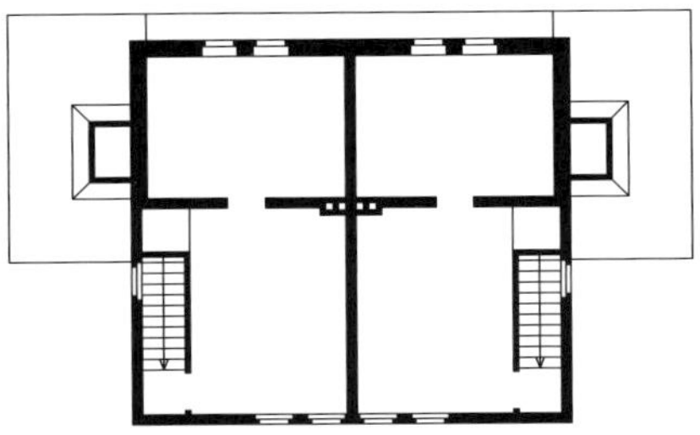

Gropius began building a granary, smithy, washhouse and workers' housing for his uncle's country estate while still a student. While most of the estate has since been destroyed, the granary still stands. The granary building stood next to Erich Gropius' villa and adopted many of its stylistic elements. It too is a picturesque, asymmetrical composition of exposed brickwork, half-timbered gables, hipped roof and rough-hewn stone base.

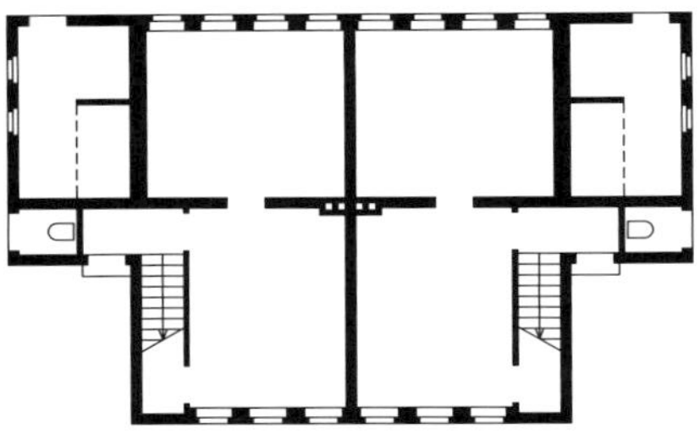

The pair of brick houses for farm workers built a few years later were, by contrast, much more rigorously classical in design. Built in 1908 after Gropius had begun working in Peter Behrens' atelier, they had clear symmetrical forms and systematic floor plans of near-industrial simplicity. The building elevations and plans are proportioned according to the Golden Section[1] and the abstract, geometric form of the buildings is underlined by the arrangement of the entrances to one side and the rhythmic rows of uniform window openings. While Behrens favoured rows of an odd number of windows, the mirrored floor plan results here in an even number of windows. A cornice and shared base emphasise the buildings' horizontality and the front face is divided by a horizontal band, while the upper floor steps back at the rear of the building. As Gropius published little of his early work, the house for the farm workers, included by Sigfried Giedion in his biography of Gropius was long thought to be his first work.

1 See Annemarie Jaeggi, *Adolf Meyer – Der zweite Mann – Ein Architekt im Schatten von Walter Gropius*, Berlin 1994, pp 237, 238. While Jaeggi analyses the design for a pair of houses for farm workers at Golzengut, the two projects are almost identical and share the same organisational scheme. Jaeggi demonstrates that their design adheres to the Golden Section. The plans shown here are reconstructions based on the plans for Golzengut in Jaeggi's book.

Upper floor plan
Ground floor plan
Semi-detached house for farm workers, entrance elevation
Semi-detached house for farm workers, garden elevation

Granary
Granary, detail

Von Brockhausen Estate

Mittelfelde/Pomerania, now Poland
1907–14

Gropius described the house for four families that he built on Heinrich Eugen von Brockhausen's country estate in 1908 as "rather opulent".[1] Comprising four symmetrically equal parts, the north and south elevations of the building are identical. Like Gropius' other buildings from this period, the corner quoins are tapered while the entire building mass and its projecting and recessed sections are covered by a single large roof. As with the Metzler House and granary at Janikow, Gropius used different window formats, but the mirrored arrangement of the building gives the house a systematic appearance.

In addition to this house for farm workers, Gropius was also entrusted with the reorganisation of the estate. He changed the entrance situation, adding large walls and a gateway. The now partially collapsed and overgrown walls are capped with glazed green tiles. In 1913–14, Gropius built further buildings for the estate of which all that remains are photos of a greenhouse from Gropius' own documents.[2]

1 Walter Gropius in a letter to his mother dated 15 February 1907, in: Reginald R. Isaacs, *Gropius: An Illustrated Biography of the Creator of the Bauhaus*, Boston 1991, p. 17.
2 Annemarie Jaeggi has speculated on whether a still existing electricity transformer building can be attributed to Gropius and Meyer. Annemarie Jaeggi, *Adolf Meyer – Der zweite Mann – Ein Architekt im Schatten von Walter Gropius*, Berlin 1994, p. 268.

House for four families, south elevation
House for four families, north elevation

Von Arnim House

Falkenhagen/Pomerania, now Poland
1910–11

The manor house on Friedrich Wilhelm von Arnim's country estate lies about a hundred metres from the road. The driveway leads directly up to the symmetrically-arranged house before dividing to lead from the left and right up a slope to the front of the house. The house's slightly elevated position is underlined by the rough-hewn stone base on which it stands, and an adjoining conservatory and entrance canopy are articulated as delicate iron and glass constructions. At the rear of the house, a flight of stairs descends in a cascade into the park-like garden. Gropius' design bears similarities to the Schroeder House that Peter Behrens had built previously in Hagen and which Gropius had "detailed almost entirely on his own"[1] while working in his office. That project was, however, the subject of a dispute between Gropius and Behrens who wanted no roof overhang, a decision that did indeed prove to be a problem later. In his design for the von Arnim House, Gropius therefore employed a mansard roof in an attempt to improve on Behrens' architecture, which he otherwise identified with.[2] Like Behrens, Gropius incorporated the drainpipe within the wall and chose a linoleum flooring with an ornamental design by Behrens for the conservatory. Like the ochre-rendered Schroeder House, the entrance hall of the von Arnim House was plastered in red, giving it a "Pompeian atmosphere".[3] The house has since been altered inside and out and the glass conservatory no longer exists.

1 As Walter Gropius wrote in a letter to Georg Hoeltje on 5 June 1958, published in: Helmut Weber, *Walter Gropius und das Faguswerk*, Munich 1961, p. 23.
2 Ibid. Gropius wrote: "For years, I spent my evenings at Behrens' and identified with all his work."
3 Fritz Hoeber, Peter Behrens, Munich 1913, p. 89. Annemarie Jaeggi also notes that the plaster of the entrance hall was red and the external render in a yellow tone. She cites a note by Gropius that describes the details as having "a cream base / black-brown bands / a little malachite green". Annemarie Jaeggi, *Adolf Meyer – Der zweite Mann – Ein Architekt im Schatten von Walter Gropius*, Berlin 1994, p. 236.

Entrance facade
Garden facade
Conservatory

Golzengut House

Dramburg/Pomerania, now Poland
1910–11, conversion, destroyed

Gropius' uncle purchased the Golzengut estate adjoining his own Janikow estate and commissioned his nephew to renovate and convert the manor house.[1] Gropius also designed a house for farm workers on the estate.[2] It is not known how much he altered the building's facades: the rusticated rendering, cornice profiling and detailing of the window surrounds was also present on neighbouring buildings from the early 1800s and Gropius may only have added a central risalit and semi-circular bay window in the middle of the end facade. The style echoed that of the architecture of Karl Friedrich Schinkel. A similarly neo-classicist architectural language can be seen in Gropius' unrealised designs for a hospital and regional councillor's office from 1912–13. The narrow end of the manor house faced the main road and the main entrance was set to one side in a single-storey side extension with roof terrace above. At the rear, the garden elevation opened onto a broad terrace raised two steps above the garden. The house was destroyed during the Second World War.

1 See Annemarie Jaeggi, *Adolf Meyer – Der zweite Mann – Ein Architekt im Schatten von Walter Gropius*, Berlin 1994, pp. 236–239.
2 Reginald R. Isaacs wrote that Gropius designed several such houses for the Golzengut estate. Reginald R. Isaacs, *Gropius: an illustrated biography of the creator of the Bauhaus*, Boston 1991, p. 17.

View from the road
Entrance facade

Kleffel Starch Factory

Baumgarten Estate, near Dramburg/Pomerania, now Poland
1911 (with Adolf Meyer), destroyed

The building was inserted into existing buildings on the country estate.[1] Partially rendered and partially left as exposed brickwork, the building fitted in with the surrounding agricultural buildings. While the base was articulated as a band of brickwork, the central section was marked by a raised tower and projecting vertically-delineated central risalit that gave the building a monumental appearance reminiscent of many of Behrens' industrial buildings. The device of concealing several narrow windows in tall vertical slots that connect several storeys was employed later by Gropius and Adolf Meyer, who had also worked in Behrens' atelier, for the factory facade at the Werkbund Exhibition Building in Cologne. The projecting vertical wall section appears to look like a colossal pilaster bearing an architrave. The loadbearing structure is a steel frame construction with Prussian vaulted ceilings. The building, which was used to turn potatoes into starch flour, was demolished in 2014.

1 The building is recorded in the list of works (Sigfried Giedion, *Walter Gropius – Work and Teamwork*, New York 1954, p. 233) as dating from 1913–14 but a letter from the client's daughter, Hildegard Kleffel, from 24 October 1957 (Bauhaus-Archiv Berlin, Inv. No. 6124/1) suggests the building was built some three years earlier.

View from the rear

Fagus Factory

Alfeld, Germany
1911–15, 1921–25 (with Adolf Meyer)

"This building was so excellent that he became, with one stroke, one of the leading architects in Europe,"[1] noted Mies van der Rohe. Gropius' commission to build a factory for shoe lasts – wooden forms for making shoes – at the age of 28 was the product of his tenacity and perseverance after writing hundreds of letters to potential clients. It was Carl Benscheidt who took the risk of employing the young, unknown architect motivated by a desire to improve on an existing more conventional design for his factory by the architect Eduard Werner. He commissioned Gropius to design the facades while retaining the existing floor plans. Gropius would later explain: "Convinced that the new architectural possibilities of building with steel, concrete and glass had not been fully recognised and that one could achieve more daring results, I attempted to find an uncompromisingly radical solution."[2]

While Gropius together with his collaborator Adolf Meyer were able to make slight modifications to the floor plan, their primary architectural innovation was the design of the main building with its glass curtain wall and transparent glazed corners. As the facade was not completely suspended from the supporting structure, it was not strictly-speaking a curtain wall but it demonstrated an architectural solution that was to influence the subsequent development of architecture as a whole. The loadbearing structure takes the form of brick piers that slope slightly inwards. In contrast to Peter Behrens' AEG Turbine Factory, which Gropius had also worked on, where the skeleton frame is upright but the glazing slants slightly inwards, the Fagus Factory did the opposite: the glazing was vertical while the masonry surfaces were slightly inclined so that the piers grow narrower towards the top, creating shadow lines.

By placing the building on a very dark brick base, Gropius wanted "to give the buildings a sense of lightness, to allow them to float above the ground". His principle of using large sections of glazing to unite several storeys into a single plane was, so he said: "a product of my tendency to combine forms or elements to achieve ever greater simplicity. In my teaching I would always tell my students that, if they had the opportunity, they should not hesitate in combining two or three elements into one. Such a design process increases the sense of scale and avoids designs becoming overly fussy and 'too much'."[3]

The complex was built in several phases, mostly between 1911 and 1914. Various outbuildings, extensions and interior fittings followed later.

1 Ludwig Mies van der Rohe on the occasion of Gropius' 70th birthday on 18 May 1953 in Chicago, cited in: Sigfried Giedion, *Walter Gropius – Work and Teamwork*, New York 1954, p. 17.
2 Walter Gropius "Vor 50 Jahren" (50 years ago), in: Helmut Weber, *Walter Gropius und das Faguswerk*, Munich 1961, p. 7.
3 Walter Gropius in a letter to Helmut Weber dated 10 May 1959, in: ibid., p. 60.

Staircase

The entire complex
Main building, view from the southwest

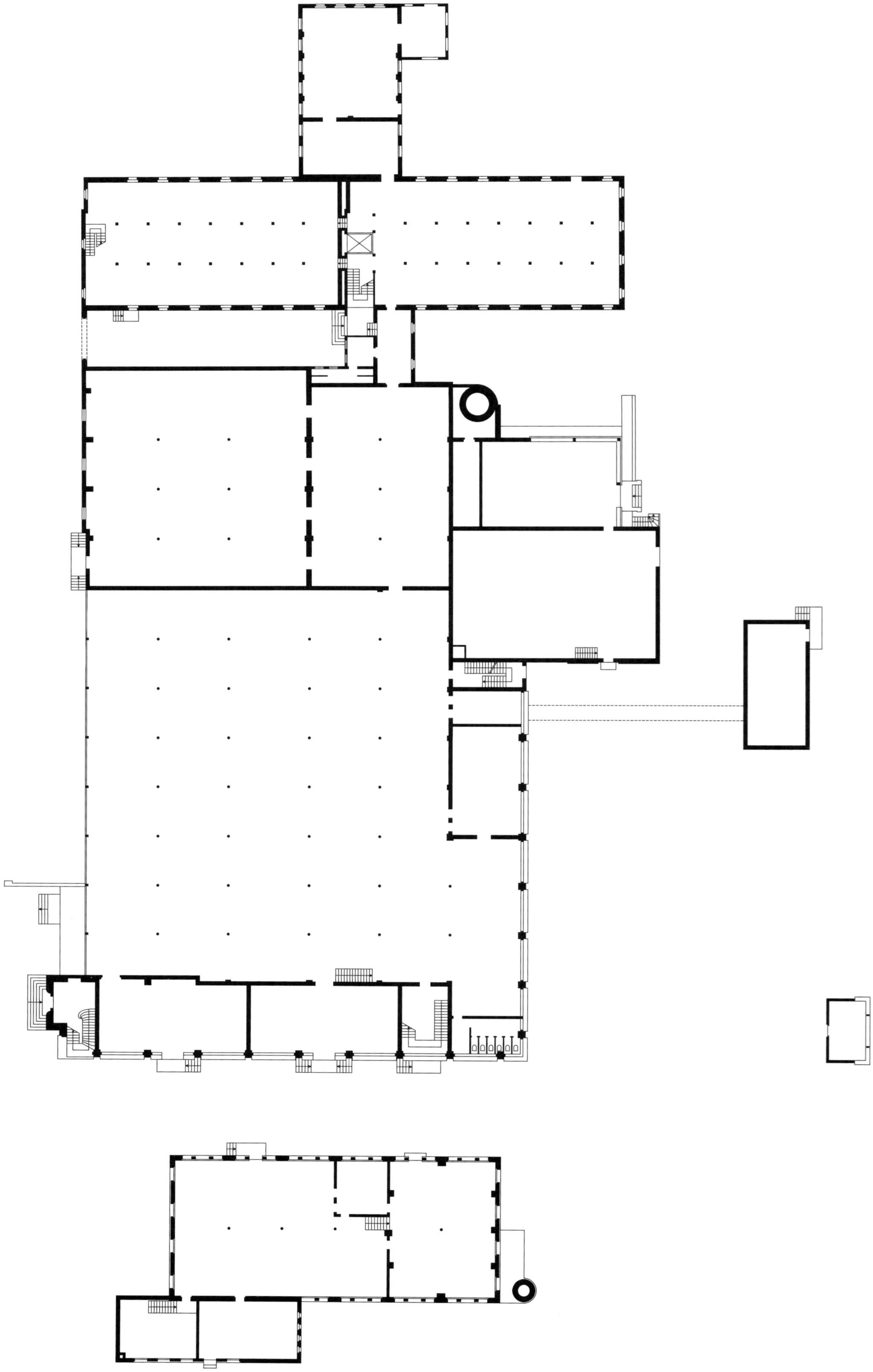

Ground floor plan

Main building, view from the northeast
View from the south
Chip and coal bunker

Storage building

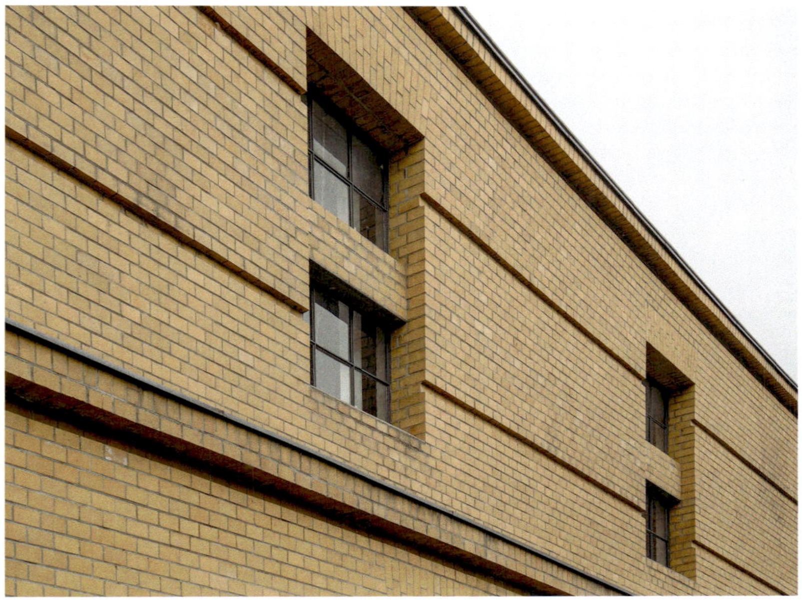

Main building, detail
Main entrance
Main building, vestibule

Main building, south corner
Southwest facade, detail
Stair detail

Workers' Dwellings for Bernburger Machine Factory

Alfeld, Germany
1912–13 (with Adolf Meyer)

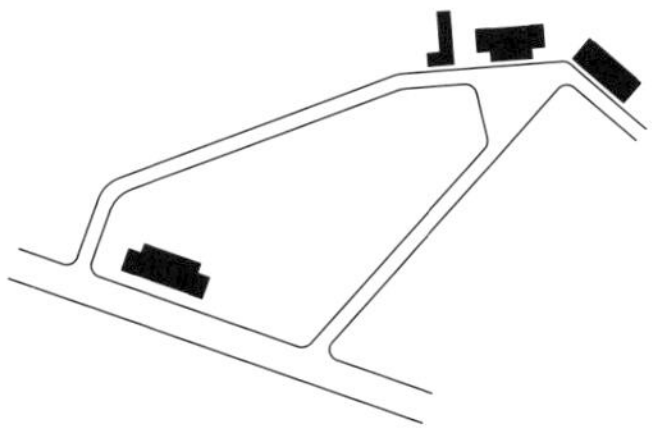

For the workers at Bernburger Machine Company, Gropius planned a group of three pairs of houses with a total of twelve dwellings. The pair of houses adjoining the main road was flanked by two lower outbuildings with space for keeping livestock. The toilets were likewise reached from outside. Simple variations to the facades and building volumes differentiate the houses, which were developed from the twin-house type fcr workers first used in Janikow. They employ, for example, the same rhythmic succession of simple, vertical-format window openings with 1:2 proportions. In a letter Gropius wrote to Karl Ernst Osthaus in 1911, he described the imminent realisation of his house type concept.[1] He would later develop this typological idea at the Bauhaus into a modular system employing variations of uniform elements, but by 1918 he had already disassociated himself from his earlier buildings.[2] The buildings and facades have since undergone significant alterations and their original design is no longer legible.

1 Walter Gropius in a letter dated 13 November 1911, cited in: Annemarie Jaeggi, *Adolf Meyer – Der zweite Mann – Ein Architekt im Schatten von Walter Gropius*, Berlin 1994, p. 266.
2 Walter Gropius in a letter dated 23 December 1918 to Karl Ernst Osthaus: "I have not built any houses in recent years and those I built in the past are so appalling that I cannot bear to look at them", cited in Winfried Nerdinger, *The Architect Walter Gropius*, Berlin 1985, p. 38.

Site plan
Semi-detached house type 1
Semi-detached house type 2

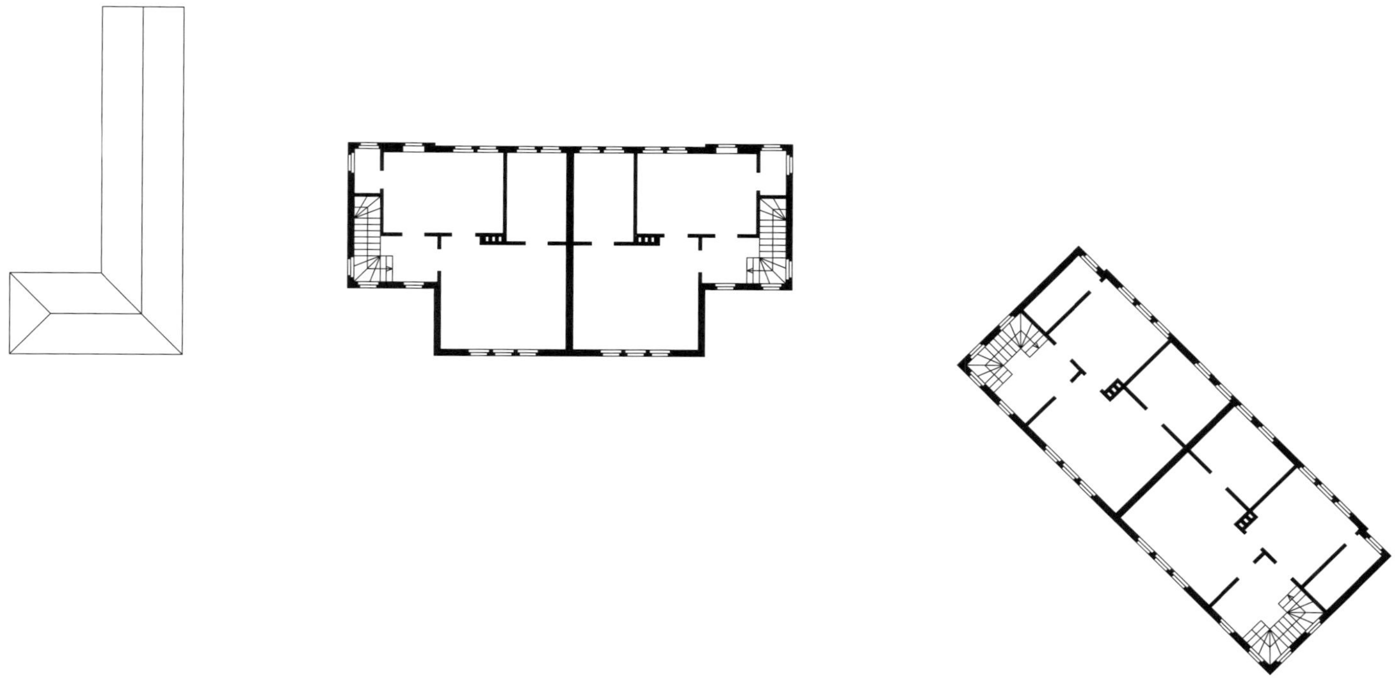

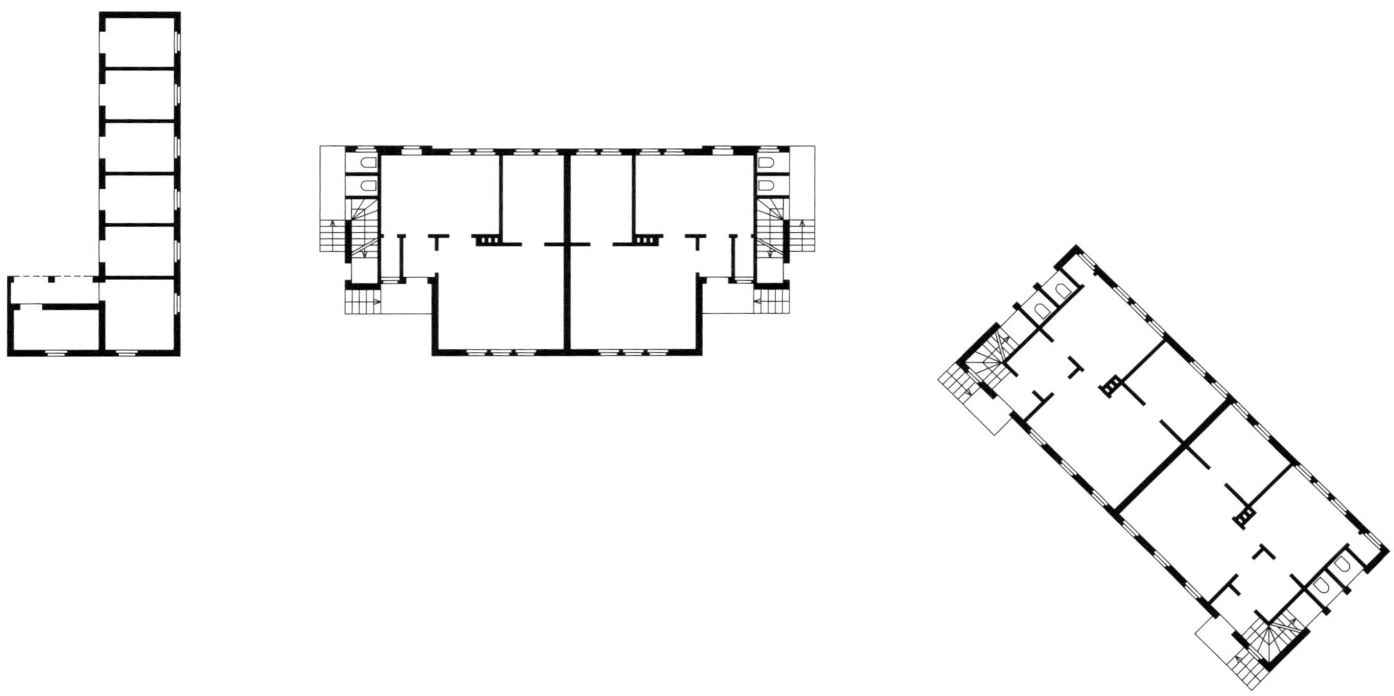

Upper floor plans
Ground floor plans

Grain Store and Housing

Märkisch Friedland/Pomerania, now Poland
1913–14

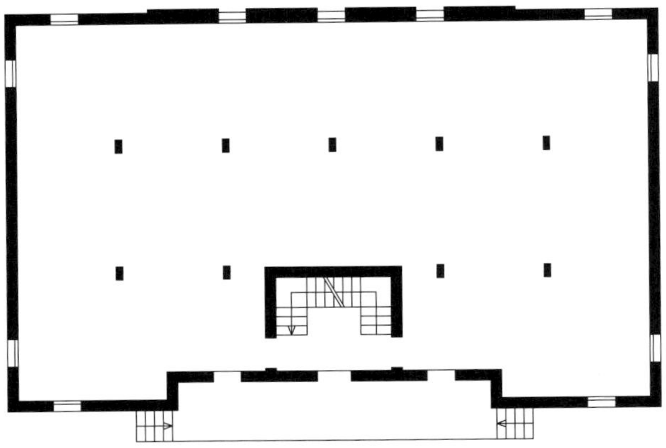

The grain store with the inscription "Agricultural Trade Association" and the building next to it enter into an architectural dialogue. While the central section of the grain store steps back, that of the house protrudes slightly forward. And while the rendered walls of the grain store are delineated by brick coursing, the brick walls of the house are crowned by a rendered band beneath the eaves. The horizontal delineation of the grain store is similar to that of the Fagus Factory, aligning with the tops and bottoms of the windows. In an early list of works, the project is listed as "Grain Store and Houses",[1] suggesting that at least one further house was planned that would most likely have stood opposite the existing house creating a symmetrical layout: the houses and grain store form an architectural ensemble. The different building masses have similarly proportioned floor plans and both buildings feature elements – a central gable and two turret-like corners – that extend above the walls out over the facades which are partially set back. The house has since been demolished and the grain store has been altered so significantly that only parts of it are still original.

1 See Annemarie Jaeggi, *Adolf Meyer – Der zweite Mann – Ein Architekt im Schatten von Walter Gropius*, Berlin 1994, p. 281.

Floor plan of the grain store
Residential building

Grain store
Detail

"Eigene Scholle" Housing Estate

Wittenberge, Germany
1913–14 (with Adolf Meyer)

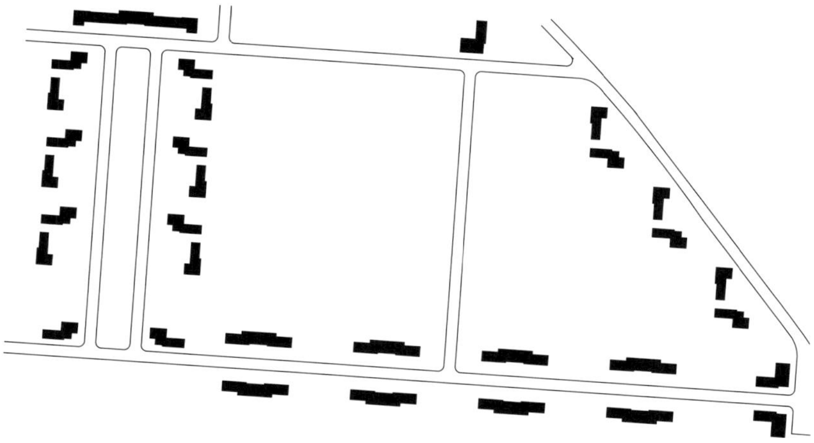

The housing estate for workers at the nearby factories comprises three different house types.[1] Along the southern edge of the site, a series of identical semi-detached houses with adjoining outbuildings for livestock lines an avenue of lime trees. To the west, along a strip of chestnut woodland, and along the road bordering the site to the east, rows of single-family houses are arranged in rhythmic L-shaped constellations that form small courtyards between them. To the north at the end of the chestnut trees, a pair of semi-detached houses are flanked by a pair of single-family houses. The housing types respond to both the linear character of the avenue as well as the more dispersed structure of the chestnut trees. To the east, two slightly larger houses are placed opposite one another to act as a gateway.

The single-family houses are likewise equipped with outbuildings for livestock and outside toilets. Those closer to the road have more elaborate facades, although the abstract classical motifs are not applied to the walls' surfaces but are articulated by modulating the wall render. The wall surface steps back slightly to create the impression of a plinth, pilasters and beams in relief. Although some of the houses have since been destroyed, the ensemble of houses around the chestnut trees still exists. All the buildings have, however, been altered and none are in original condition.

1 The houses were built by the "Landgesellschaft Eigene Scholle" for workers at the Singer Factory and German Railways. While the semi-detached houses and large single-family houses sold well, the most common smaller single-family house type was obviously too expensive for its size and proved hard to sell. See Annemarie Jaeggi, *Adolf Meyer – Der zweite Mann – Ein Architekt im Schatten von Walter Gropius*, Berlin 1994, pp. 276–280.

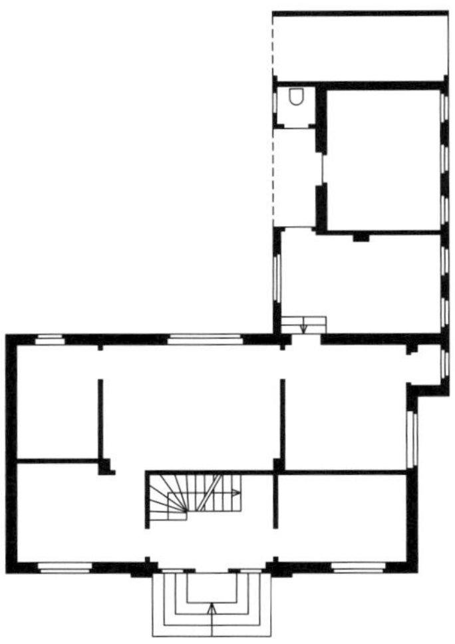

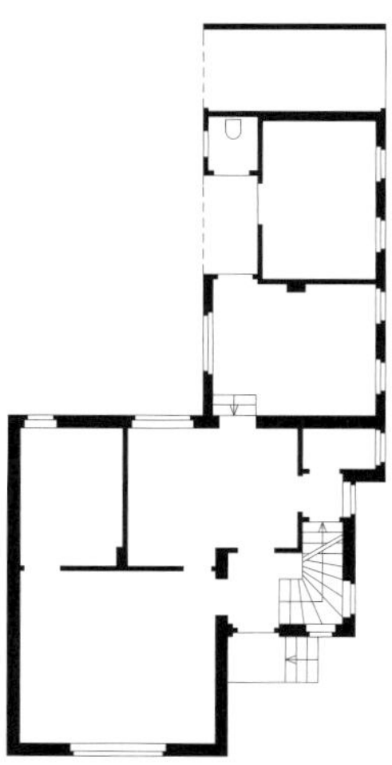

Site plan
Large single-family house, floor plan
Single-family house, floor plan
Single-family house with outbuildings

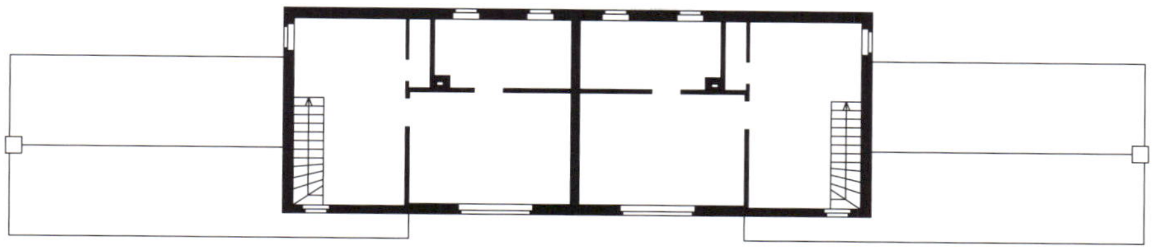

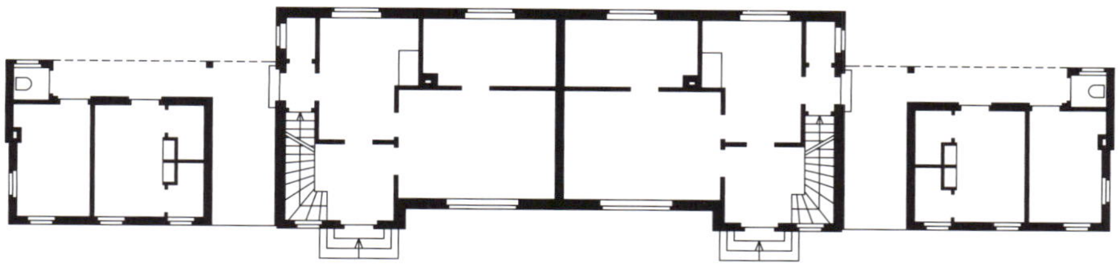

Semi-detached house, upper floor plan
Semi-detached house, ground floor plan
Chestnut grove
Semi-detached house with outbuildings

Model Factory at the Werkbund Exhibition

Cologne, Germany
1913–14 (with Adolf Meyer), destroyed

For the Werkbund Exhibition in 1914 in Cologne, Gropius and Adolf Meyer designed a model factory that, unlike most of the other exhibition buildings, was to be permanent and built of "real" materials sponsored by companies. Hans Poelzig was originally selected to build the factory but withdrew from the commission. Although Gropius and Meyer would rather have designed a "factory complex in its entirety",[1] they were obliged to incorporate a pre-existing dismantlable machine hall designed by the engineer Hans Schmuckler, to which they only made design adaptations. Despite making changes to the building's massing, Gropius described the construction of the hall as "excellent" and "the best formal solution of this kind that I have seen."[2] A long narrow office building demarcated the southern end of the complex while a pavilion for Deutz Motor Factory stood to one side at the northern end of the machine hall.

The rigorously symmetrical office building, taking cues from Frank Lloyd Wright's architecture, had a large roof terrace and was clad with light yellow and very dark bricks. The ends and north-facing facade were clad with glass curtain walling, its curved glass panes wrapping gracefully and membrane-like around the rounded staircases at each end. While the front face of the building with its monumental entrance portal and long access corridor on the upper floor was shielded by a monolithic facade, the more private facade to the rear was entirely open, allowing light to flood into the extremely tall office spaces. The experience of passing from the dark entrance areas with their painted walls and ceilings and decorative reliefs and figurines[3] to the light-filled "neutral" space of the work areas behind was dramatic.

Like the machine hall, the iron structure of the Deutz Pavilion was encased so that its open trusses looked like solid beams and columns, heightening, in the manner of Peter Behrens, the physical presence of the pavilion. The walls of the pavilion interior were faced with ornamental ceramic panels.

1 Walter Gropius in a letter to Karl Ernst Osthaus dated 15 July 1913, cited in: Annemarie Jaeggi, *Adolf Meyer – Der zweite Mann – Ein Architekt im Schatten von Walter Gropius*, Berlin 1994, p. 270.
2 Ibid.
3 Including work by Gerhard Marcks who later became a Master at the Bauhaus.

Deutz Pavilion, interior

Entrance elevation of office building
End elevation
Rear elevation of office building

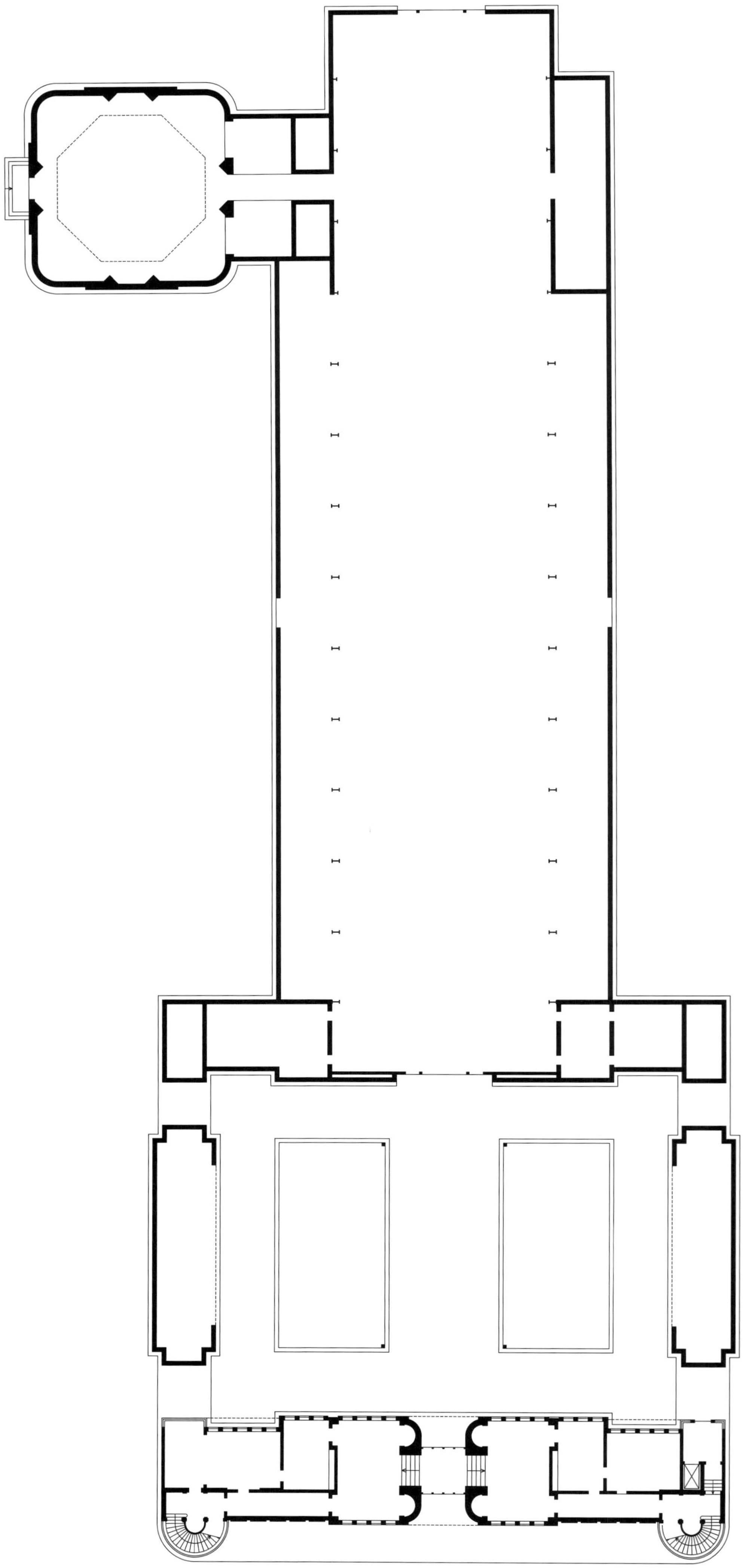

Ground floor of the entire complex

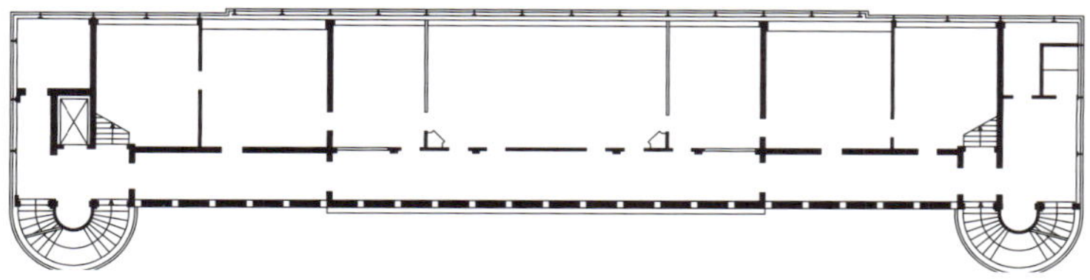

Office building, top floor plan
Office building, upper floor plan
The entire complex

Monument to the March Dead

Weimar, Germany
1920–22, reconstructed

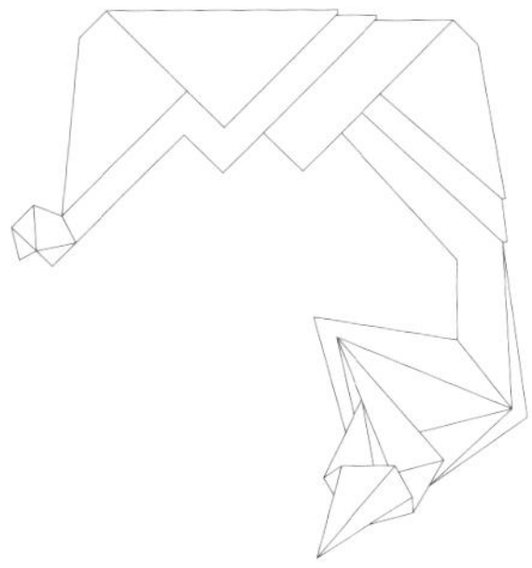

The monument was built to commemorate those killed in the right-wing Kapp Putsch to overthrow the new democratic Weimar Republic. In March 1920, ten young workers were killed during a general strike and the workers' union organised a competition for a memorial to be erected next to the graves in Weimar's central cemetery, which Gropius won. His design for a crystalline sculpture made of concrete was at once gravestone and monument, a dynamic object that framed a space that was intended to be "open to everyone"[1] and not a fenced-off area. Gropius stated that "the bolt of lightning from the bottom of the grave is a symbol of the living spirit!!"[2] His idea was "to erect a symbol which would express the spirit of freedom",[3] though he would later state: "I hesitate to offer any literary explanation for the monument. It should be left to the observer to interpret how they will."[4]

While limestone was originally specified, the monument was eventually made of concrete with local limestone and black and white terrazzo aggregate mixed in.[5] The surface was then hammered to create a uniform worked appearance. Gropius, who from 1919 was the Director of the Bauhaus, worked with the sculpture workshop at the Bauhaus on the design where a plaster model of the monument was made. In 1936, the Nazis blew up the jagged part of the monument, but it was reconstructed again in 1946 in a slightly modified, less angular form.

1 Walter Gropius' own description of the design from December 1920. See Klaus-Jürgen Winkler und Herman van Bergeijk, *Das Märzgefallenen-Denkmal in Weimar*, Weimar 2004, p. 29.
2 Ibid.
3 Walter Gropius in a letter to Dietrich Clarenbach dated 1 August 1968, cited in: Reginald R. Isaacs, *Walter Gropius – Der Mensch und sein Werk*, Berlin 1983, p. 465.
4 Walter Gropius in a letter to Dietrich Clarenbach dated 24 December 1968, cited in: ibid.
5 See footnote 1, p. 45.

Top view
Monument shortly after completion

Reconstructed monument
Memorial slab

Sommerfeld House

Berlin-Lichterfelde, Germany
1920–22 (with Adolf Meyer), mostly destroyed

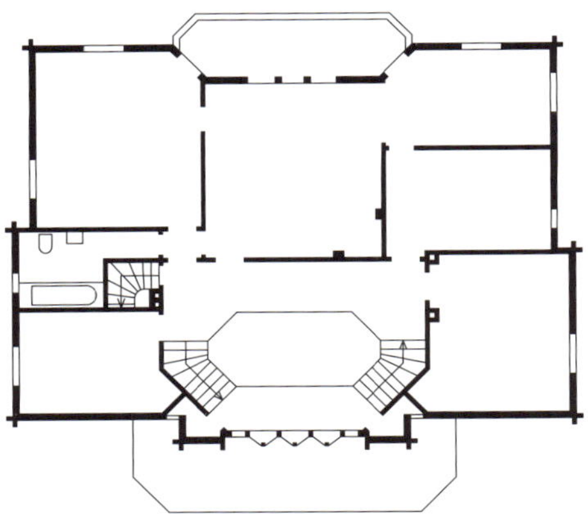

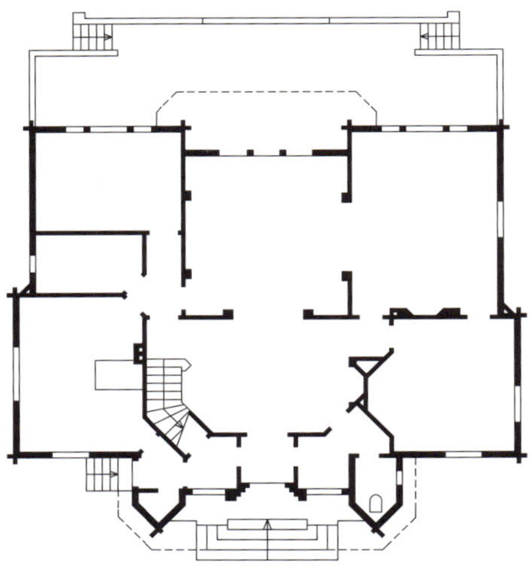

Gropius worked on the design for this house not just with Adolf Meyer but also with many of the workshops at the Bauhaus. Josef Albers contributed a coloured glazed window over the entrance, Marcel Breuer furniture, Joost Schmidt wood engravings on the timberwork and Hinnerk Scheper the colours of the interior.[1] Metalwork and textiles for the house were also made in the Bauhaus workshops. "Architects, sculptors, painters – we all must return to craftsmanship," wrote Gropius in his programme for the Bauhaus in 1919. "Let us strive for, conceive and create the new building of the future that will unite every discipline, architecture and sculpture and painting."[2] The joint project was commissioned by the Jewish building industrialist and timber merchant Adolf Sommerfeld.

The design of the rigorously symmetrical house bears obvious similarities to the work of Frank Lloyd Wright but has a more conventional floor plan. The structure was a twin-skin timber block construction method devised by Sommerfeld and the interior was clad with teak panelling salvaged from a wrecked ship. "Wood is the building material of the present," proclaimed Gropius in 1920, "Wood is the original building material of men, sufficient for all the structural parts of building; walls, floor, ceiling, roof, columns and beam."[3] Gropius had previously employed wood in the loadbearing structure of the grain store in Märkisch Friedland and the Fagus Factory but the spirit of this house – much like that of the "Dombauhütte" built around the same time by Peter Behrens — is more expressionist and mystical than rational and technical. Like Behrens, Gropius turned away from the neo-classicist style from 1918 onwards, though his approach to floor plans changed little. Adolf Sommerfeld emigrated to Palestine in 1933 and later to England. The house was destroyed during the Second World War and all that remains is the house built for the chauffeur and the gateway to the garden.

1 Celina Kress, *Adolf Sommerfeld/Andrew Sommerfield – Bauen für Berlin 1910–1970*, Berlin 2011, pp. 104–105.
2 Hartmut Probst and Christian Schädlich, *Walter Gropius – Band 3: Ausgewählte Schriften*, Berlin 1987, p. 72.
3 Walter Gropius, "Neues Bauen" (New Building), in: *Der Holzbau – Mitteilungen des Deutschen Holzbau-Vereins*, a supplement to the Deutsche Bauzeitung, 1920, Vol. 2, p. 5.

Upper floor plan
Ground floor plan
Entrance gate
Chauffeur's house, facade detail

Front elevation
Vestibule

Sommerfeld Row Houses

Berlin-Lichterfelde, Germany
1920–22 (with Adolf Meyer)

The articulation of the row of four single-family houses built for the employees of Adolf Sommerfeld's company with its side extensions and recessed sections creates the impression of a single large house. The mirroring of the floor plans, the emphasis given to the protruding central section in which two house entrances are incorporated and the single large roof that, like its four-dwelling predecessor in Mittelfelde, covers all four houses, further heighten this impression. The building was erected on the same site as the Sommerfeld House and here, too, wood features prominently on its facades. The building rests on a traditional rough-hewn stone base while the upper floor projects forward like a traditional half-timbered house, the gable projecting even further forward. Like historical half-timbered houses, the exposed ends of the beams are also decoratively carved. Gropius drew inspiration from historical examples, explaining: "The medieval timber frame houses in Germany and France, the wooden houses in Tyrol, Lithuania, the Balkan countries, Russia and Scandinavia all bear testimony to the endless possibilities of the decorative treatment of wood."[1]

During the renovation of the building, many of the details were omitted, such as the slight upswing of the eaves at the corners reminiscent of Chinese or Japanese temples. Further houses were originally planned for the site, along with an administrative building that extended over the roadway like a bridge.

1 Walter Gropius, "Neues Bauen" (New Building), in: *Der Holzbau – Mitteilungen des Deutschen Holzbau-Vereins*, a supplement to the *Deutsche Bauzeitung*, 1920, Vol. 2, p. 5.

View from the road

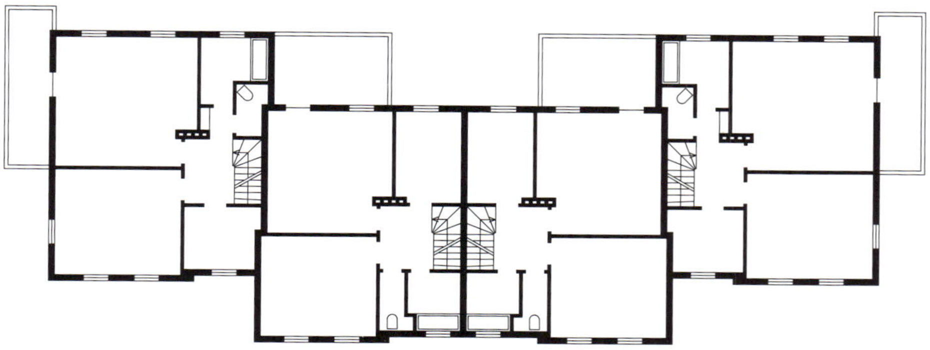

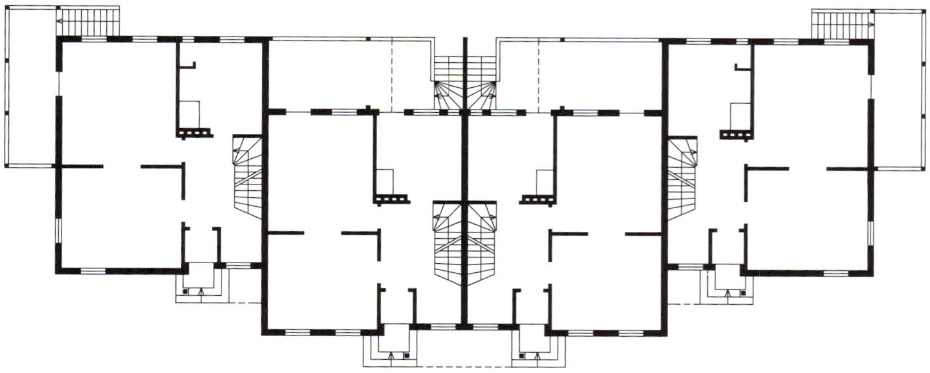

Upper floor plan
Ground floor plan
View from the garden
Front side

Mendel House

Berlin-Wannsee, Germany
1921, conversion (with Adolf Meyer)

The project encompassed the conversion of a Wilhelmine-era villa on a large site adjoining Wannsee lake in Berlin for the clothing factory owner Albert Mendel. Gropius had previously designed furniture and interiors for his home in the centre of the city and when Mendel decided in 1921 to move to his summer residence, several rooms in the house as well as the veranda were deemed in need of radical alterations and the furniture needed incorporating.

"The virtually square porch was converted by Gropius and Meyer into an eight-sided polygon with a tent-like ceiling formed of pointed triangles. From its centre, they hung an opal glass lamp in the form of an inverted pyramid, its tip pointing downwards. A series of steps led from the porch to the upper vestibule, the showpiece of the converted villa."[1] Annemarie Jaeggi goes on to describe a "fireplace with a brass fire hood, likewise with pointed triangles, that mirrors the shape of the ceiling above the eight-sided porch in miniature."[2]

The motif of the triangle also recurs in the design of the ceiling, the stair balustrade and top of the window in the vestibule. Rows of bare light bulbs on the ceiling accentuate the pointed sections of the ceiling recess. Gropius seems to later have disassociated himself from this Expressionist phase, omitting all the Berlin projects between 1920 and 1922 from his list of works.[3] The client died shortly after the conversion was completed and Gropius also designed his tomb at the Jewish Cemetery in Berlin-Weißensee.

1 Annemarie Jaeggi, *Adolf Meyer – Der Zweite Mann – Ein Architekt im Schatten von Walter Gropius*, Berlin 1994, pp. 404–405.
2 Ibid., p. 405.
3 See Sigfried Giedion, *Walter Gropius – Work and Teamwork*, New York 1954, p. 233.

Stoeckle House

Berlin-Zehlendorf, Germany
1921–22 (with Adolf Meyer), destroyed

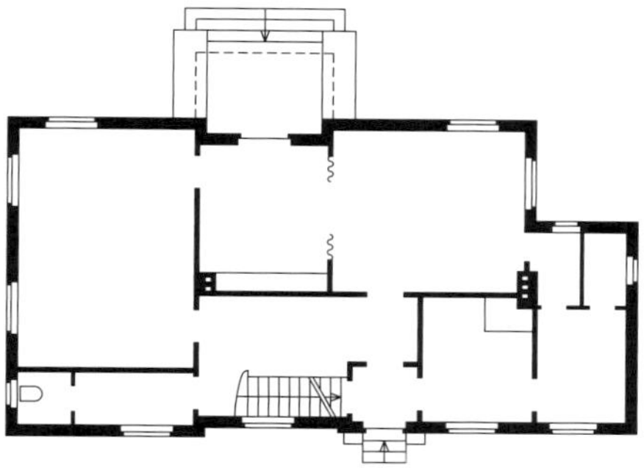

The building contractor Adolf Sommerfeld not only undertook the building's construction but also provided the land through his property company.[1] Like the row houses for Sommerfeld, built at the same time, the timber cladding at the top of the gable switches to a diagonal pattern. This Expressionist device is the only moment of extravagance in an otherwise modest and solidly constructed house with a steep pitched roof and window shutters that would be worthy of Heinrich Tessenow.[2] The colour scheme for the interiors was designed and undertaken by the wall-painting workshop at the Bauhaus and a carpet was also made at the Bauhaus weaving workshop.[3] At the rear facing the garden was a terrace crowned by a centrally-arranged balcony that, like Gropius and Meyer's other single-family houses, emphasised the centrality of the building. The house was badly damaged during the war and in 1959 completely demolished.

1 Annemarie Jaeggi, *Adolf Meyer – Der zweite Mann – Ein Architekt im Schatten von Walter Gropius*, Berlin 1994, pp. 144–146, 302–304.
2 Fred Forbát, who worked on the project at the time, wrote in a letter to Wolfgang Pehnt dated 24 July 1969 that the house "could almost have been by Tessenow". Wolfgang Pehnt, "Gropius the Romantic", in: *The Art Bulletin*, Sept. 1971, p. 383.
3 The design of the walls and colours was developed by Hinnerk Scheper. See Annemarie Jaeggi, op. cit., p. 303.

Ground floor plan
View from the road

Otte House

Berlin-Zehlendorf, Germany
1921–22 (with Adolf Meyer)

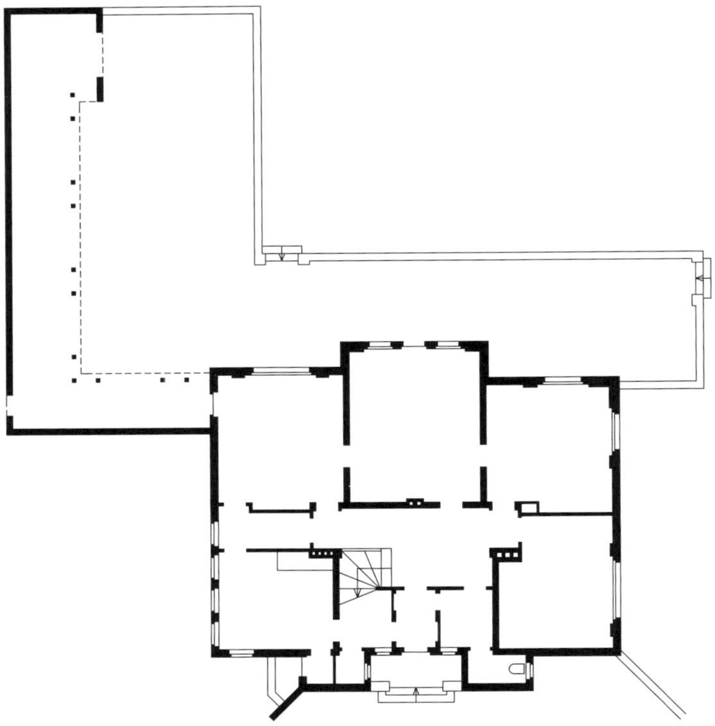

The house is similar in type to the Sommerfeld House and its design began just as the latter was nearing completion. In both cases, a two-storey villa is fronted by a single-storey extension for the entrance that replicates the form of the house in miniature. And in both cases, Josef Albers designed a large coloured window above the entrance, lending the tall dark-coloured vestibule an almost sacred atmosphere. The photo of the vestibule shows a lighter wall colouring added later by the owner who was evidently less partial to the room's original mystical atmosphere.[1] While the tectonic timber block construction of the Sommerfeld House reflects the early Bauhaus ideals of craftsmanship in construction, the smooth, membrane-like render of the Otte House already heralds the sober rationalism of the later Bauhaus. The rust-red wooden window frames and roof form were traditional, with the exception of the broken eaves line over the entrance. The floor plan and the adjoining pergola that framed one side of the garden likewise follow traditional patterns. After numerous alterations over the years, the building has since been restored to its original condition. In place of the destroyed glass window by Josef Albers is now a coloured window by Gerhard Richter.

1 See Annemarie Jaeggi, *Adolf Meyer – Der zweite Mann – Ein Architekt im Schatten von Walter Gropius*, Berlin 1994, p. 309. The wall-painting workshop at the Bauhaus was likewise responsible for the colour scheme of the walls of this house.

Ground floor plan
Entrance hall

Front view
Rear view

Municipal Theatre in Jena

Jena, Germany
1921–22, conversion (with Adolf Meyer), destroyed

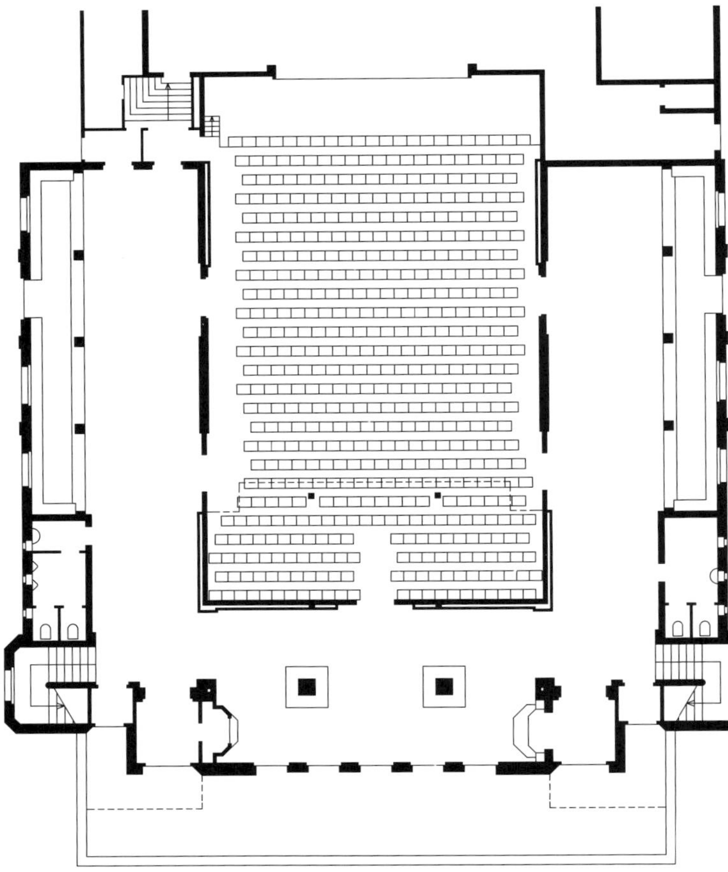

Gropius' conversion radically altered the appearance of the original theatre from 1872. Both the classicist facade with its central triangular pediment as well as the public areas of the interior were converted while the stage area and general floor plan was retained. Gropius had involved the Bauhaus workshops in the project, who produced decorative wood ornamentation. Over time, however, the project took on a "completely"[1] new form. This change reflected the shift in design sensibilities underway in the Bauhaus at that time. While the original design of the main entrance envisaged a two-storey opening with classically proportioned pillars, the final design featured a broad low portal with an entirely unbroken surface on the upper half of the facade. Similarly, Gropius had an already completed figurative ceiling mural by Oskar Schlemmer painted over, possibly in response to scathing criticism from the De Stijl proponent Theo van Doesburg after a visit to the theatre.

The interiors were eventually painted in very strong colours. "The building's only decoration is its colour," wrote a reporter at the time, before proceeding to describe the auditorium: "A dark grey colour allows the disproportionately large balcony to recede while bright salmon-red emphasises the central area which is in turn demarcated by the grey colour of the stage area. [...] With exquisite taste, the colours of the individual rooms have been carefully coordinated, establishing intimate connections, for example with the blue of the stage curtain."[2] A second article describes the two lobbies as being blue, the foyer light yellow, the cloakrooms violet, the staircase terracotta-coloured and the curtain as deep blue.[3] The geometric abstraction of the architecture is mirrored by the cubic light fittings in the building and entrance portal. In 1948, the building was once again completely altered eradicating Gropius' design in the process.

1 Adolf Meyer in a letter to Fred Forbát dated 4 December 1921, cited in: Annemarie Jaeggi, *Adolf Meyer – Der zweite Mann – Ein Architekt im Schatten von Walter Gropius*, Berlin 1994, p. 305.
2 R. Seubert, "Theater der Stadt Jena", in: *Das Volk*, 26 September 1922.
3 Oskar Rhode, "Das neue Theater der Stadt Jena," (The New Theatre in Jena) *Jenaische Zeitung,* 2 October 1922, cited in: Ulrich Müller, *Walter Gropius – Das Jenaer Theater*, Cologne 2006.

Floor plan
Entrance

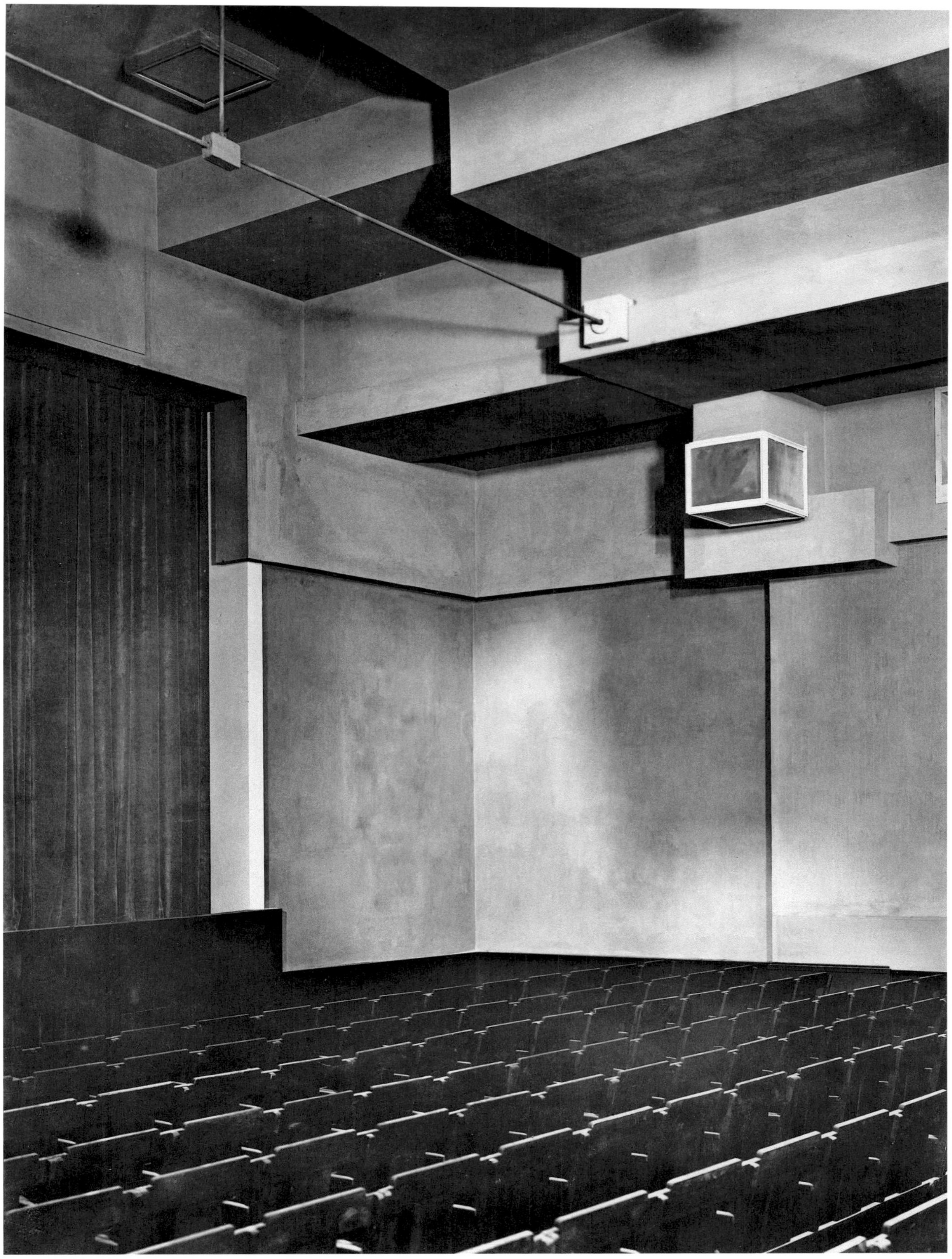

Kappe Storage Warehouse

Alfeld, Germany
1922–24 (with Adolf Meyer)

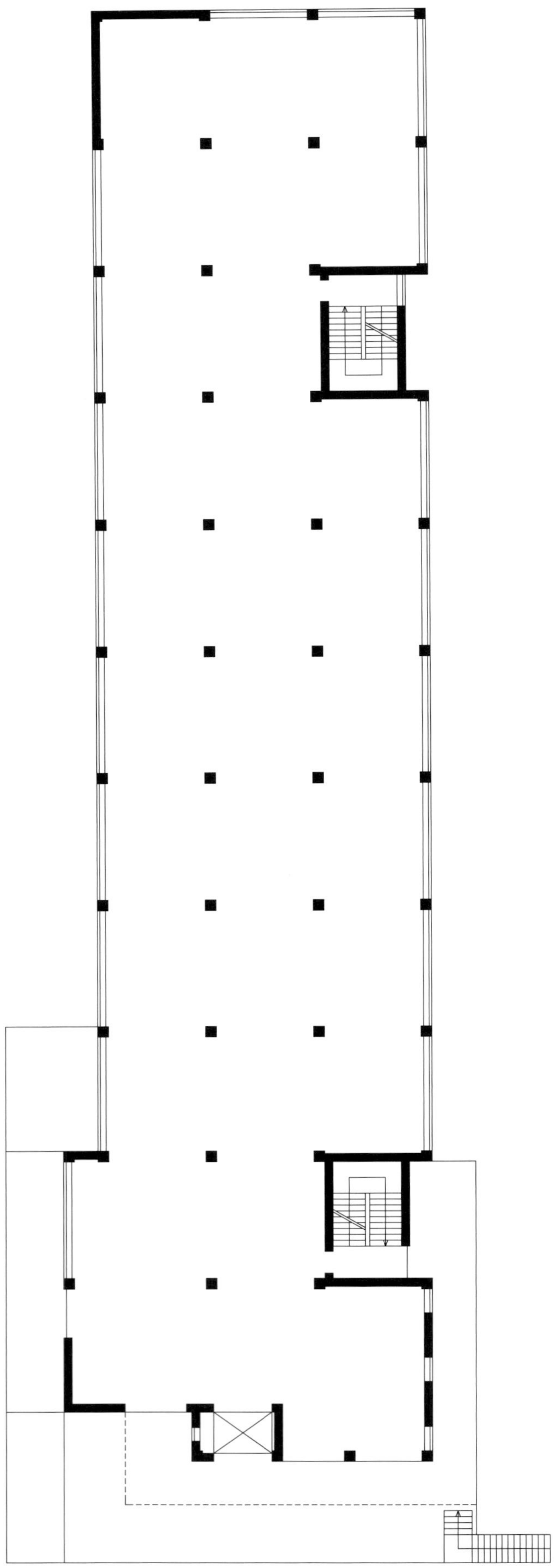

The building was used to house and exhibit agricultural machines produced by the Brothers Kappe & Co. The factory in which the machines were made, not far from the Fagus Factory, likewise had a loading bay served by the railway line. The structure, its skeleton frame, beams, ceilings and walls are made entirely of reinforced concrete. Initially, only the iron profiles of the windows were painted red[1] and the walls were rendered later. Later still, the southern end of the building was also redesigned. While Gropius described the design process as "straightforward" and "of no special significance",[2] Ernst Neufert, who was working for Gropius at the time explained that "this building was typical of the way Adolf Meyer and Gropius worked together. Adolf Meyer came almost every day with new ideas for the overall concept until Gropius turned up and chose the one he thought most appropriate. But even then, the project underwent constant revisions."[3]

1 A note from the office written in 1923 states: "concrete, naturally grey/guttering, black/window frames, minium red/doors, black (sheet metal)". Annemarie Jaeggi, *Adolf Meyer – Der zweite Mann – Ein Architekt im Schatten von Walter Gropius*, Berlin 1994, p. 314.
2 Walter Gropius in a letter to Helmut Weber dated 18 April 1960, cited in: ibid.
3 Ernst Neufert in a manuscript dated 12 May 1976, cited in: ibid., p. 314–315. His colleague Fred Forbát likewise claimed to have worked on the project. See ibid., p. 313.

Floor plan
View from the northeast

West side
Facade detail

Hanover Paper Factory

Alfeld, Germany
1922–24, conversion (with Adolf Meyer)

Gropius designed an extension for the Hanover Paper Factory that was, however, only partially realised. Situated next to a water course, the building remained unrendered for a long time and later underwent such extensive alteration that little of its original architectural design remains.[1] The plans show light-coloured facades with red doors. The wall panels between the upper and lower windows are slightly recessed giving the wall a vertical structure not unlike that of the Fagus Factory nearby. The concrete skeleton frame had brick masonry infill with barrel-vaulted sections on the roof. This building and the Otte House were the first of Gropius' works not to rest on an explicitly articulated base. This kind of functional industrial architecture served as a vehicle in his shift towards ever more geometric abstraction in which configurations of white-rendered cubes were assembled to reflect the internal functional processes, often appearing to be pushed into each other, so that only the clear proportions of the building volumes and the openings cut into them determine their architectural expression.

1 A few years later, without Gropius' involvement, the building, which still serves as a paper factory, was given an additional storey and the windows much reduced in size. See Karin Wilhelm, *Walter Gropius Industriearchitekt,* Braunschweig, Wiesbaden 1983, p. 107.

View from the east

Tomb for Albert Mendel

Berlin-Weißensee, Germany
1923

The tomb for Albert Mendel, whose house in Berlin Gropius had converted just two years before, lies in the Jewish Cemetery in Berlin-Weißensee.[1] Made of travertine, its inscription and inlaid Star of David on the sarcophagus are made of brass. The five-sided monolithic travertine block of the stylised sarcophagus is part of an asymmetrical overall composition. The stone frame of the rear panel continues as a meandering ribbon along the ground. Unlike the classical tomb that Mies van der Rohe designed for Laura Perls in the same cemetery in 1919, Gropius' tomb has a Constructivist formal language that defines an architectonic space and also incorporates the Expressionist triangular motif so prominent in the interiors of Mendel's house. The realisation of the tomb was undertaken in conjunction with the stone sculpture workshop at the Bauhaus.[2]

1 Landesdenkmalamt Berlin and Technische Universität Berlin (Ed.), *115.628 Berliners – The Weissensee Jewish Cemetery – Documentation of the Comprehensive Survey of the Burial Sites*, Berlin 2013, pp. 54–55.
2 See Annemarie Jaeggi, *Adolf Meyer – Der zweite Mann – Ein Architekt im Schatten von Walter Gropius*, Berlin 1994, p. 417. Annemarie Jaeggi has shown that Adolf Meyer was involved in this project, but the list of works (Sigfried Giedion, *Walter Gropius – Work and Teamwork*, New York 1954, p. 233) records the tomb as a work by Gropius on his own.

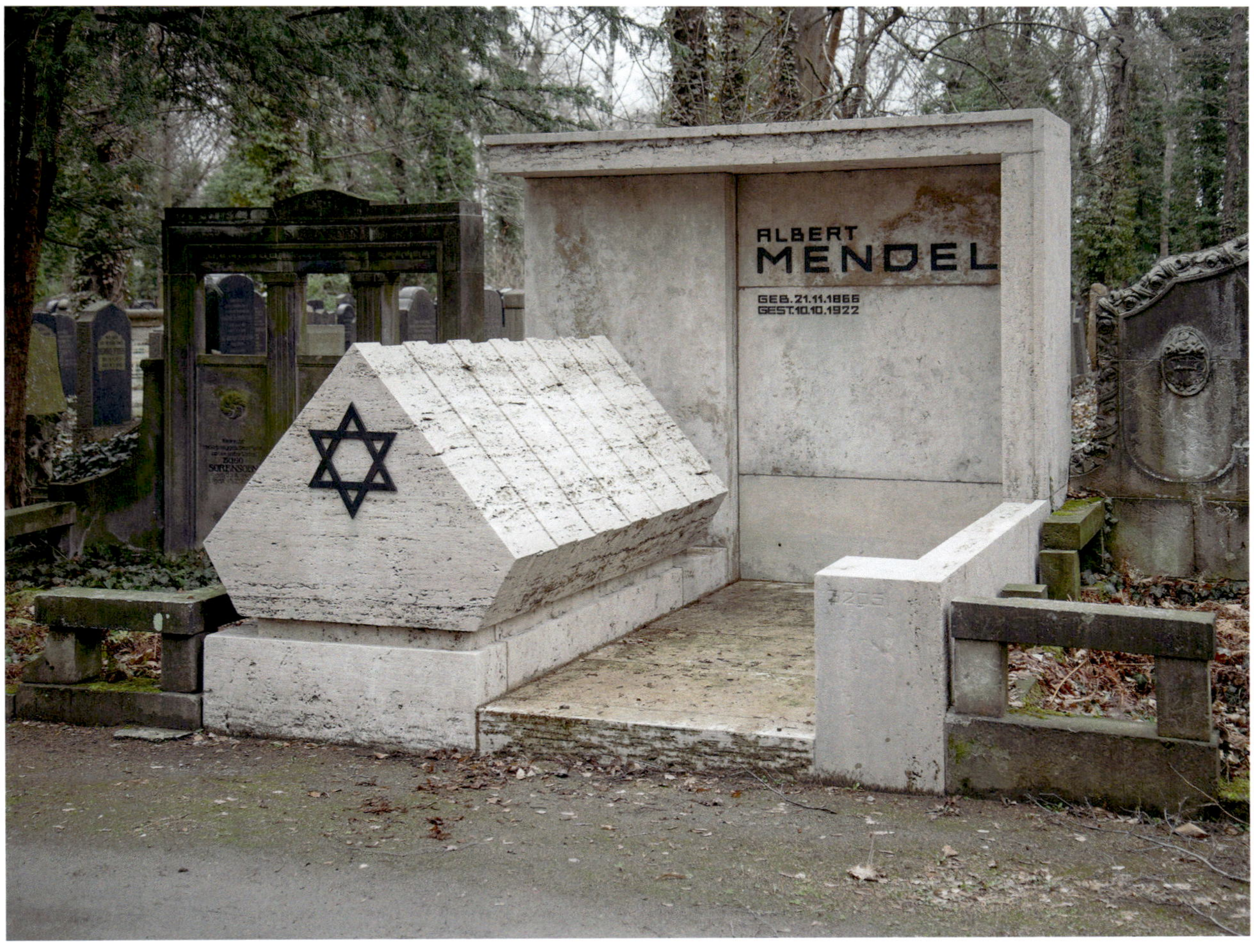

Director's Office at the Bauhaus

Weimar, Germany
1923, reconstructed

For the first Bauhaus exhibition in 1923, Gropius as its director proposed a model office that would be designed and built by the different Bauhaus workshops. Only later did the room in Henry van der Velde's school building become Gropius' own office. The design embraced the idea of a Gesamtkunstwerk and the unity of architecture and furniture. "The Bauhaus strives to coordinate all creative effort, to achieve, in a new architecture, the unification of all training in art and design. The ultimate, if distant, goal of the Bauhaus is the collective work of art,"[1] wrote Gropius, who also considered himself an artist.[2]
The design inscribed an imaginary cube measuring 5 × 5 × 5 metres as a 'room in room' inside the rectangular space, marking its boundaries with an abstract suspended lighting fixture, a wall hanging and a carpet. The room itself was divided according to the Golden Section. The Constructivist lighting fixture shows the influence of the artists' group De Stijl.[3] Quadratic and cubic were also the central table and armchair. Adjoining the desk is a letter tray that lies directly in the sightline between the seated person and the point of entry into the room, inviting visitors to enter and move about the room. The desk is framed by a dark meandering line that runs asymmetrically around the table before rising behind the table to act as a holder for the glass shelves of the letter tray.
When the Bauhaus relocated to Dessau, Gropius took the furniture with him and incorporated them partially into his new office, which was less expressive. In 1997, the director's office was reconstructed. The original desk is now in Gropius' former house in Lincoln in the USA.

1 Walter Gropius, *Idee und Aufbau des Staatlichen Bauhauses Weimar*, Munich, 1923, p. 3. Published in English as "The Theory and Organization of the Bauhaus", in: Herbert Bayer, Walter Gropius, and Ise Gropius (Eds.), *Bauhaus 1919–1928*, New York, 1938, pp. 24–25.
2 See Reginald R. Isaacs, *Walter Gropius – Der Mensch und sein Werk*, Berlin 1983, p. 249.
3 Gerrit Rietveld had originally developed this concept for a lighting fixture, which Gropius had previously used in a modified form for the Otte House. The isometric drawing of the room produced by Herbert Bayer is likewise influenced by the style of the De Stijl group.

Reconstructed director's office

Auerbach House

Jena, Germany
1924 (with Adolf Meyer)

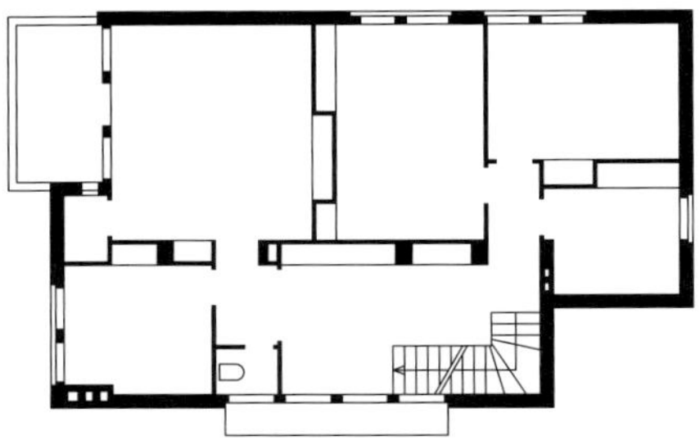

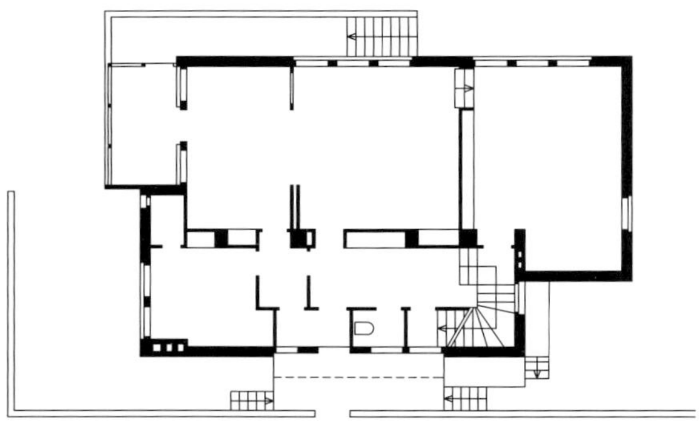

The building consists of two different-sized cubic volumes that have been pushed – slightly offset – into each other. The section facing the street contains ancillary functions such as the kitchen, bathroom, corridor and stairs, while the south-facing volume overlooking the garden houses the main space of the living room and bedrooms. The clear division between the private and public zones inside the house is not apparent from outside. Instead the facades are given rhythm by grouping windows into sets of two, three or four openings. As with Gropius and Meyer's earlier houses, a classical floor plan arrangement prevails but is given a dynamic asymmetry through the placement of the door to the garden and the stairs to the upper floor at opposite corners.

The dynamic character of the succession of spaces is further heightened by the use of colour. While the smooth external render was painted uniformly white, with only the blue window frames and red metal balustrades adding colour accents, the walls of the interior were richly coloured. The original colour scheme devised by the Bauhaus student and later Master Alfred Arndt was restored as part of comprehensive renovation works in 1995.[1] Over 30 different colours, predominantly light pastel colours but also dark red for the handrails and dark blue for the smaller spaces, create a polychromic interior that highlights the different roles of the architectural elements. In some cases, elements were also combined by painting adjoining wall surfaces or ceiling panels the same colour.

This last building to be designed together with Adolf Meyer[2] bears no trace of the expressive motifs of past buildings. The uncompromisingly orthogonal building with its flat roofs, used partially as roof terraces, appears disconnected from the ground due to its stepped-back base and the fact that its position on a sloping site entailed entering via a walkway. The external walls were porous slag blocks that were made with cement on site, while the internal walls are mostly double-skin partitions which often also serve as interior fittings with built-in cupboards and shelves. Similarly, the living and dining room can be divided off by a sliding glass wall that disappears into the wall.

The client, Felix Auerbach, a renowned professor of physics at the University of Jena, and his wife Anne were of Jewish descent and took their own lives shortly after the Nazis came to power in 1933.

1 The new owners of the house describe the building and its renovation in a book: Barbara Happe and Martin S. Fischer, *Haus Auerbach von Walter Gropius mit Adolf Meyer*, Tübingen 2003.
2 Little is known about the separation of the two architects. After the closure of the Bauhaus in Weimar and its relocation to Dessau, Meyer decided to continue running an office under his own name in Weimar. Gropius had, it seemed, never offered him equal partnership in the office.

Upper floor plan
Ground floor plan

View from the southeast
View from the east

Stepped-back base
Door to the conservatory
Entrance area

Staircase
Wall unit
Sliding door between the living and dining room

Müller Factory

Kirchbrak, Germany
1925–26

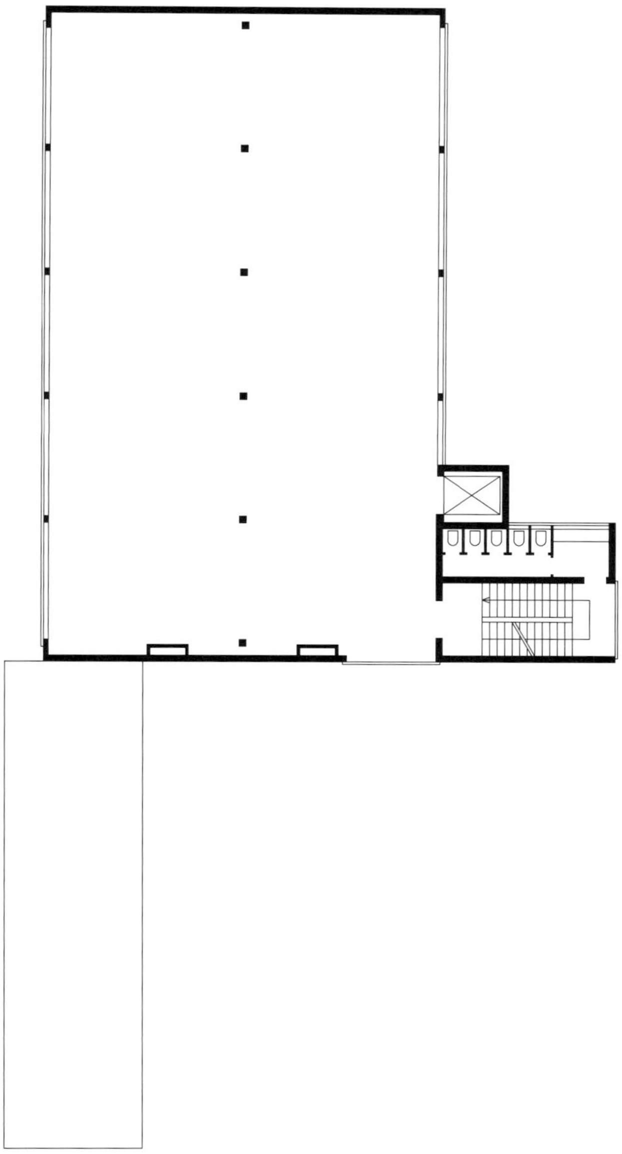

Gropius' first commission after moving with the Bauhaus from Weimar to Dessau arose through a recommendation by Carl Benscheidt, the owner of the Fagus Factory. It was for an extension to a wood product factory for August Müller & Co.[1] The production hall for manufacturing wooden furniture parts was a reinforced concrete skeleton frame construction with white-rendered masonry walls and blue painted window profiles. Next to the main section, its floor plan proportioned according to the Golden Section, was an access tower with lift, staircase and sanitary facilities and a second lower single-storey building. The fact that Ernst Neufert signed the plans for the planning permission indicates that Gropius had evidently entrusted him with a degree of autonomy. The building has since been altered several times.

The design is objective in the sense that it fulfilled its practical purpose. A building "can lay claim to beauty as long as it remains objective,"[2] wrote Gropius at the time and employed smooth, even surfaces in an attempt to strive for geometric clarity rather than tectonic expression. "The effect of the surface is so powerful because the subtle subdivisions create no contrast between light and shadow."[3] Proportions played a central role in this process of abstraction, and Gropius, like Mies van der Rohe recognised its spiritual value: "Proportion is a matter of the spiritual world: material and construction appears as its bearers with the help of which it manifests the spirit of its master. It is tied to the function of the structure, gives evidence of its substance and gives it its suspense – spiritual life over and above the value of its usefulness."[4]

1 Karin Wilhelm, *Walter Gropius Industriearchitekt*, Braunschweig, Wiesbaden 1983, pp. 107–111.
2 Walter Gropius, "Grundlagen für Neues Bauen", in: Hartmut Probst and Christian Schädlich, *Walter Gropius – Band 3: Ausgewählte Ausgewählte Schriften*, Berlin 1987, p. 109, originally in: *Bau- und Werkkunst*, 1925–26, pp. 134–147.
3 Ibid., p. 108. Gropius was referring here to skyscrapers in the USA.
4 Walter Gropius, "Die neue Baugesinnung", in ibid., p. 95, originally in: *Innendekoration*, No. 36, 1925, pp. 134–137.

Upper floor plan
View from the north

Bauhaus

Dessau, Germany
1925–26

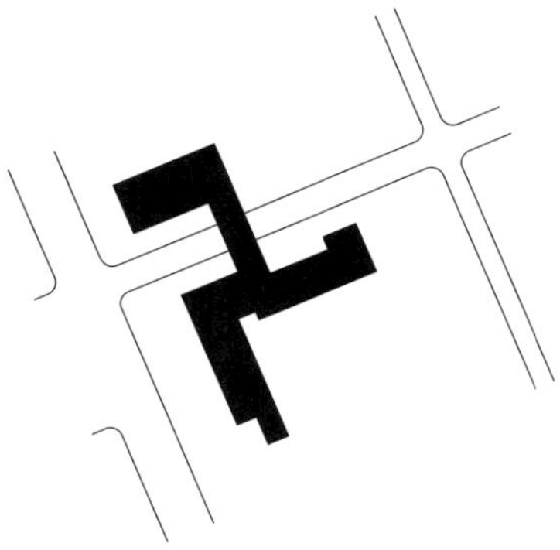

The Bauhaus building comprises three parts: a workshop wing, a studio building with student accommodation and roof terrace and a wing for the technical school. Despite the quite different design of the three wings, which extend outwards in pinwheel fashion, they read as parts of a whole. The almost completely glazed workshop wing with the main entrance extends out over the road with a bridge-like office section and connects to the studio building via a single-storey element. This low-rise section contains communal spaces such as the auditorium and adjoining stage area that also opens onto the canteen. Gropius also showed aerial photographs with a bird's eye view of the building, emphasising that it should also appear designed when seen from this perspective. "One must walk around this building in order to understand the three-dimensional character of its form and the function of its parts."[1]

The design and manufacture of the furniture, the lighting and the colours of the interior was undertaken in the Bauhaus workshops. Gropius utilised many construction details previously used in his industrial buildings. The exposed concrete construction bearing the section

Site plan
The entire complex with workshop wing and studio building

bridging the road bears similar detailing to his factory buildings from that time. The supporting concrete beams, for example, widened to meet the columns, forming diagonal brackets.[2] In contrast to the factory buildings, however, the concrete surfaces were subsequently worked. The columns are also cruciform with indented edges and grow more slender towards the ground. Although the architecture celebrates its technical form, it is not entirely free of classical elements, such as the monumental staircase and the articulated base of the building.
Despite having embraced the romantic call for a return to craftsmanship only a few years earlier, here he declared craftsmanship as obsolete. "Modern architecture hand in hand with technology has developed a characteristic face that is considerably different from that of the old crafts-oriented building arts. Its typical traits are clear, well-proportioned features."[3] The primary criteria for a "good floor plan" according to Gropius were a clear separation of different functional areas and the flexibility afforded by a skeleton frame construction.[4]

One parallel to the Expressionist phase of innovation that emerged in the post-war years is the excessive – but also climatically unfavourable – use of glass. "Glass architecture, until recently a poetic utopia, is now becoming reality unconstrained," wrote Gropius.[5] Later he would say: "This transparency aims at producing the illusion of a floating continuity of space. The building appears to float and space flows through it."[6] The skeleton frame construction with cantilevered floor slabs made it possible to create vertical window bands and a glass curtain wall with transparent glazed corners.

1 Walter Gropius, *Bauhausbauten Dessau*, Munich 1930, p. 19.
2 This efficient construction had already been tried and tested in the Hanover Paper Factory, the Kappe Storage Warehouse and the Müller Factory.
3 Walter Gropius, op. cit., p. 83.
4 Ibid., p. 20.
5 Walter Gropius, "glasbau" (Glass Architecture), in: Hartmut Probst and Christian Schädlich, *Walter Gropius – Band 3: Ausgewählte Schriften*, Berlin 1987, pp. 103 & 105, originally in: *Die Bauzeitung*, May 1926, pp. 159–162.
6 Walter Gropius, *Architektur – Wege zu einer optischen Kultur*, Frankfurt am Main, Hamburg 1956, p. 39.

Workshop wing, view from the south

Northern wing
Trade school facade

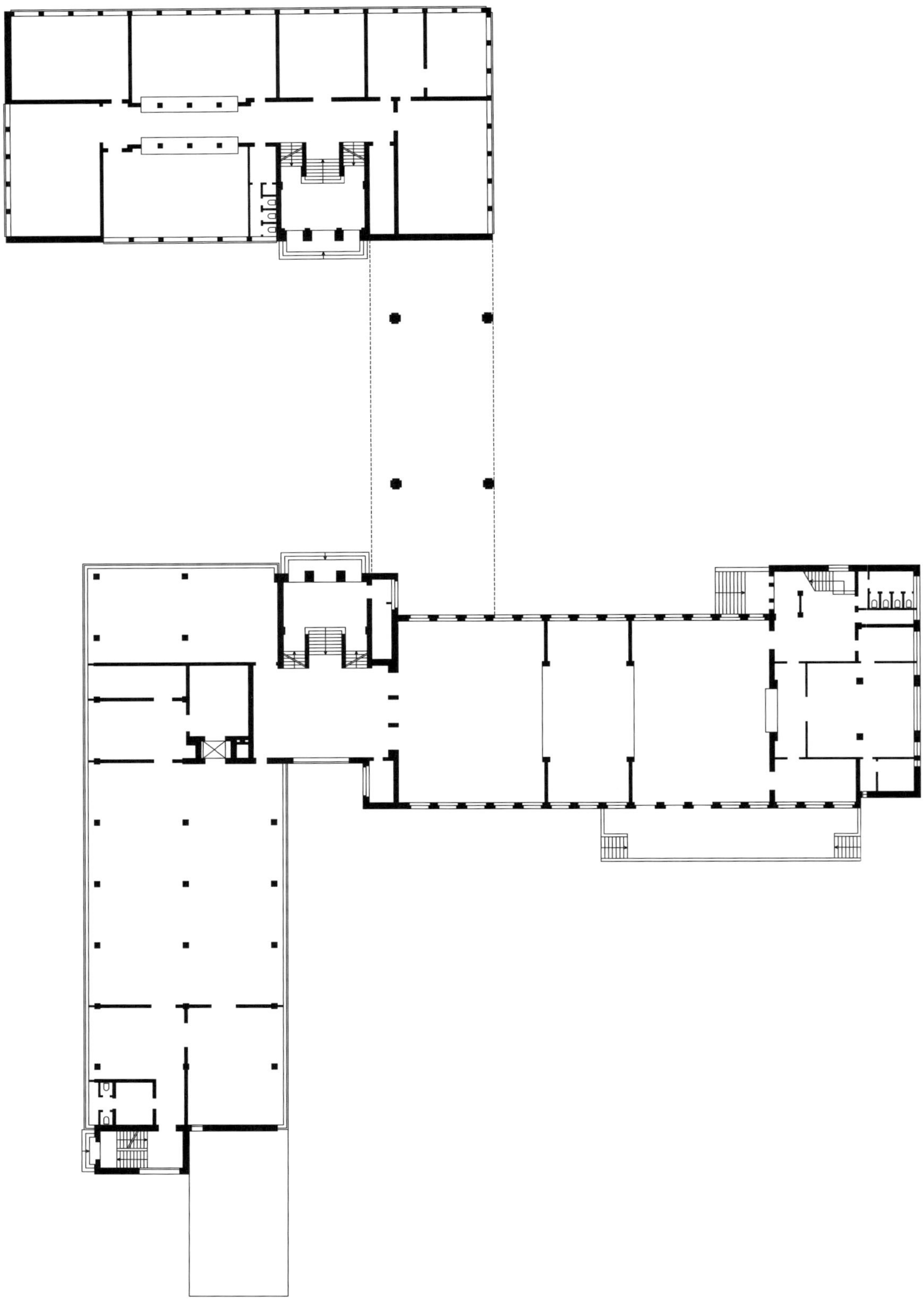

Ground floor plan

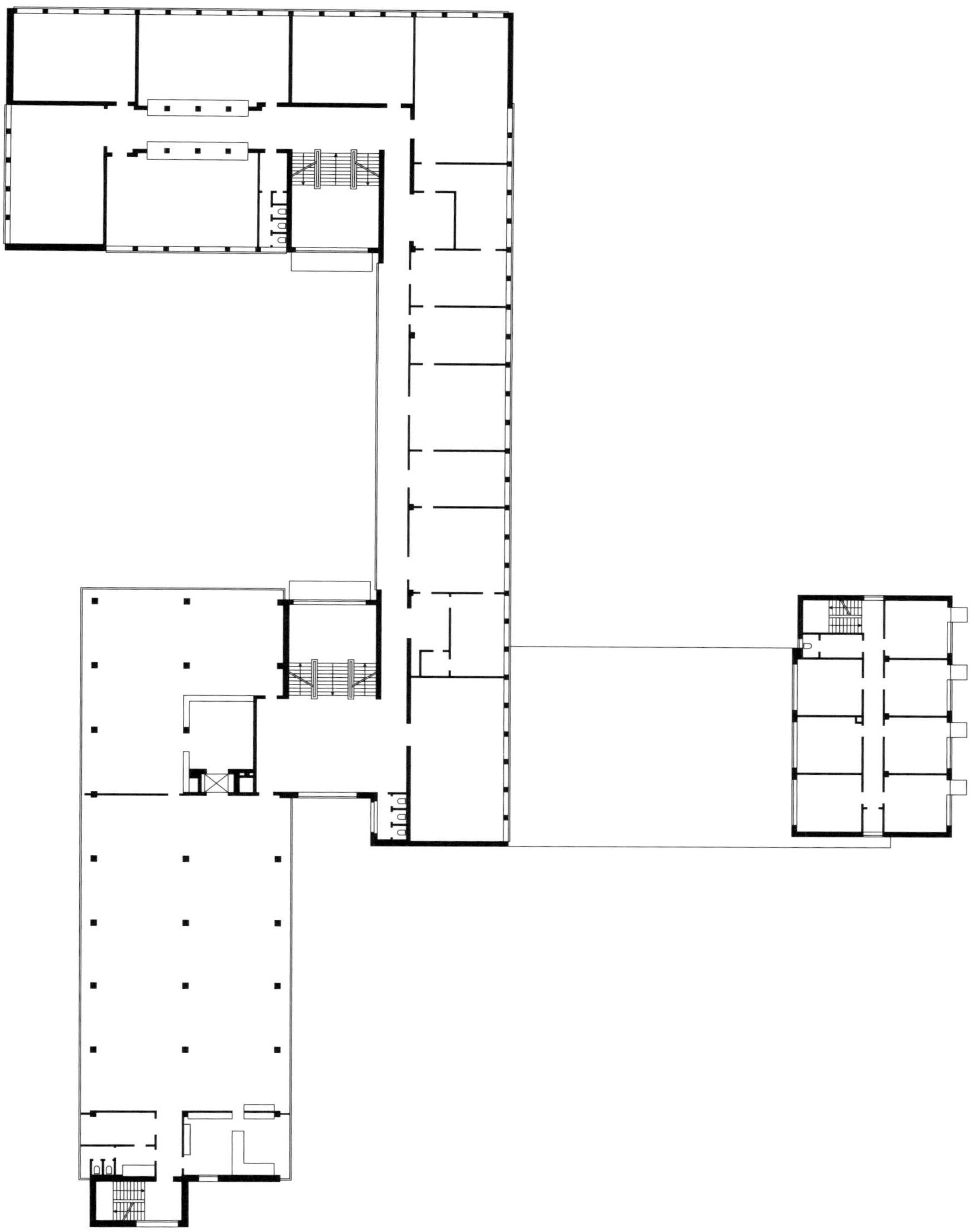

Upper floor plan

Construction over the road
Southern and eastern wings of the building

Workshop wing
Curtain wall

Corner of the building
Connecting corridor

Studio building
East-facing facade

Entrance hall of the studio building
Main stairs
Lighting by László Moholy-Nagy

Staircase of the studio building
Entrance to the main hall
Main hall with furniture by Marcel Breuer

Masters' Houses

Dessau, Germany
1925–26

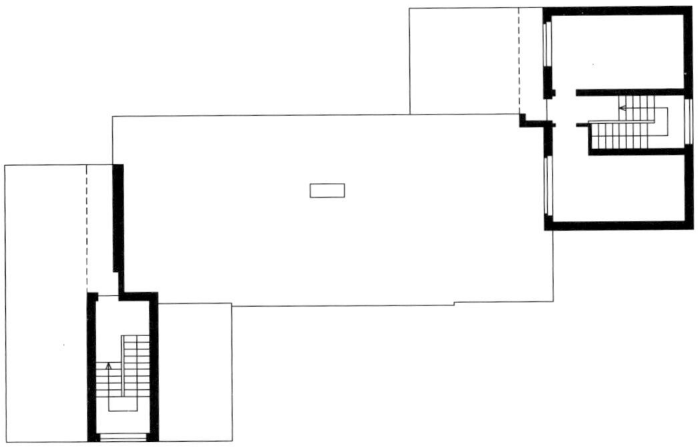

Not far from the Bauhaus building, Gropius was able to build a series of houses embedded in pine woodland for the Bauhaus masters. Three pairs of houses were built for László Moholy-Nagy, Lyonel Feininger, Georg Muche, Oskar Schlemmer, Wassily Kandinsky and Paul Klee along with a single house for the director which Gropius moved into. The rent and running costs were above-average and the fact that housing had been provided only for the senior Bauhaus masters became the cause of some discontent. The design and colour of the interiors were developed together with the artists who moved into the houses with their families.

"All six dwellings in the three double houses are the same but different in the impression they make," explained Gropius.[1] The asymmetrical composition of the interlocking volumes is a product of the mirroring and 90-degree-rotation of the plan of one of the halves. Not only the balconies and roof slabs cantilever outwards but also the upper storeys, which, like Gropius' earlier houses, are larger than the ground floors.[2] The central area of the house is the studio on the upper floor, which is higher than the other rooms. On entering, the houses appear small and fragmented: the number of doors create the impression of being convoluted, in stark contrast to the expansive spaciousness of the studios with their floor-to-ceiling glazing.

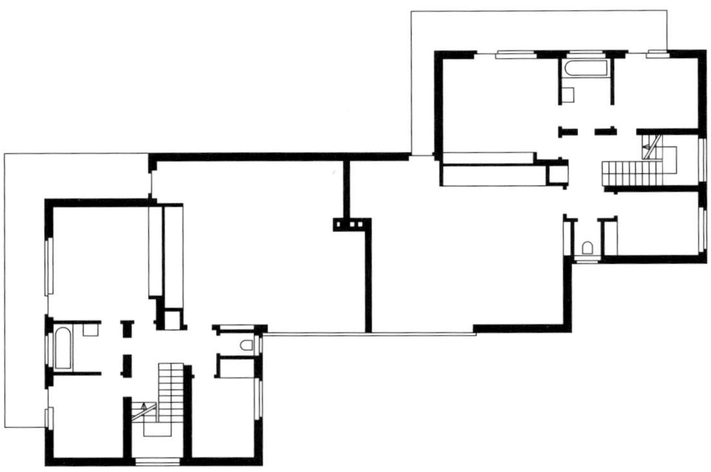

More than in any other of his works, Gropius draws here on the design concepts of De Stijl as proclaimed by Theo van Doesburg in his 16-point manifesto "Towards a Plastic Architecture" published in 1924.[3] Mirror-image arrangements should be avoided, as should encapsulating all functions in a single cubic form. The forward-facing planes of protruding elements were painted in the primary colours red, yellow and blue.

The house for Moholy-Nagy at the eastern end was destroyed in 1945 and the remaining five houses were drastically altered over the years. Since then, all the existing buildings have been restored to their original state while the house for Moholy-Nagy and Gropius' house next to it have been reconstructed as abstract 1:1 'models' by the architects Bruno Fioretti Marquez in 2010

1 Walter Gropius, *Bauhausbauten Dessau*, Munich 1930, p. 86.
2 The Sommerfeld House, the Sommerfeld row houses, the Stöckle House and the unrealised project for an estate in Berlin-Haselhorst (1929) all feature cantilevered upper storeys.
3 Published in: *De Stijl*, No. 6/7, 1924.

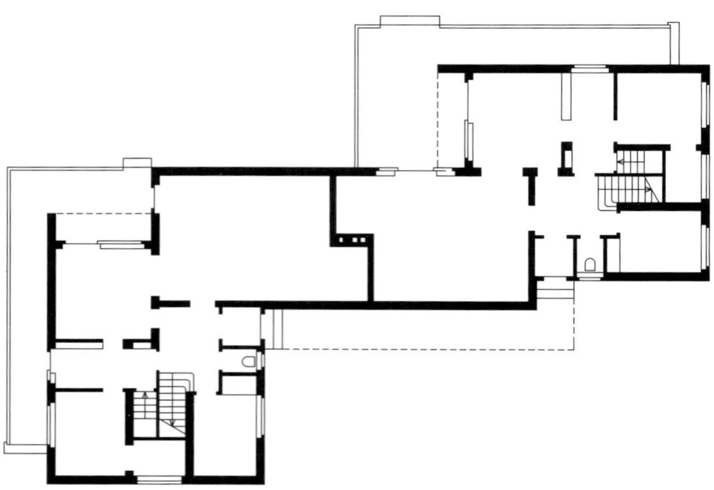

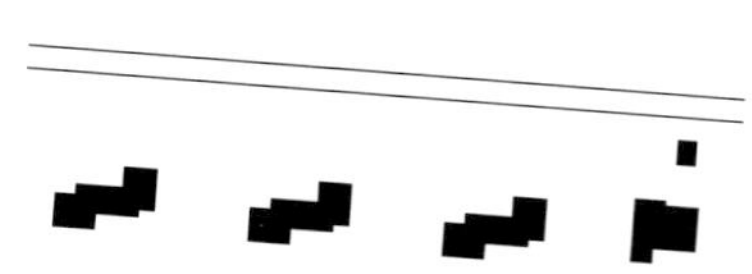

Roof-level floor plan
Upper floor plan
Ground floor plan
Site plan

East elevation of a pair of houses
László Moholy-Nagy's house

Pair of houses for Georg Muche and Oskar Schlemmer
View from the southeast

View from the north
View from the northeast

Paul Klee's house, upper floor
Paul Klee's house, ground floor

Paul Klee's house, bedroom
Paul Klee's house, stair to the roof
Wassily Kandinsky's house

Gropius House

Dessau, Germany
1925–26, reconstructed

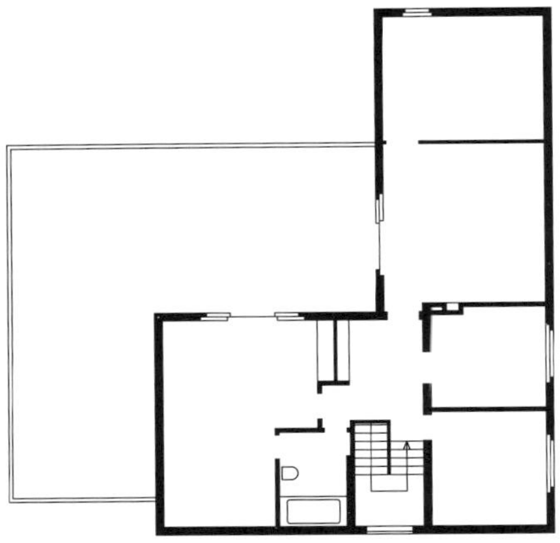

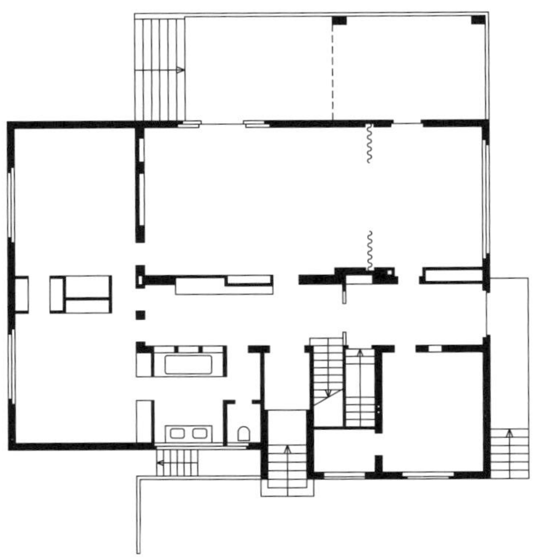

Gropius planned the house for himself as director of the Bauhaus at the eastern end of the row of Masters' Houses. While the latter stand on an open grassy site without any fencing, the garden of this house is surrounded by a wall.[1] Like the pairs of Masters' Houses, the house is a configuration of interlocking cubic forms. Although the upper floor does not actually cantilever outwards, the dark, reflective cladding of the corner pillar creates the impression that it does. The use of a dark-coloured base on some sections of the building further heightens the impression of floating elements. While the Masters' Houses are only minimally raised above the garden, the ground floor here lies significantly higher.

The ground level of the house is very clearly divided into separate functional zones. The serving spaces – bathroom, WC, larder and kitchen – face the road while the living and dining areas face south and the bedroom west. As was customary for upper-middle-class villas at that time, the house also contains rooms for a maid and janitor. The interiors were partitioned by shelving elements which, like the tubular steel furniture and wall colouring, were designed by Marcel Breuer[2] with whom Gropius would later enter into an office partnership. In the tradition of the total work of art, the furniture and architecture were part of the same composition: "The dissolution of the loadbearing walls into pillars made it possible to use the wall depth for fitted cupboards."[3] While the living room was given a more discreet colour, the curtains of the roof terrace were orange.[4] The living and dining area could also be separated off by a curtain. Gropius strove here, as with the Masters' Houses, to "make

Upper floor plan
Ground floor plan
Reconstructed house

it possible to go outside from every room".[5] He additionally created a strong connection between indoors and outdoors by glazing one side of the terrace, creating an outdoor room.

In the book *Bauhausbauten Dessau* Gropius presented the house in numerous sequences of film stills that demonstrated the use and flexibility of the built elements, such as the opening and closing of cupboard doors, sliding elements, the collapsing of a twin sofa and the handling of the walk-in wardrobe. He wanted to demonstrate its function: "Building means designing life processes. The organism of a building results from the course of processes that play out within it. In a residence these are the functions of dwelling, sleeping, bathing, cooking, which necessarily lend form to the overall shape of the house."[6] The house was destroyed in 1945 and in 2010 reconstructed in an abstract form by the architects Bruno Fioretti Marquez. The volume of the building was erected on the foundation and base of the original while the interior serves as an exhibition space.

1 Mies van der Rohe later inserted a kiosk, the "Trinkhalle" (refreshment stand), into the wall.
2 Walter Gropius, *Bauhausbauten Dessau*, Munich 1930, p. 102.
3 Ibid.
4 Ibid., p. 97.
5 Ibid., p. 134.
6 Ibid., p. 92.

Entrance facade
Garden elevation

Törten Housing Estate

Dessau, Germany
1926–28

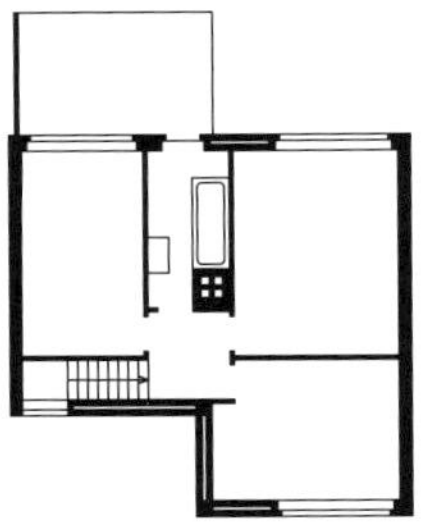

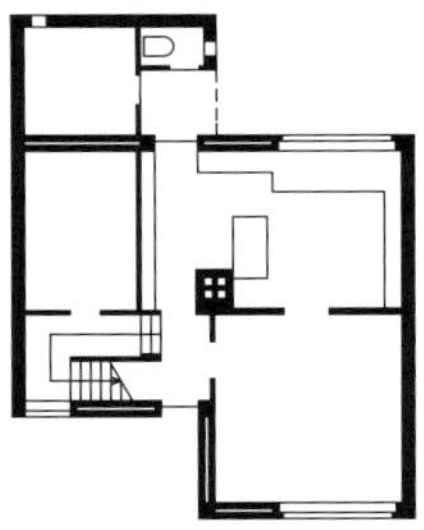

Although Gropius already had prior experience of designing workers' housing, the buildings for this estate were experimental prototypes with a radical intention: "The objective was the rationalisation of all construction processes under the primary consideration of reducing costs."[1] The floor plans of these low-income houses were so compact that a sitting bathtub was located in the kitchen, though this was later enlarged in subsequent apartment types in 1927. As with Gropius' previous workers' housing, the toilets were not connected to the drains, a choice he justified by citing the possibility of waste usage for self-sufficiency: "As this is a semi-rural estate, with kitchen gardens of 350–400 m^2 per household, only waste water from the kitchen and rainwater will feed into the drains while toilet waste will be collected for using as compost for the kitchen gardens."[2] The estate similarly featured outbuildings for keeping livestock.

A central aspect of the drive for cost-effectiveness through rationalisation was the organisation of the construction process like a production line. While the founding manifesto of the Bauhaus had advocated the skills of the craftsman, Gropius noted with respect to Törten that: "the existing crafts-oriented character of construction is gradually shifting towards large-scale industrial manufacture."[3] In the publication *Bauhausbauten Dessau* he showed the building process using sequences of film stills, presenting a site plan that depicted a mobile crane on railway tracks as justification for the housing blocks' linear layout. Like the Masters' Houses, large-format slag concrete blocks were used. The floor joists were pre-cast concrete elements from which the steel windows were hung before the non-loadbearing wall panels were filled with brick masonry. In a later variant of the building type from 1927 onwards, the strip windows were made longer. One hundred and thirty complete rendered dwellings were produced in just 88 work days: "that is, 0.67 days per dwelling unit or 5½ work hours per unit."[4]

Like the Masters' Houses, the buildings stood on an open grassland site while the colour scheme for the interior walls was developed at the Bauhaus along with typical items of furniture by Marcel Breuer. The blocks were augmented by a tower-like building, the so-called Konsumverein, with several apartments and series of shops. Alterations made by subsequent residents have all but eradicated the original appearance of the estate. However, a few houses have been carefully restored or returned to their original condition.

1 Walter Gropius, *Bauhausbauten Dessau*, Munich 1930, p. 153.
2 Ibid., p. 155.
3 Ibid., p. 158.
4 Ibid., p. 155.

Floor plan type 1927, upper floor
Floor plan type 1927, ground floor
Houses type 1927

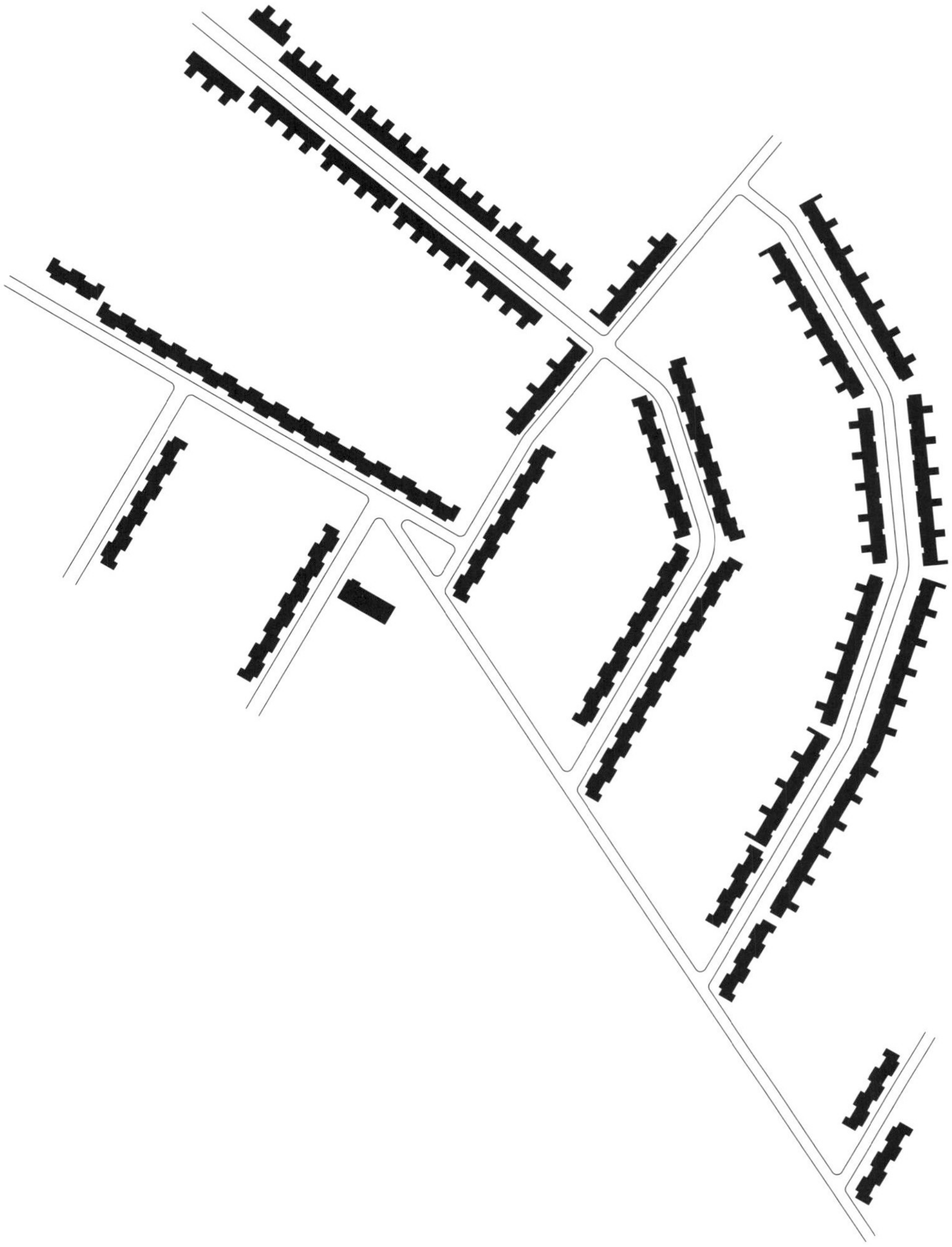

Site plan

House type 1928, street elevation
House type 1928, garden elevation

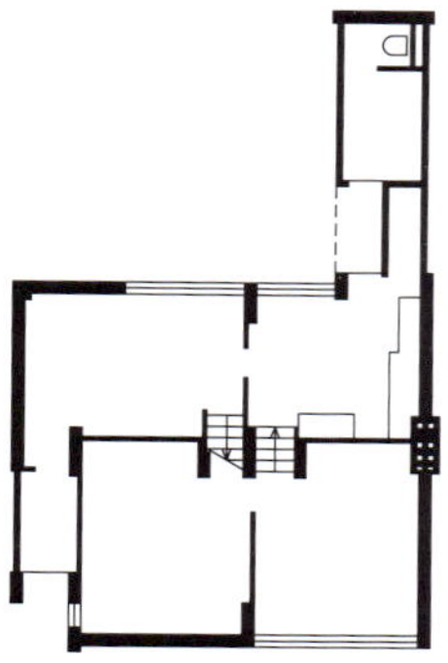

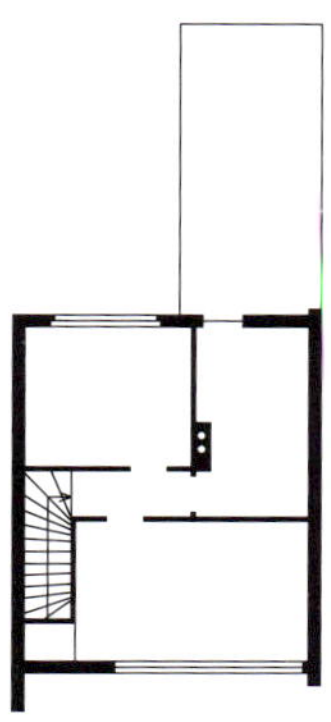

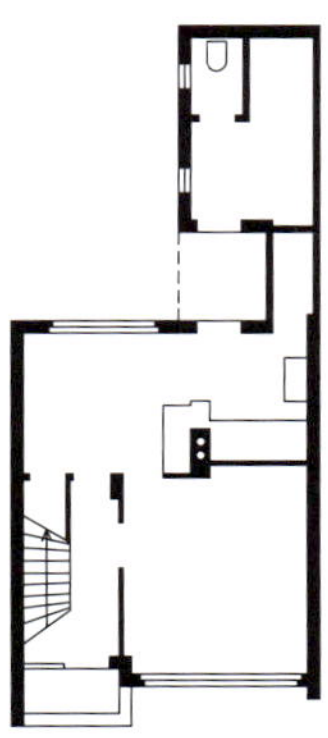

Floor plan type 1928, ground floor
Floor plan type 1926, upper floor
Floor plan type 1926, ground floor
House type 1926
House type 1926, entrance

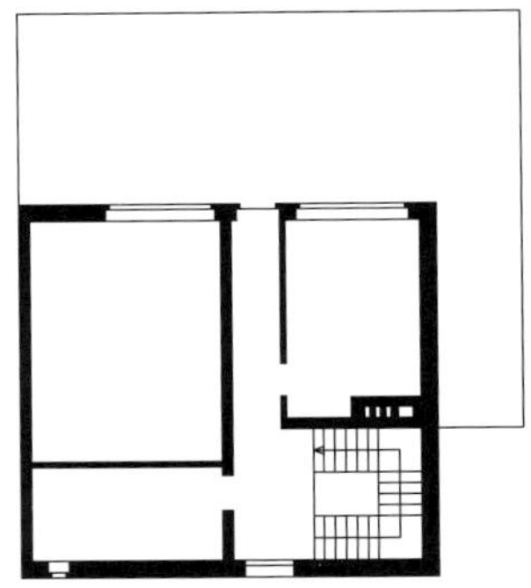

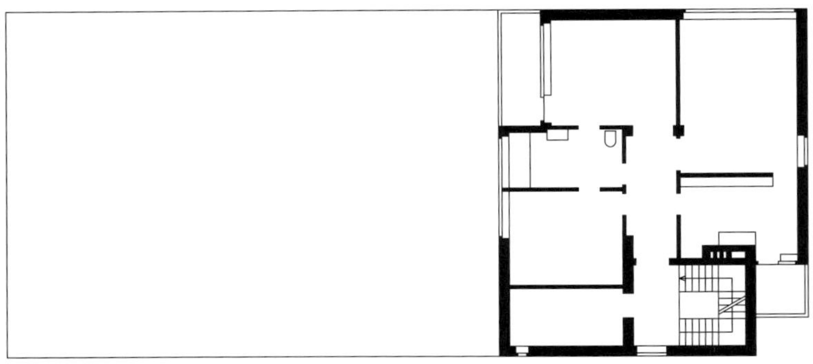

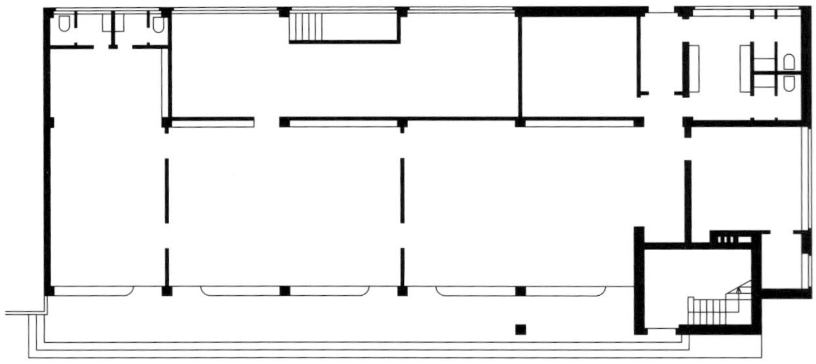

Floor plan of Konsumverein building, roof level
Upper floor
Ground floor

Konsumverein building, view from the northeast
View from the southwest

Weissenhofsiedlung Houses

Stuttgart, Germany
1927, destroyed

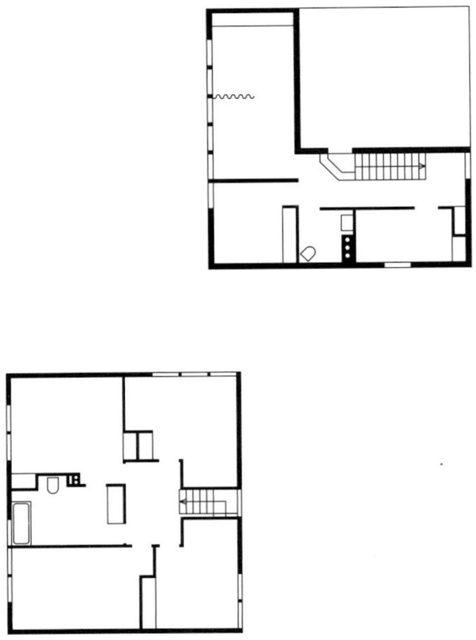

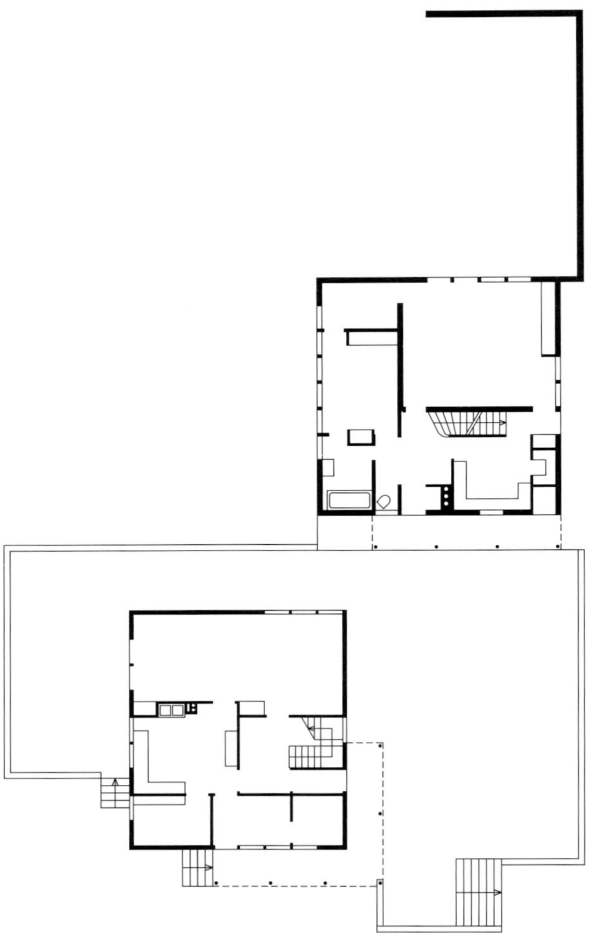

Gropius designed two houses for the German Werkbund's housing exhibition which Mies van der Rohe, as the organiser, described as "the most interesting houses in the exhibition".[1] Like Mies, Gropius experimented with a steel skeleton frame construction. While House 16 to the south was a masonry structure with traditional render, House 17, which was set back further down from the road, was made of pre-cast elements. Clad with Eternit panels and insulated with cork, this "experimental house"[2] had much thinner walls than a conventional house. The tubular steel furniture was designed by Marcel Breuer.

Although just a few years earlier Gropius had described his "large-scale building kit" as an "additive system of connected cellular rooms"[3] for achieving maximum flexibility, these houses contained all functions in a simple cubic volume from which one corner was subtracted to function as a roof terrace. The incorporation of different spaces into a single block that Theo van Doesburg and De Stijl so vehemently opposed is here the product of an efficient loadbearing structure whose 1.06-metre grid was calculated to ensure that normed door sizes could be used. The window profiles were made of metal. The lightweight construction of House 17 can be seen in the exposed panelling inside and outside and the placement of a window at the corner of the facade.

1 Ludwig Mies van der Rohe in a speech held on 18 May 1953 in Chicago, in: Sigfried Giedion, *Walter Gropius – Work and Teamwork*, New York 1954, p. 18.
2 Walter Gropius, "wege zur fabrikatorischen hausherstellung" (The path to industrialised house building), in: Deutscher Werkbund (Ed.), *Bau und Wohnung*, Stuttgart 1927, p. 60.
3 Walter Gropius in a description of a "honeycomb architecture" on an exhibition panel from 1923. See Winfried Nerdinger, *The Architect Walter Gropius*, Berlin 1985, p. 59.

Floor plans of the two houses, upper floor
Floor plans of the two houses, ground floor

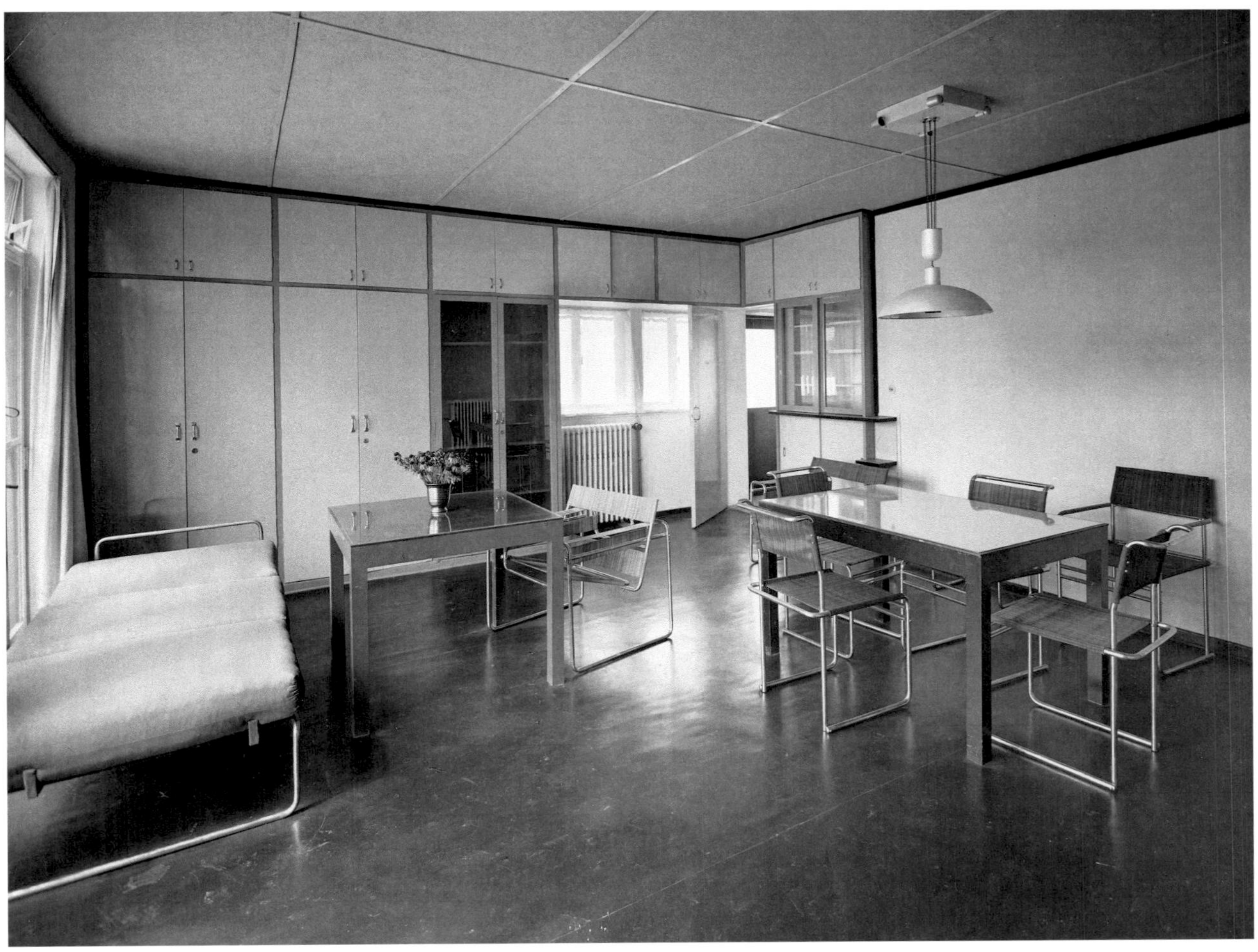

House 16, view from the road
House 16, living and dining room

Municipal Employment Office

Dessau, Germany
1927–29

Arranged around the outside of the freestanding building are a series of doors. The numerous entry points and semi-circular floor plan are a direct response to the task of providing "employment services for a large number of job-seekers of various vocational areas with the lowest possible number of civil servants."[1] While the waiting rooms for the various vocations are arranged in segments around the periphery of the building, the individual consultation rooms lie within. "The semi-circular form resulted in the illumination of the inner rooms with the help of concentric rings of saw-tooth roof glazing,"[2] explained Gropius, and described the role of the architect as a "co-ordinating organiser, whose business it is to resolve all the formal, technical, sociological and commercial problems, and combine them in a comprehensive unity."[3] The floor plan was for him a means of designing life processes.

The low-rise section adjoins an administrative wing not accessible to the general public. A trench in front of this wing allowed light into the lower ground floor. The reinforced concrete skeleton frame structure is divided by concentric internal walls lined with white glazed tiles and the entire interior has a continuous glass ceiling. Additional light fittings were designed by Marianne Brandt at the Bauhaus and the furniture and colour scheme of the rooms were designed in the Bauhaus workshops, now under the directorship of Hannes Meyer who Gropius had proposed as his successor in 1928. As the new director of the Bauhaus, Meyer argued that building "has to become a collective affair".[4] At the time of its building, Meyer's ideological position seemed to echo that of Gropius, as he too declared that "building is only organisation: social, technical, economic, psychological organisation."[5]

The employment office building has since been restored, although the introduction of windows in the rounded external wall has somewhat diminished the monumental character and abstract clarity of the building's geometry.

1 Walter Gropius, *Bauhausbauten Dessau*, Munich 1930, p. 202.
2 Ibid.
3 Ibid., p. 216. English translation: Walter Gropius, *Scope of Total Architecture*, New York, 1962, p. 65.
4 Hannes Meyer, "bauen", in: *Bauhaus*, Vol. 2, 1928, pp. 12-13.
5 Ibid.

View from the north
View from the south

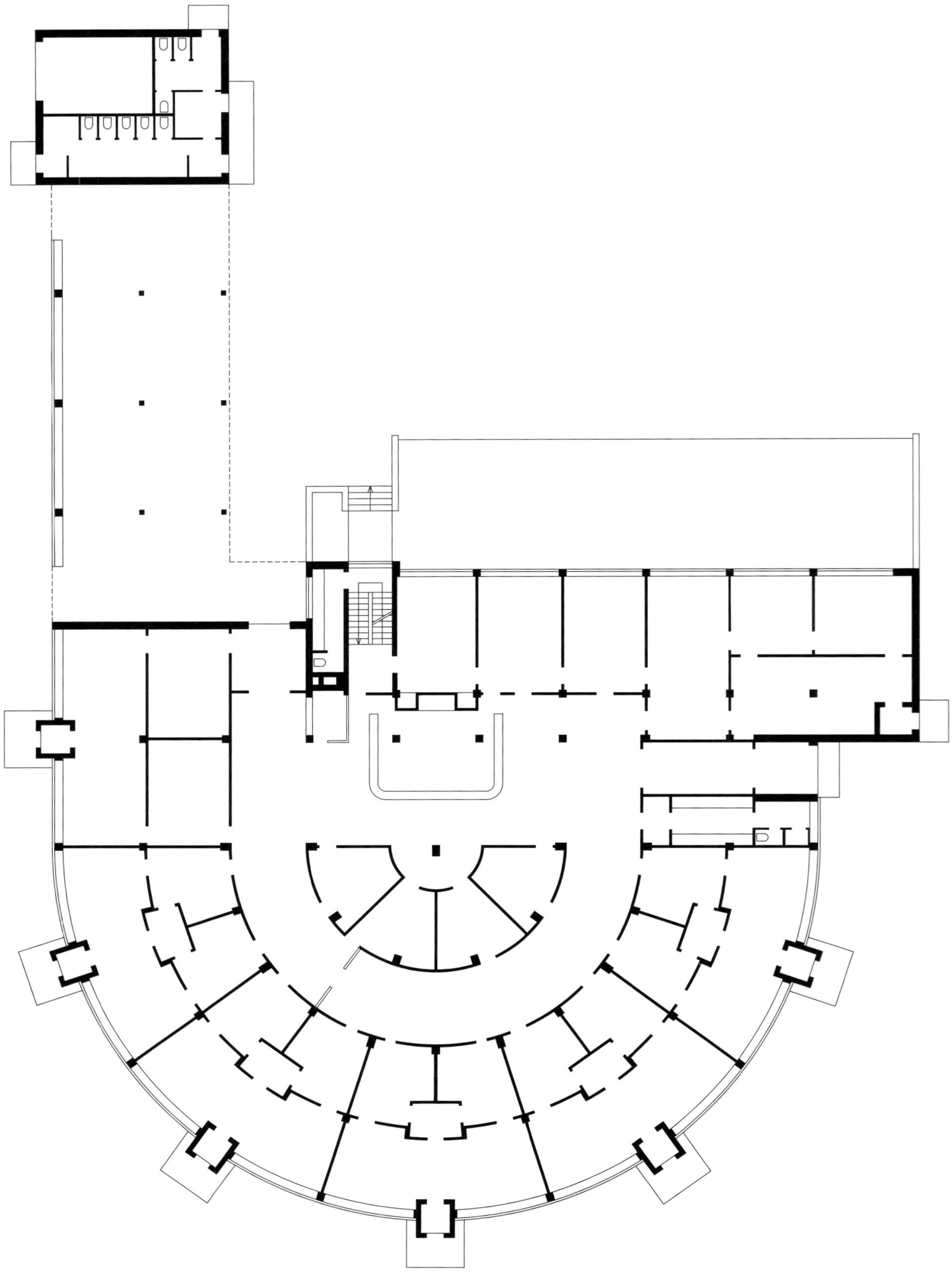

Ground floor plan

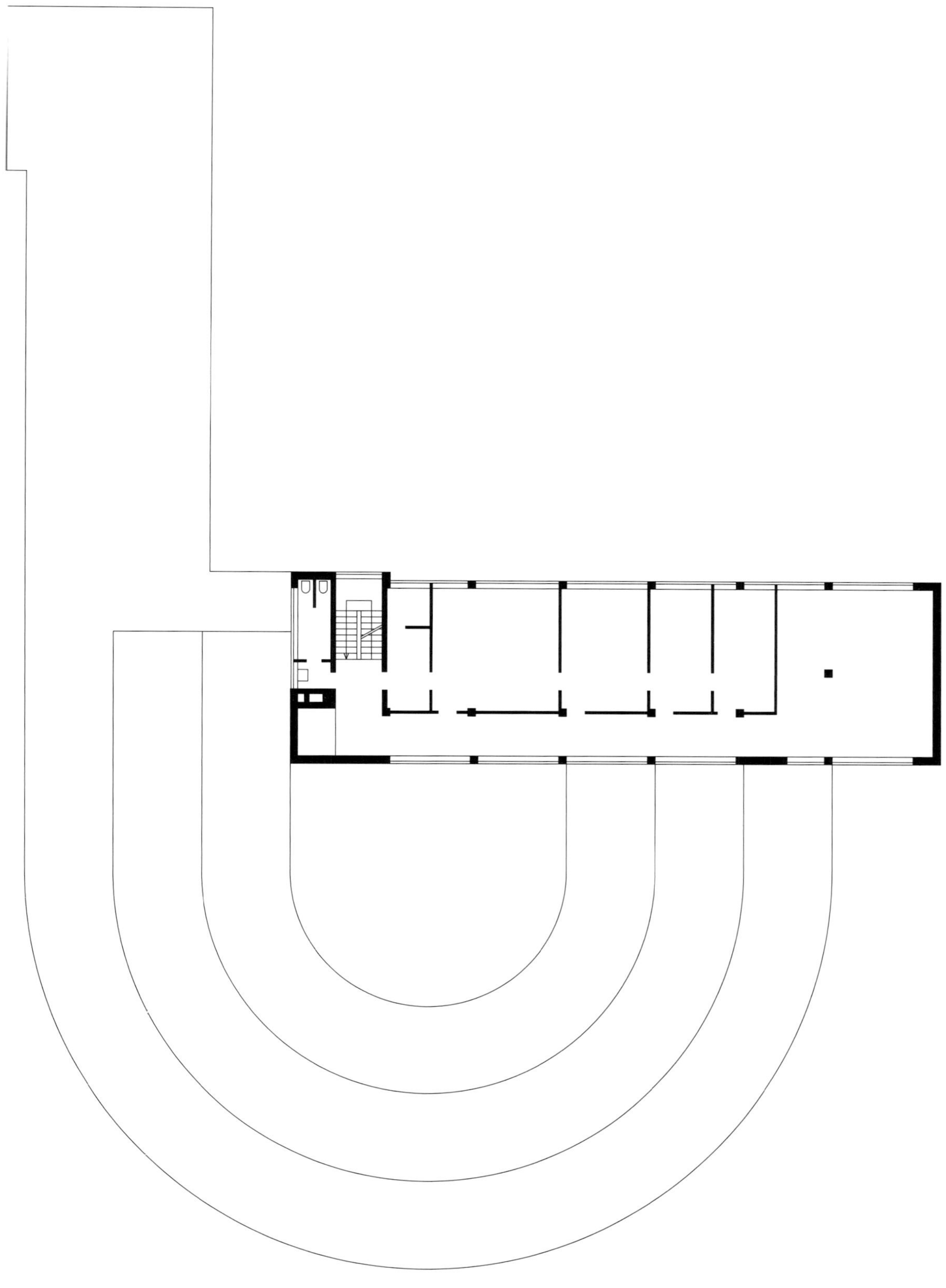

Upper floor plan

South side
North side

Inner corridor
Central register area

Zuckerkandl House

Jena, Germany
1927–29

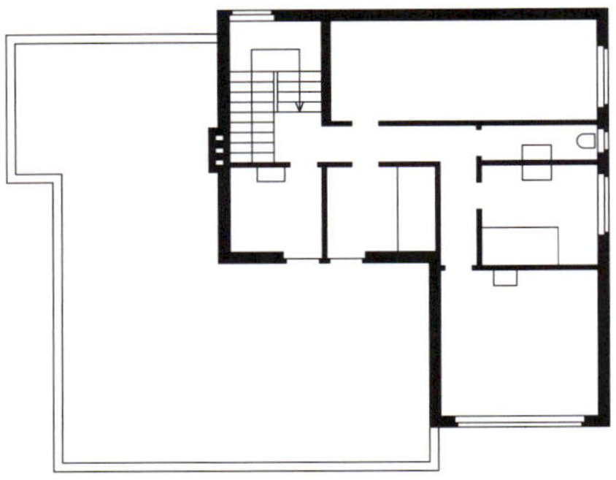

The white-rendered building rests on a dark-coloured base that is simultaneously the ground floor and entrance to the house. As with the nearby Auerbach House, which also lies on a slope, Gropius made the glass winter garden protrude forward from the base so that the house itself appears to float. Here, too, various interlocking volumes with roof terraces create an asymmetrical composition. The geometric clarity of the abstract cubic volumes is a product of the use of flat roofs, which at the time were controversially discussed. The interior walls are designed as wall cupboards and the drawers and cupboard compartments between dining room and kitchen open in both directions. While the floor covering is a light-coloured linoleum, other elements were given strong colours, such as the red lacquered metal balustrade of the staircases.

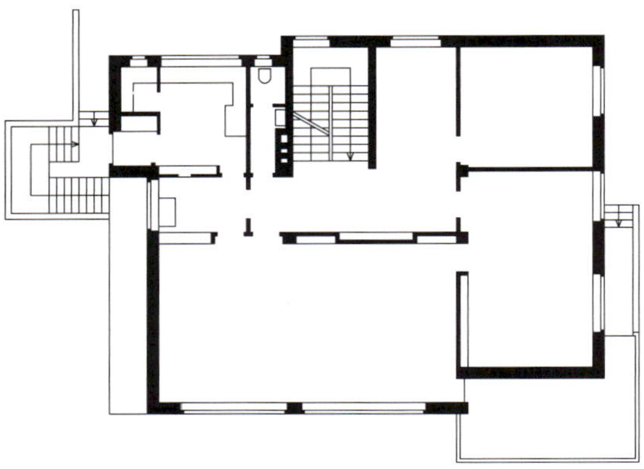

"We want to create a clear, organic architecture, whose inner logic will be radiant and naked, unencumbered by lying facades and trickeries; we want […] an architecture whose function is clearly recognizable in the relation of its form." For Gropius, the design goal was to "balance contrasts" through "an asymmetrical but rhythmical balance".[1]

The client was the widow of Professor Robert Zuckerkandl, who came from a Jewish family and worked in Vienna and Prague. When Therese Zuckerkandl received a deportation notice in 1942, she took her own life.[2]

1 Walter Gropius, *Idee und Aufbau des staatlichen Bauhauses Weimar*, Munich 1923, p. 9. Published in English as "The Theory and Organization of the Bauhaus", in: Herbert Bayer, Walter Gropius, and Ise Gropius (Eds.), *Bauhaus 1919–1928*, New York, 1938, pp. 29–30.
2 Thorsten Büker, "Jenaer Bauhaus-Villa steht zum Verkauf für zehn Millionen", in: *Ostthüringer Zeitung*, 24 October 2017.

Roof-level floor plan
Upper floor plan
Front elevation with winter garden
View from the road

AHAG Sommerfeld Exhibition

Berlin-Zehlendorf, Germany
1928 (with László Moholy-Nagy), destroyed

When Gropius left the Bauhaus in 1928, Adolf Sommerfeld, who continuously supported the Bauhaus financially, commissioned him to produce an exhibition on the Berlin housing situation and social housing construction in Berlin-Zehlendorf where Sommerfeld and his company, Allgemeine Häuserbau A.G., were heavily involved in housing construction. The exhibition was directed by László Moholy-Nagy, who Gropius valued for his artistic versatility and whose Constructivist tendencies are reflected in the architecture.

The exhibition pavilion was open to the courtyard. A linear sequence of bays opened alternately to the courtyard and the street. The roof over the garden café was also designed as a temporary timber construction. The design included words such as "Light Air Sun" in large letters that lent the exhibition the character of a Russian Constructivist project.

"The AHAG exhibition," wrote Adolf Behne, "is a new type of exhibition. Here [...] the exhibition organizes the path of the attentive visitor, and the path they take past certain objects in a certain unambiguous direction and sequence is identical with the train of thought of the exhibitors. Here, the principles of modern book direction are applied for the first time to an exhibition."[1]

1 Adolf Behne, "AHAG-Ausstellung", in: *Internationale Revue i10*, Vol. 17–18, 1928, p. 94.

Garden café
Entrance area

Lewin House

Berlin-Zehlendorf, Germany
1928–29

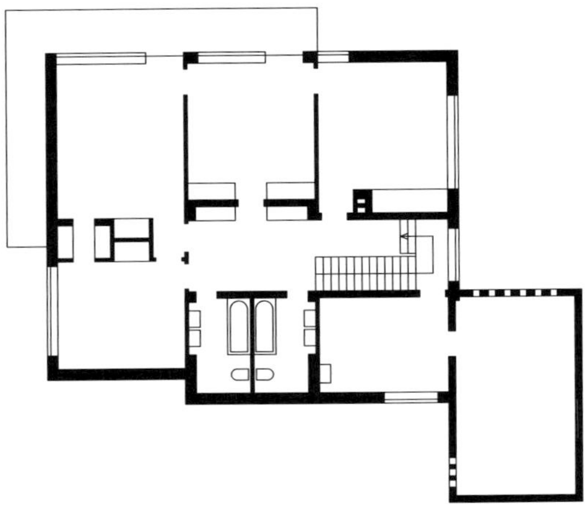

Gropius received the commission to build the residential building for the publishing director Josef Lewin through a recommendation from Adolf Sommerfeld.[1] The building, which was originally planned as a skeleton frame construction but was eventually constructed as a conventional masonry building, takes the form of a composition of blocks of different height, with a dark base and cantilevered corners.[2] The horizontal windows with metal profiles are dimensioned according to uniform modules. The central room of the house, the living and dining room, opens to the east and onto a terrace to the south. The living area, furnished only with Wassily chairs, could be separated from the dining area by a curtain, which was also furnished with chairs designed by Marcel Breuer. The rooms have a red linoleum floor and the surfaces of the built-in wall cupboards had the same wood grain as the doors. The clarity of the spaces is underlined by the flush positioning of the door and wall cupboards and their uniform veneer.

In 1933, Josef Lewin fled Germany and the house was expropriated. The composition of the house was later altered by the addition of a side extension.

1 Winfried Nerdinger, *The Architect Walter Gropius*, Berlin 1985, p. 110.
2 The completed building was published showing a floor plan that was not built, and included a grid of columns with movable partitioning walls. Cf.: "Ein Wohnhaus in Berlin-Zehlendorf", in: *Die Form*, Vol. 18, September 1929, pp. 496–499.

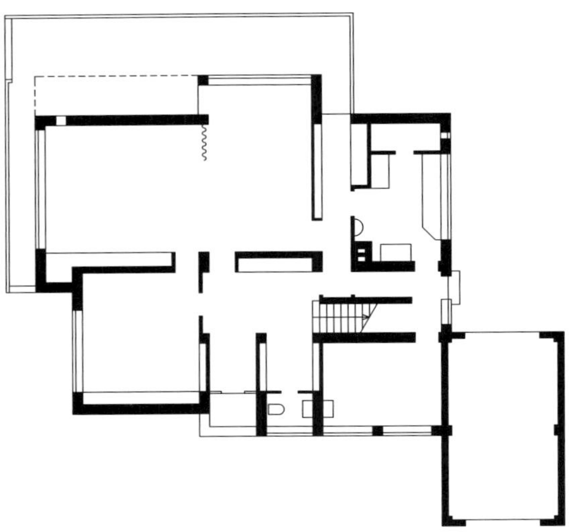

Upper floor plan
Ground floor plan
View from the garden

View from the road
Entrance facade

Dammerstock Housing Development

Karlsruhe, Germany
1928–29

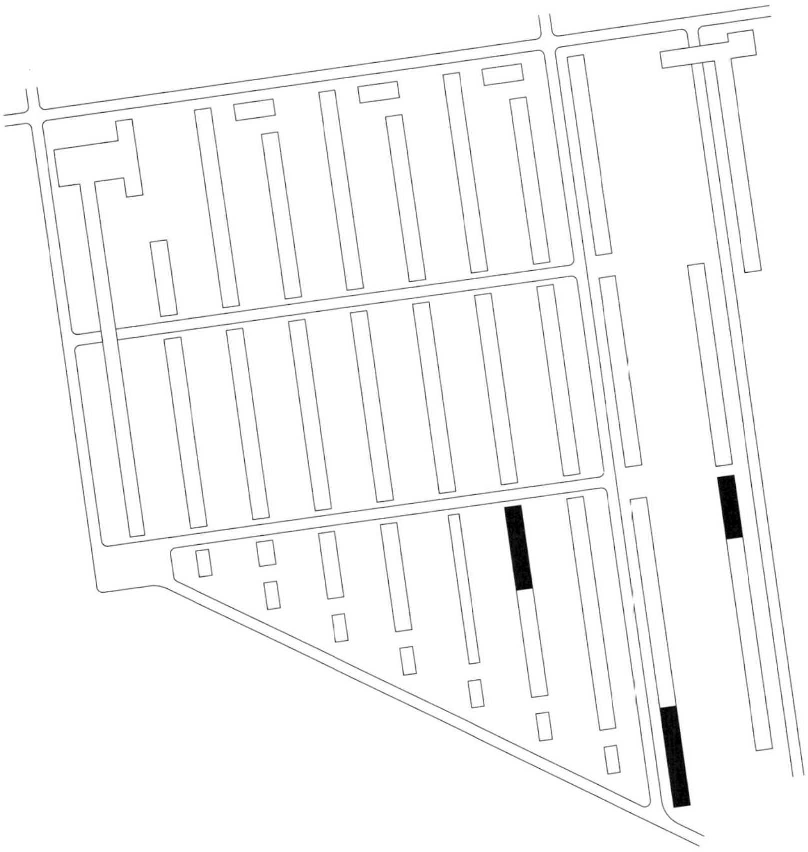

The radically linear row construction was a requirement of the competition and Gropius was commissioned with the master plan because he had most consistently implemented this principle in his design. He designed a gallery-access block, an apartment building and a row of terraced houses, while the other buildings were realised by various architects, including Otto Haesler and Wilhelm Riphahn. The global economic crisis of 1929 put a halt to the project and the second construction phase was not carried out.

Gropius' urban design concept provided pedestrian access to the terraced houses between every second row, and the floor plans are therefore mirrored with the house entrances facing sometimes west and sometimes east. This scheme, which Gropius regarded as "disadvantageous",[1] made it possible to create a private garden zone between the rows, which are laid out consistently in a north-south direction. The schematic dogmatism of this approach, in which no rooms can face south, was controversial. "The Dammerstock method is a dictatorial method," criticised Adolf Behne after completion. "The advantages of row construction are excellent and should continue to be utilised. But it can only serve urban development as a means of urban design, not in place of urban design."[2]

Although the planning intention was to achieve greater construction efficiency through the use of standard floor plans from the Reichsbauforschung, the construction costs were still above average.[3] As with the Weißenhofsiedlung in Stuttgart in 1927, various furnished show apartments could also be viewed by the general public.

1 Walter Gropius, "bebauungsplan und wohnformen der dammerstock-siedlung", in: Hartmut Probst and Christian Schädlich, *Walter Gropius – Band 3: Ausgewählte Schriften*, Berlin 1987, p. 138, originally published in: *Ausstellung Karlsruhe Dammerstock-Siedlung "Die Gebrauchswohnung"*, Karlsruhe 1929, pp. 8–9.
2 Adolf Behne, "Dammerstock", in: *Die Form*, Vol. 6, 1930, p. 165.
3 Winfried Nerdinger, *The Architect Walter Gropius*, Berlin 1985, pp. 112–114.

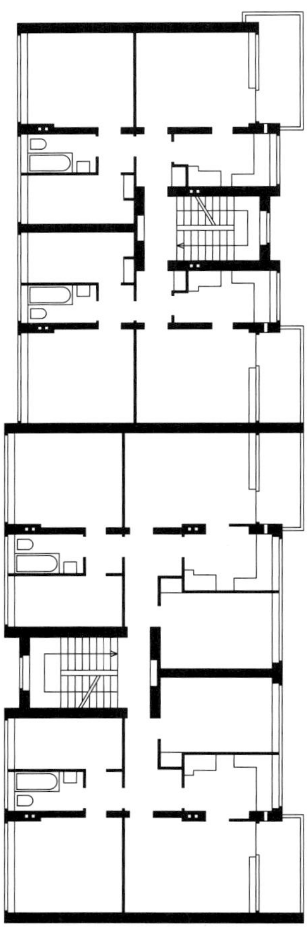

Site plan
Floor plan of apartment building
View of the entire first phase

Apartment building
West side

Gallery-access block , east side
Facade detail, west side

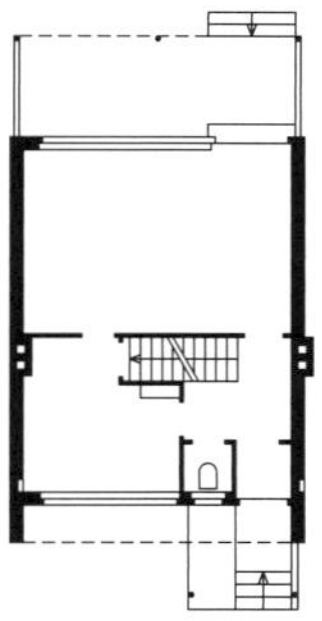

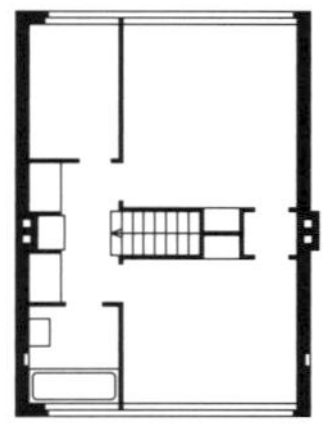

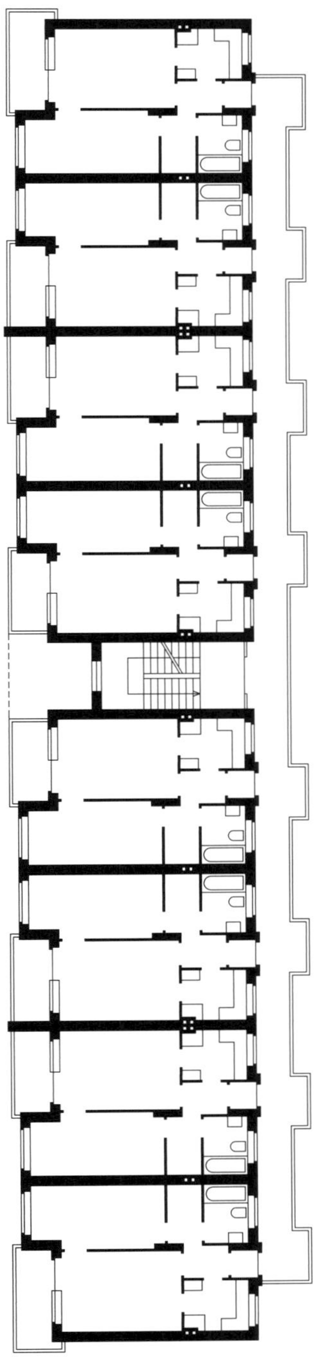

Floor plan of terraced house, ground floor
Floor plan of terraced house, upper floor
Floor plan of gallery-access block
Terraced house, east side
West side

Am Lindenbaum Housing Development

Frankfurt am Main, Germany
1929–30

The housing development along the street Am Lindenbaum was part of the "Das Neue Frankfurt" urban planning programme established by the city architect Ernst May. The long rows are capped by an end building at right angles, enclosing long U-shaped green areas between them. "Row construction has the undisputed advantage over block construction," wrote Gropius, "that the poorly ventilated corner apartments do not occur."[1] In this development, row buildings and block perimeter layouts are combined while the corners are left out for "hygienic" reasons. The originally white-painted buildings, with dark red brick-clad bases, comprised different types of "minimal apartments".

At the second CIAM congress (Congrès internationaux d'architecture moderne) in Frankfurt in 1929 on the subject of "The Minimum Dwelling", Gropius explained his conviction that "a smaller but well-disposed floor plan is of greater value to its inhabitants than a larger, irrationally distributed floor plan of the old kind."[2] At the same time, he added, "if the provision of light, sun, air and warmth is culturally more important and, with normal land prices, more economical than an increase in space, then the rules dictate: enlarge the windows, reduce the size of rooms."[3]

1 Walter Gropius, "bebauungsplan und wohnformen der dammerstock-siedlung", in: Hartmut Probst and Christian Schädlich, *Walter Gropius – Band 3: Ausgewählte Schriften*, Berlin 1987, p. 138, first published in: *Ausstellung Karlsruhe Dammerstock-Siedlung "Die Gebrauchswohnung"*, Karlsruhe 1929, pp. 8–9.
2 Ibid., p. 140.
3 Walter Gropius, "Die soziologischen Grundlagen der Minimalwohnung für die städtische Industriebevölkerung", in: ibid., p. 134.

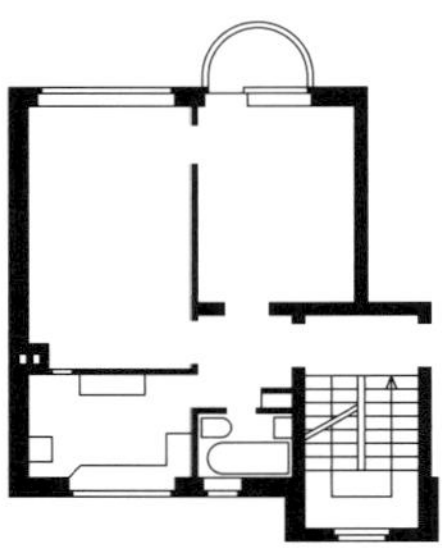

Site plan
Floor plan of apartment
Bird's-eye view from the east

View from the south
View from the east
Northeastern block

Siemensstadt Housing Development

Berlin-Siemensstadt, Germany
1929–30

In the Siemensstadt housing development, masterplanned by Hans Scharoun, Gropius designed two rows of buildings in a north-south orientation with green roof gardens as well as an adjoining gallery-access block at right angles to it. As in the Am Lindenbaum project in Frankfurt, the block corners have been left out with the exception of a single-storey shop built at one corner. Each row of buildings with their rhythmically structured facades and different-coloured staircases is designed differently. Despite appearing extremely restrained, the facades have been carefully composed, as can be seen in the classical grouping of windows on the gallery facade. While for the photos of the Dammerstock project, Gropius requested that "the white pairs of pillars of the large window groups should be retouched! They should be almost as dark as the windows themselves",[1] here he had the pillars clad with the same dark brick of the building's base. This creates the impression of horizontal window bands and made the small dimensions of the minimal apartments appear more generous.

The orientation of the bedrooms to the east and the living rooms to the west is identical in both north-south blocks, resulting in bedrooms that overlook the gardens to the rear on one block and the street on the other. "What is more important for the average person: absolute peace and quiet at night or afternoon and evening sunshine on the balcony,"[2] Gropius asked himself. The apartments of the gallery-access block also overlook the street, turning their back on the large park-like open space behind.[3]

1 Handwritten note on the back of photo 6740/5 in the Bauhaus-Archiv in Berlin. Cf. Annemarie Jaeggi, "'brauchbare typen sind ständig zu verbessern' – Die Dammerstocksiedlung im Werk von Walter Gropius", in: Brigitte Franzen, Peter Schmitt, *Neues Bauen der 20er Jahre – Gropius, Haesler, Schwitters und die Dammerstocksiedlung in Karlsruhe 1929*, Karlsruhe 1997, p. 97.
2 Ibid., p. 95, cited in: Ise Gropius, "Die Gebrauchswohnung" in: *Neue Hauswirtschaft*, 11, 1929, p. 180.
3 The situation is better on the opposite side of the street where Hans Scharoun later built a gallery-access block. The apartments in his block open on to the green space and are shielded from the road.

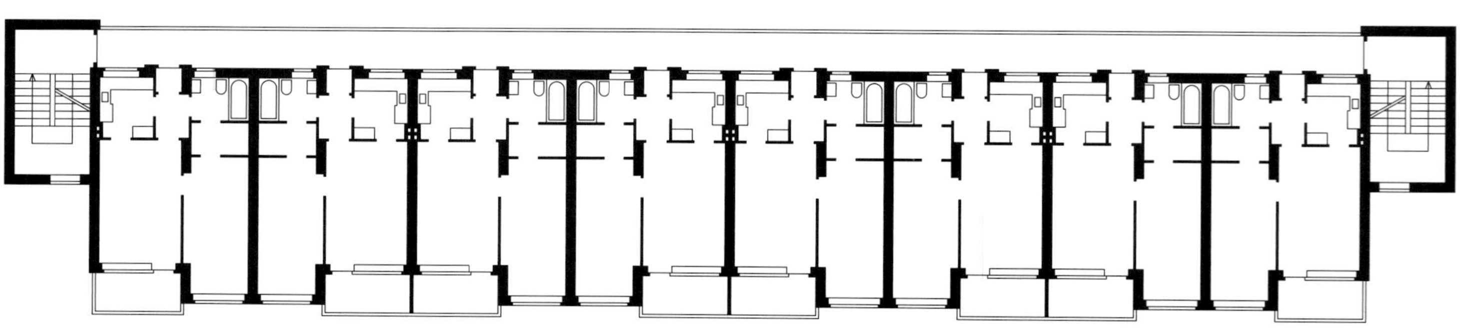

Site plan
Floor plan of gallery-access block

Gallery-access block, north side
Gallery-access block, staircase

West facade with entrances
East facade

North-south block, entrance side
North-south block, west facade

Copper-plate Houses

Finow and Potsdam, Germany
1931–32

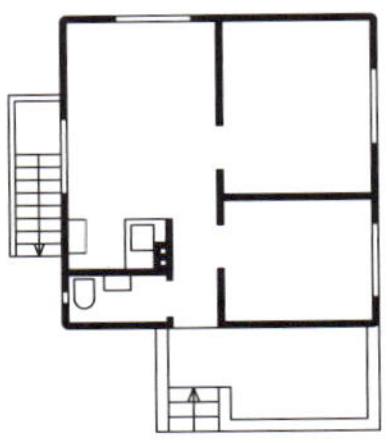

Gropius came into contact with Hirsch Kupfer- und Messingwerke, a copper and brass production company, after they presented two prototypes of industrially prefabricated copper-plated houses at the Berlin Building Exhibition in 1931. The patent for the prefabricated building system, which had been developed for serial production, came from Friedrich Förster and Robert Kraft. Gropius initially entered into a collaboration with the company after providing an expert assessment, but soon became head of its architectural development section. Together with various experts, he designed a smaller simplified copper-plate house type, which was erected as a pilot project next to the works in Eberswalde-Finow. This building, which Gropius listed as an "experimental object"[1] in his office records, had a square floor plan with an edge-length of 6.3 metres.

The panels, which comprised a thin copper-plate skin on a wooden frame construction, were very light and could be assembled within one day. Windows and doors were pre-installed, and the panels then screwed together with a specially-developed copper-clad rounded element for the building corners. The panels were insulated using air pockets sealed in aluminium foil. Although the system was designed for industrial mass production, only one more specimen of the house is known to exist in Potsdam because the company stopped developing Gropius' building type after 1932. Later, the Jewish owners of the company sold copper-plated houses to refugees, who packaged them up as part of their removal to Palestine, where some still stand today, albeit not the building type designed by Gropius.[2]

1 Note in Walter Gropius' office files from 19 November 1931, Bauhaus-Archiv Berlin, cf.: Karsten Thieme, *Kupferhäuser in Berlin und Brandenburg und der Einfluss von Walter Gropius auf ihre Entwicklung*, Dissertation Technische Universität Berlin, 2012, p. 79.
2 Friedrich von Borries and Jens-Uwe Fischer, *Heimatcontainer – Deutsche Fertighäuser in Israel*, Frankfurt am Main 2009.

Floor plan of prototype K in Finow
House of type K in Potsdam

The Growing House

Kleinmachnow, Germany
1933

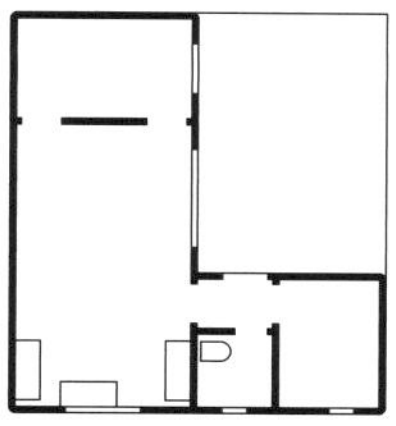

For the exhibition "Sun, Air and House for Everyone!" two prefabricated copper-plated houses were built on the Berlin Exhibition Grounds.[1] Gropius collaborated here with Hirsch Kupfer- und Messingwerke, presenting an additive system of modules that could be successively extended to meet changing needs. The larger of the two houses was an extended variant of the smaller house rotated by 180 degrees so that the terrace faced south-west. The south side of the larger house type featured an adjoining greenhouse with inclined glazing, as also seen in Hans Scharoun's "Growing House" in the same exhibition. Another development over the previous copper-plate house type was the use of a horizontally grooved copper skin and a flat roof.

Although designed for industrial mass production, the houses were never mass-produced. Gropius nevertheless did not abandon the idea of building standardized houses in factories, an idea he had first voiced in 1910: "Only through mass production can really good products be provided," he wrote at the time. [2]

1 The houses are documented in: Martin Wagner, *Das wachsende Haus – ein Beitrag zur Lösung der städtischen Wohnungsfrage*, Berlin 1932, pp. 65–68, and Hartmut Probst and Christian Schädlich, *Walter Gropius – Band 1: Der Architekt und Theoretiker*, Berlin 1985, pp. 155–157.
2 Walter Gropius, "Programm zur Gründung einer allgemeinen Hausbaugesellschaft mit künstlerisch einheitlichen Grundlagen m.b.H." (programme for the founding of a general housing-construction company following artistically uniform principles), manuscript in the Bauhaus-Archiv Berlin. Published in: Hartmut Probst and Christian Schädlich, *Walter Gropius – Band 3: Ausgewählte Schriften*, Berlin 1987, p. 19.

Floor plans of two houses opposite one another
View from the small house to larger house with winter garden
Patio

Bahner House

Kleinmachnow, Germany
1933

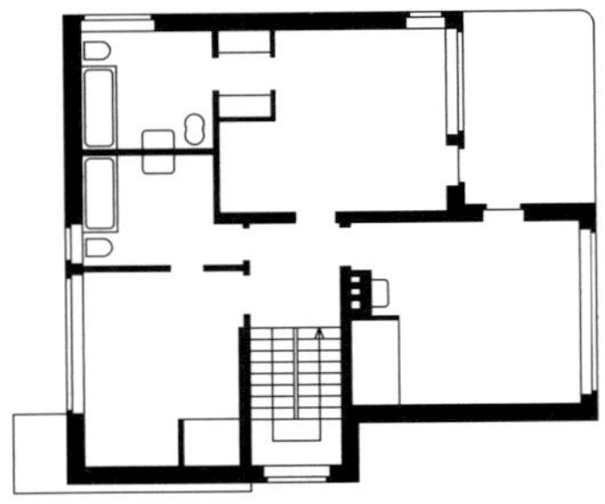

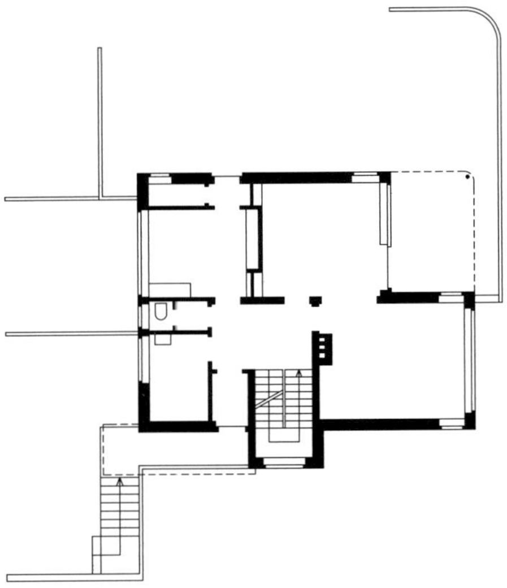

The ground floor of the house is elevated half a storey above street level so that a flight of cantilevered steps lead up to the entrance and a ramp down to the garage. The house for the factory owner Johannes Bahner[1] is positioned directly on the step in the terrain close to the street and has large windows opening on to the south-facing garden at the rear. The windows are comprised of several identical panes, expressing the concept of modularity, and a continuous window cornice groups the windows into horizontal bands, an effect further heightened by the setting back of the pillars between the windows. The building's dynamic composition is a product of cutting away a section of the clear cubic volume at the entrance, causing the corner above to protrude forward. Even though the conventionally constructed house has a hipped roof with projecting eaves, its pitch is so shallow that it looks like a flat roof and its eaves line echoes the forward edge of the roof slab over the entrance.

Sigfried Giedion saw the specific historical significance of Gropius' house designs in the "unity of building and interior design".[2] Although he was referring primarily to the collaborative input of the various Bauhaus workshops, this house does exemplify this principle in that the cabinets, wardrobes, door fittings and furniture were all designed as part of the overall concept.

1 The history of the design is unknown as earlier versions of the design are labelled "Gass House". See Winfried Nerdinger, *The Architect Walter Gropius*, Berlin 1985, p. 182, and Hartmut Probst and Christian Schädlich, *Walter Gropius – Band 1: Der Architekt und Theoretiker*, Berlin 1985, p. 194.
2 Sigfried Giedion, *Walter Gropius – Work and Teamwork*, New York 1954, p. 70.

Upper floor plan
Ground floor plan

Street elevation
Entrance area

Maurer House

Berlin-Dahlem, Germany
1933

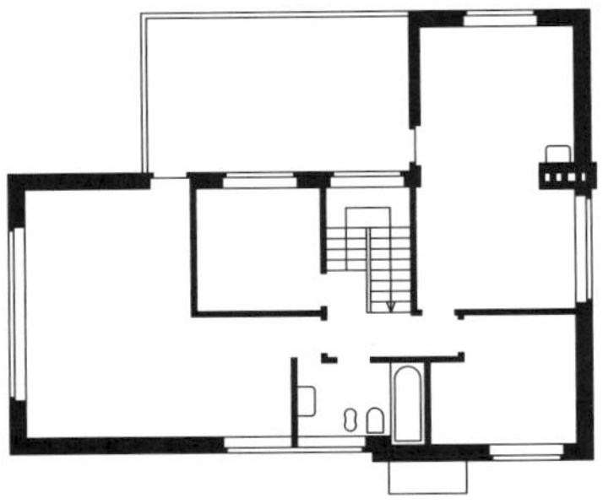

As the entrance to the house is from the south, it is shifted back from the street with the entrance placed to one side. The house for the lawyer Otto Heinrich Maurer is situated opposite a park but appears modest compared to the representative villas next to it. Its outward appearance is very restrained[1] and, as with the Bahner House built at the same time, the pitched roof prescribed by the National Socialists is all but invisible due to its shallow incline. The complicated incorporation of the gutter into the roof further underlines the impression of a flat roof. Considerable effort was invested in achieving the impression of maximum simplicity.

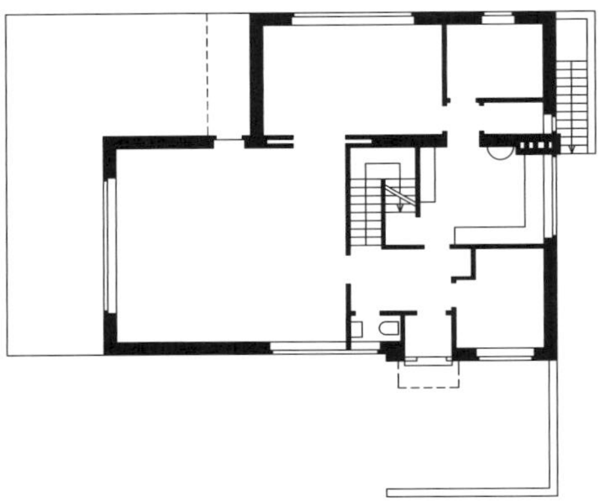

In the L-shaped floor plan, the serving rooms such as the vestibule, kitchen and maid's room are minimised, while the living room – linked to the dining room by a sliding door – is open and spacious. The dynamism of Gropius' earlier residential buildings, achieved by pushing together different-sized building volumes, is put aside in favour of the "classical" stability of a symmetrical frontage.

Th Maurer House is the last building that Gropius built in Germany before emigrating to England in 1934 and then to the USA. From exile, he resisted the accusation that his architecture was anti-traditional because he saw himself as standing in the tradition of Karl Friedrich Schinkel.[2]

1 The clarity of the building volume came about during the design process. Earlier plans show a projecting bay, a pergola on one side and a garage extension. See Winfried Nerdinger, *The Architect Walter Gropius*, Berlin 1985, p. 183.
2 Walter Gropius, *Die neue Architektur und das Bauhaus*, Mainz 1965, p. 74, originally published as: *The New Architecture and the Bauhaus*, London 1935.

Upper floor plan
Ground floor plan
View from the road

Levy House

London, Great Britain
1935–36 (with Edwin Maxwell Fry)

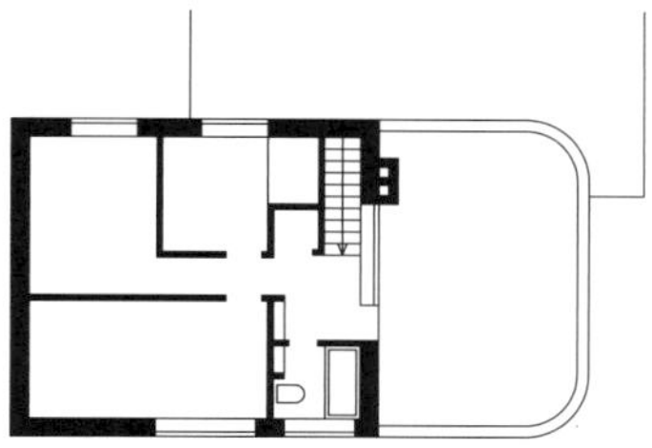

The house for the playwright Benn Levy[1] and the actress Constance Cummings forms part of an overall composition together with the neighbouring house designed by Erich Mendelsohn. The architects agreed on the building heights, facade design and massing of the two adjoining houses. While Mendelsohn's building for Levy's nephew Dennis Cohen is arranged parallel to the street and appears rigorously orthogonal, the Levy house stands at right angles to the street and has curved sections, also on its street elevation. The Levy House, with numerous rooms for domestic staff, opens onto a shared garden with large south-east facing sliding glass panes. Sliding doors between the dining room and living room likewise make it possible to combine them into a single large space.

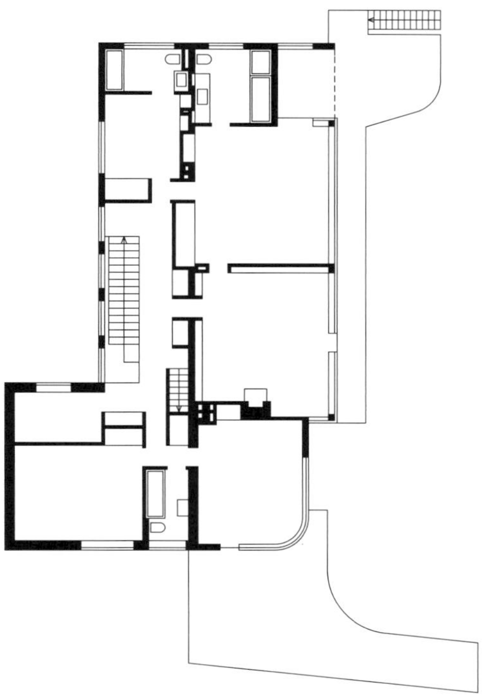

A storey was later added to the house and the roof terrace built over. In addition, the house was clad in a dark colour due to the air pollution in central London. Gropius later explained that he had drawn the client's attention to the problem of facade discoloration: "I was in favour of a brick building, but Levy wanted to have a white house."[2]

1 Benn Levy wrote the dialogue for the first British "talkie", directed by Alfred Hitchcock, who also produced a film that Levy directed. Levy also represented the Labour Party as a Member of Parliament.
2 Walter Gropius in a letter to Edwin Maxwell Fry on 25 April 1938, RIBA Archive, cited in: Ian Jackson, Jessica Holland, *The Architecture of Edwin Maxwell Fry and Jane Drew – Twentieth Century Architecture, Pioneer Modernism and the Tropics*, Farnham 2014, p. 73.

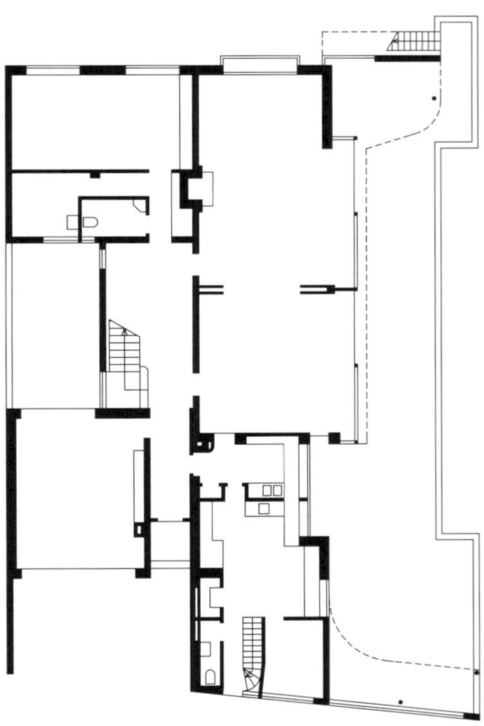

Second floor plan
First floor plan
Ground floor plan
Detail of view from the road

View from the road
View from the garden

Mortimer Gall Electrical Centre

London, Great Britain
1936, conversion (with Edwin Maxwell Fry)

The conversion of a shop on Cannon Street contrasts with the historicist columned facade of the five-storey building.[1] The front of a second shop in the same building remained unchanged with Corinthian pilasters. The facade of the new section was supported by a beam resting on a slender iron column. The newly created shopfront runs flush with the front of the building before curving inwards to lead to the recessed entrance. Black glass, glass blocks and the curved shop window are arranged flush on the front face of the shop making it appear like a thin membrane. Gropius highlighted its non-loadbearing character by offsetting the column from the window front so that it stands apart. The display-case character of the shop serves as a showroom for electrical appliances by AEG, and like their counterparts in Berlin designed by Peter Behrens, the architecture and graphic treatment of the lettering are part of the same overall composition.[2]

1 The showroom was published in the *Architect's Journal*, 5 August 1937, pp. 229–230, after Gropius had already left England for America. Although Gropius and Maxwell Fry, with whom he had an office partnership, are both named as the architects, the project is not recorded by Giedion (1954) in his list of works. In Ian Jackson and Jessica Holland's book, *The Architecture of Edwin Maxwell Fry and Jane Drew – Twentieth Century Architecture, Pioneer Modernism and the Tropics*, Farnham 2014, p. 336, a second Electricity Showroom in London's Regent Street dated 1937 is mentioned that is attributed to Gropius together with Maxwell Fry and László Moholy-Nagy.
2 The lettering no longer exists.

View of the shop
Facade details

Denham Film Laboratories

Denham, Great Britain
1936 (with Edwin Maxwell Fry)

As part of the extensive Denham Film Studios complex, Gropius and Maxwell Fry built a laboratory building for developing films. They were, however, only commissioned after construction had already begun and the loadbearing structure had already been erected as a skeleton frame construction.[1] The building's cubature was therefore already defined, and the architects also had only limited influence on the design of the facades because the escape routes and fire stairs were likewise prescribed. As a result, Gropius did not publish this building, which he saw as "offering limited artistic potential".[2]

Like Gropius' other buildings in England, and in contrast to his previous buildings in Germany, this building features striking curves. The rounded corners as well as the detailing of the facades lend the building the character of a ship with outdoor perimeter decks. The land around the building has since been redeveloped as housing and apartments have been inserted into the gutted shell of the laboratory building.

1 I would like to thank the architect John Pardey for his survey plans which served as the basis for the plan shown here.
2 Reginald R. Isaacs, *Walter Gropius – Der Mensch und sein Werk*, Frankfurt am Main, Berlin 1986, p. 774. A member of the office, Jack Howe, describes the project in a letter to Jack Pitchard dated 12 July 1969 as a 'bread and butter' project and also described Gropius' displeasure with the client, in: ibid., p. 773.

View from the southwest

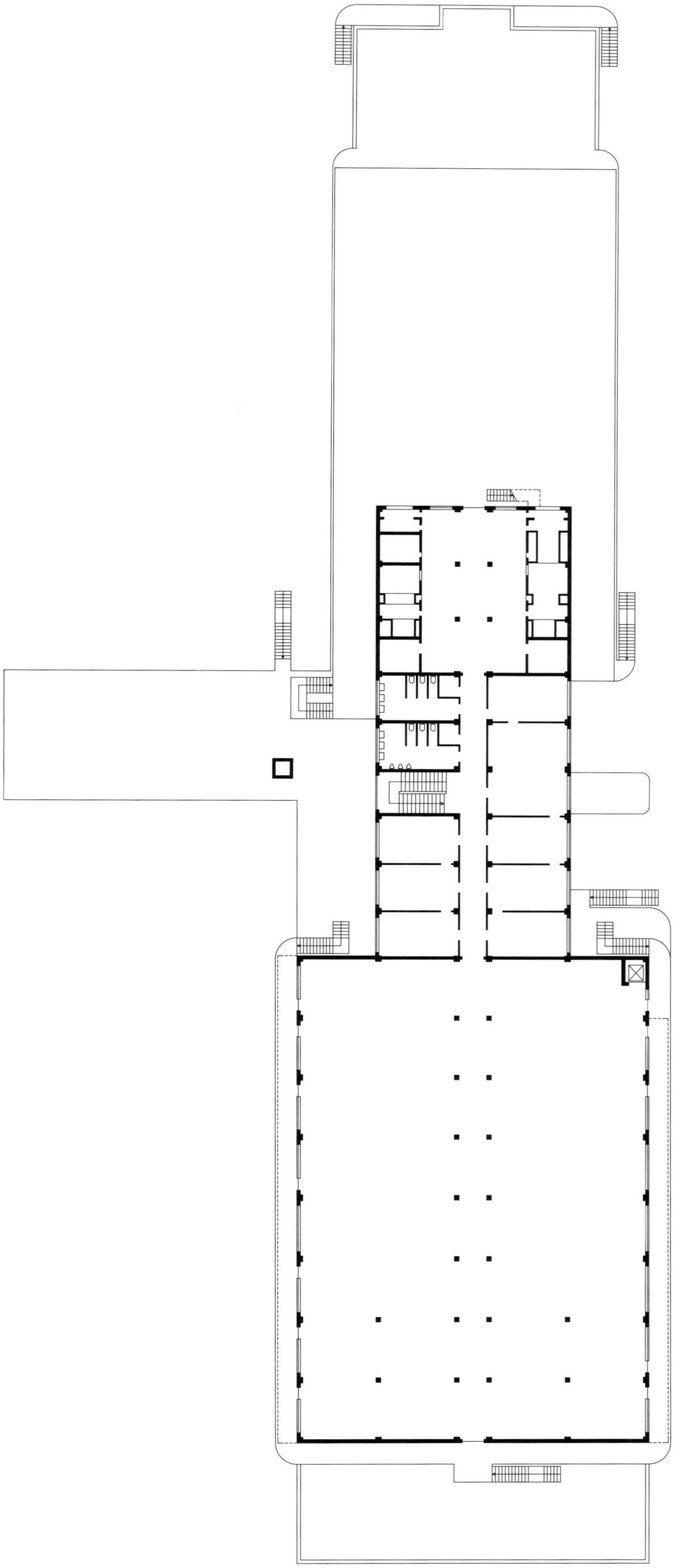

Upper floor plan

Donaldson House

Shipbourne, Great Britain
1936–37 (with Edwin Maxwell Fry)

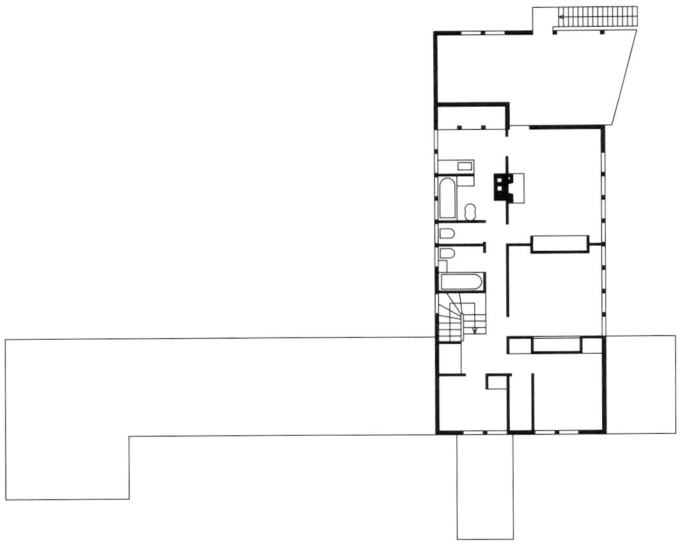

The L-shaped building, known as Wood House, stands freely in the landscape with its entrance on the west.[1] The living area is located in the south wing of the building, with the bedrooms in the north wing and on the upper floor. The eastern end of the upper floor is designed as an "open-air bedroom".[2] As with the Gropius House in Dessau, glass panes have been installed outside to shield the space from wind and give it the character of a room, creating a fluid transition from inside to outside. From the client's perspective, Frances Donaldson described Gropius as an architect who "was [...] anxious to find out exactly what one wanted and to design the house accordingly."[3]

The wooden skeleton frame construction is clad with horizontal cedar shiplap, with the window bands placed flush with the outer surface. The austere severity of the clear structure, which is crowned by a shed roof, is broken by a freestanding curved glass wall that encloses the terrace as a wind screen. As the terrain slopes away to the south, the terrace rises as a stone podium above the garden, making it look like a base on which the lightweight pavilion-like architecture stands.

1 "A Timber House in Kent", in: *Architectural Review*, February 1938, pp. 61–63.
2 Ibid., p. 61.
3 Frances Donaldson, *A Twentieth-Century Life*, London 1992.

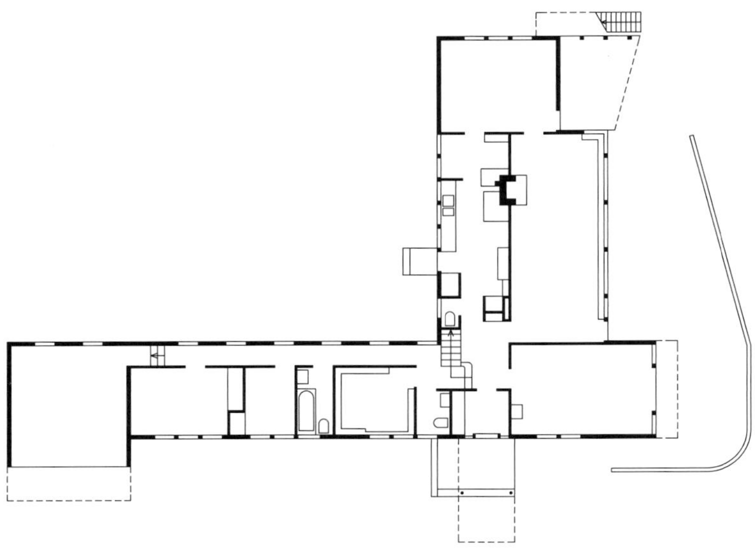

Upper floor plan
Ground floor plan
View from the south

Impington Village College

Impington, Great Britain
1936–39 (with Edwin Maxwell Fry)

The aim of the building was to create a combined school and cultural centre in a rural region.[1] In addition to the classrooms, the building also encompassed adult education facilities and a multifunctional auditorium with theatre stage. As with the Bauhaus building, the wings, which vary in shape depending on their function, extend in different directions. The college stands at the edge of the village overlooking the landscape and is embedded in an existing park, emphasising its public character. The form of the building was arranged to preserve as many of the existing mature trees as possible. Access is from the north-west in the direction of the fan-shaped auditorium, with an entrance next to the auditorium that leads off into a promenade that connects the wings of the classrooms and the wings of the communal facilities. Some of the school rooms are also used in the evenings for extracurricular activities.

The classrooms open to the south-east and have a view across the fields through glazed frontages that have sliding sections to allow semi-open-air teaching. The common rooms, on the other hand, have typical English bay windows. The exterior walls, as well as some of the indoor areas, are faced with yellow and dark brown bricks with a very rough texture. The structural elements of the interiors are painted blue while the walls are a light grey-green with "sulphur yellow" curtains.[2] Mahogany panels were used on the walls.

Even though the building was considered radically modern in England at the time, in retrospect it is also characterised by regional design elements. Gropius already lived in the USA during the planning phase and was building his own house there in a style that Sigfried Giedion described as "New Regionalism".[3]

1 The concept of the Village College was developed in the 1920s by Henry Morris, who was responsible for education in Cambridgeshire. The intention was to help stem the flow of people leaving rural areas by providing local facilities. See "The Village College Idea", in: *Architectural Review*, December 1939, pp. 225–226.
2 "Impington Village College", in: ibid., p. 234.
3 Sigfried Giedion, *Walter Gropius – Work and Teamwork*, New York 1954, p. 70.

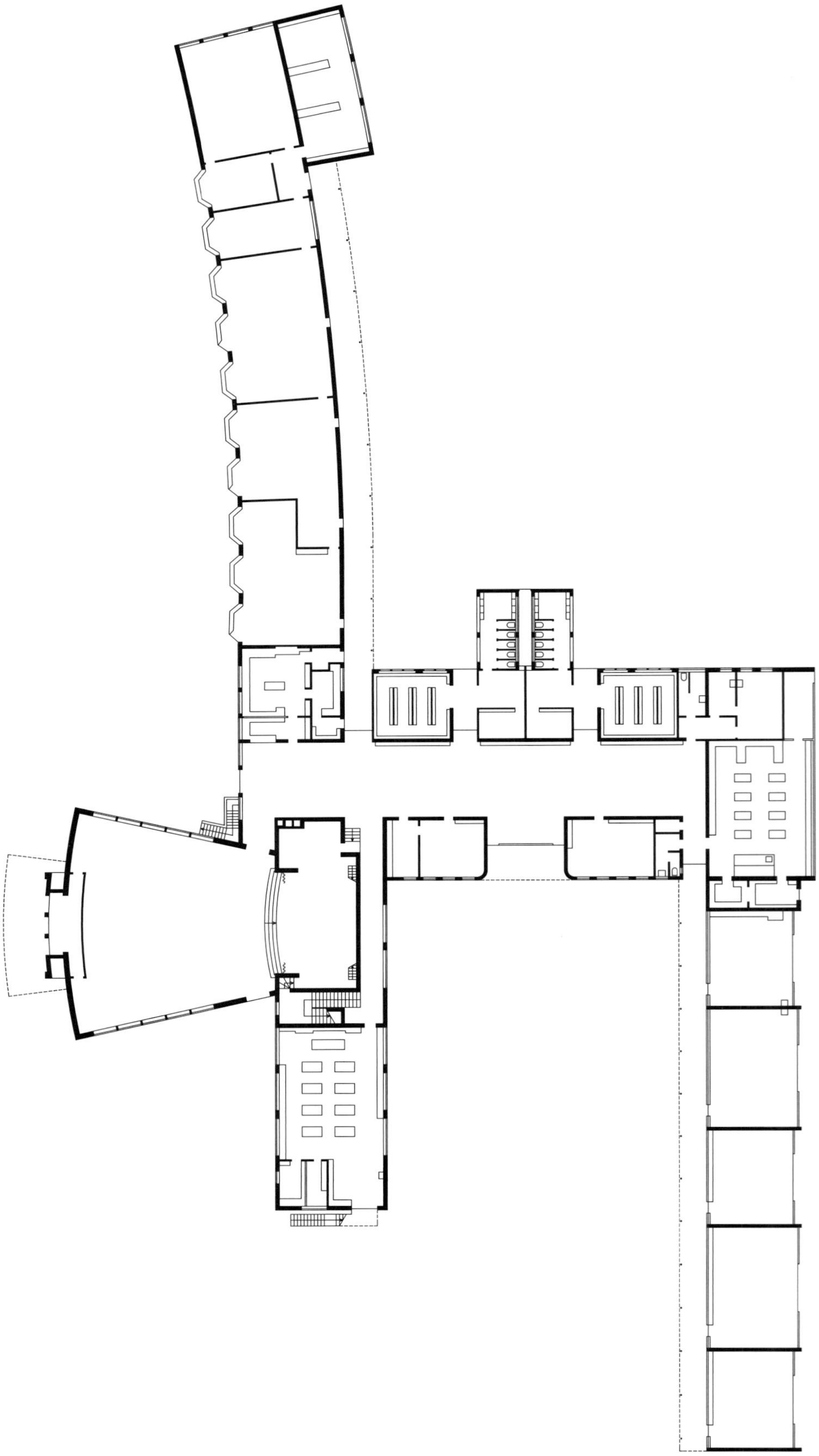

Ground floor plan

Wing with common rooms and auditorium
Classroom wing, view from the south

Gropius House

Lincoln, Massachusetts, USA
1938 (with Marcel Breuer)

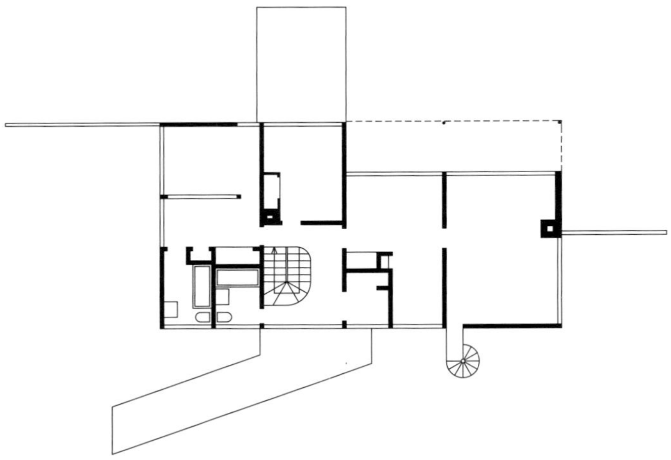

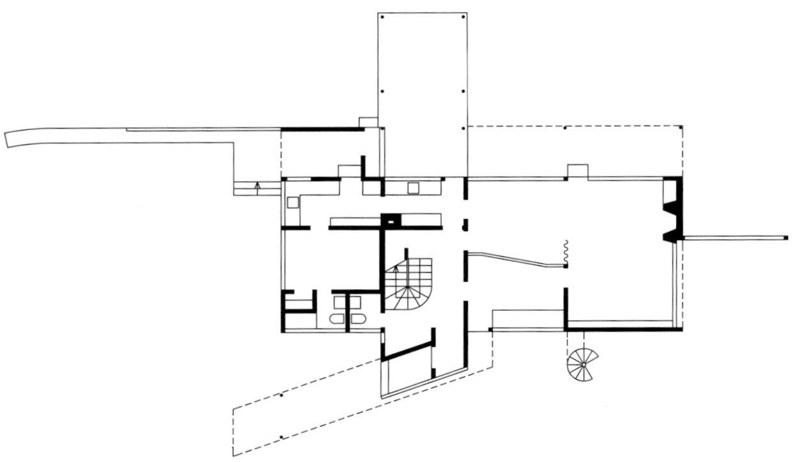

For the second time, Gropius was able to build a house for himself without having to raise the finances for it thanks to the generosity of a patron.[1] As with his house in Dessau, he worked with Marcel Breuer, with whom he also established an office partnership. Gropius chose a location in the Boston area after taking up a professorship at Harvard University. The freestanding building crowns a hill in the landscape near Walden Pond, made famous by the writer Henry David Thoreau.

From the entrance side, the building appears as a pure white cube with horizontal window bands, similar to Gropius' buildings from the late 1920s. On entering, however, its character is more akin to that of a house by Alvar Aalto in Finland than to the New Objectivity propagated in America as the International Style. The house is constructed of wood and the painted wood panelling is visible both outside and inside. Sigfried Giedion wrote: "Within Gropius' house at Lincoln there is nothing that stresses its modernity. Living has simply, in some new and subtle way, become pleasanter. The flow of space through the studio, living-room and dining space on the ground floor is agreeably relaxing."[2]

Gropius explained that he had drawn on the architectural tradition of New England in the design of the house: "The blending of the genius loci with my modern concept of architecture allowed me to create a house that I never would have built under the completely different climatic, technical and psychological conditions in Europe".[3] In a letter to Breuer, he described his enthusiasm for the historical houses of the area. These houses are "entirely in our spirit in simplicity, functionality, and uniformity".[4]

Gropius drew not only on traditional construction methods, but also typological elements, such as the porch in front of the house, which he reinterpreted. In his time at the Bauhaus he had used the principle of "life-size building blocks" to join different volumes together, but here the design process is better described as subtractive because different volumes have been removed from the primary form, creating a freer, more "relaxed"[5] architecture.

1 Helen Storrow procured the site and paid for the building's costs. She rented the house to Gropius and gave him the option to purchase it later.
2 Sigfried Giedion, *Walter Gropius – Work and Teamwork*, New York 1954, p. 72.
3 Walter Gropius, *Architektur – Wege zu einer optischen Tradition*, Frankfurt am Main, Hamburg 1959, p. 11.
4 Walter Gropius in a letter to Marcel Breuer dated 17 April 1937, cited in: Winfried Nerdinger, *The Architect Walter Gropius*, Berlin 1985, p. 194.
5 This is how Sigfried Giedion characterized the architecture. See footnote 2.

Upper floor plan
Ground floor plan

Front elevation
View from the west

View from the west
View from the southwest

View from the dining area into the living room
View of the dining area

Hagerty House

Cohasset, Massachusetts, USA
1938 (with Marcel Breuer)

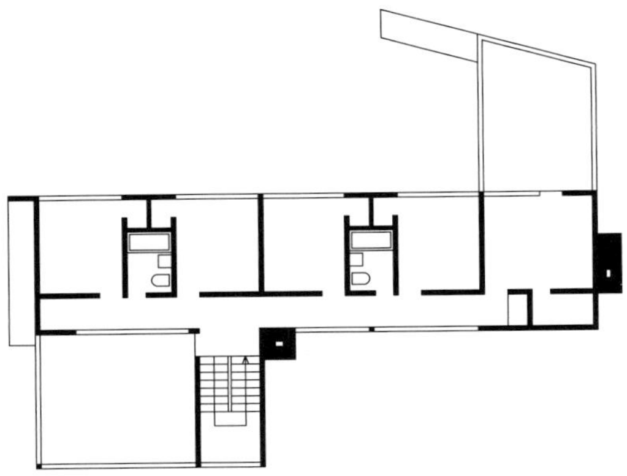

The building looks different from each side. Approaching the entrance, one sees a white cubic volume looking out over the sea. The house is partially elevated, and at the same time embedded in the rocky coastal landscape, walls of rough stonework anchoring it firmly to the ground. Resting on this massive foundation is a lightweight timber construction with membrane-like walls. In its detailing, some elements of the building are reminiscent of naval architecture, while others have an extremely archaic character. Marcel Breuer, who claimed primary authorship of the design,[1] had previously used similar rustic walls in his designs for a pavilion in England and a hotel in Austria.

Even though the client Josephine Hagerty accused the architects of having ignored her personal preferences,[2] Gropius and Breuer tried to adapt their principles to the regional context.

1 Marcel Breuer in a letter to Walter Gropius dated 10 September 1946, quoted in: Joachim Driller, *Breuer Houses*, London 2000, p. 102. This house was completed in 1938. See "Hagerty Completion Statement" from 5 December 1938, Marcel Breuer Archive, Syracuse University, ID 11319-001.
2 Josephine Hagerty in a letter to Walter Gropius and Marcel Breuer dated 26 January 1939, Marcel Breuer Archive, Syracuse University, ID 11329-008. "You insisted on your own preconceived ideas without considering their adaptability to the existing conditions or the likes and dislikes of your client."

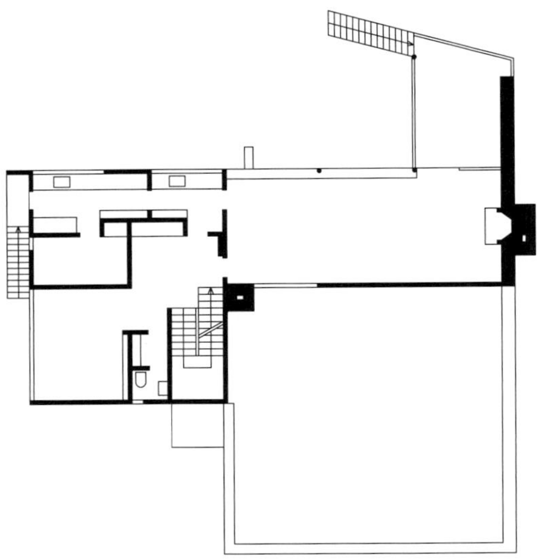

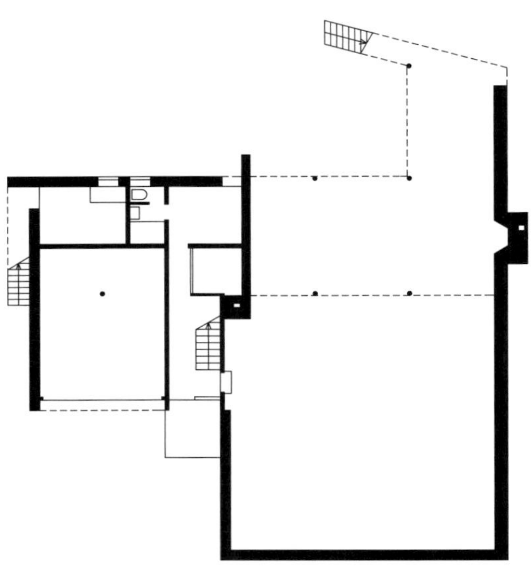

Second floor plan
First floor plan
Ground floor plan

West elevation
East elevation

Breuer House

Lincoln, Massachusetts, USA
1938–39 (with Marcel Breuer)

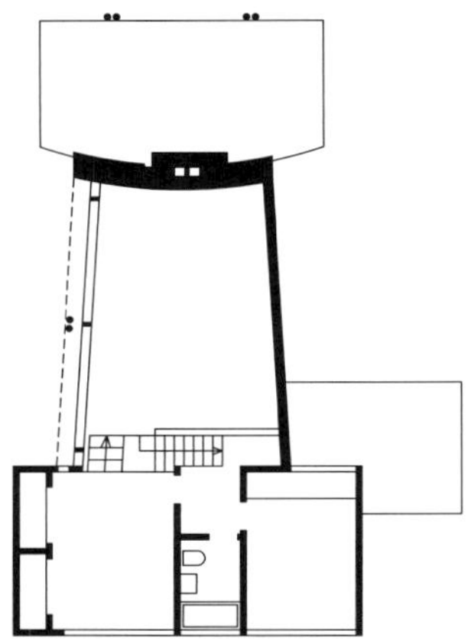

The house stands within sight of the Gropius house, and like Gropius, Marcel Breuer was given the opportunity by the owner of the site to design a house for himself without having to finance it.[1] Although Breuer designed the house independently, it also appears in Gropius' list of works, as it was designed as part of their office partnership.

The open centre of the house is a trapezoidal, two-storey living room around which the other rooms are arranged: a slightly lower-lying dining room, a west-facing veranda and a bedroom separated only by a curtain. Breuer chose different materials for the walls and also designed the furniture. As with the Hagerty House, a fireplace is embedded into a wall of rough stonework that is visible both inside and out and defines the character of the house. The heavy wall plane, which serves as an anchor for the light timber construction of the rest of the building, is curved like the plywood of the furniture.

In contrast to the cubic volume of the Gropius House, this house looks like an additive assembly of different volumes, reflecting the different characters of the functional areas.[2] The house was later extended.

1 Joachim Driller, *Breuer Houses*, London 2000, pp. 124–131.
2 The figures of the floor plans of the individual building volumes are clearly proportioned. The eastern area is designed in the proportions of 1:2. See ibid., p. 131.

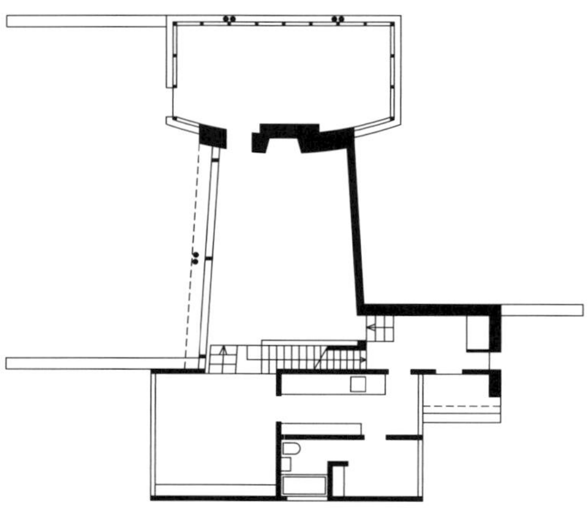

Upper floor plan
Ground floor plan
View from the south
Living room

View from the east

Ford House

Lincoln, Massachusetts, USA
1938–39 (with Marcel Breuer)

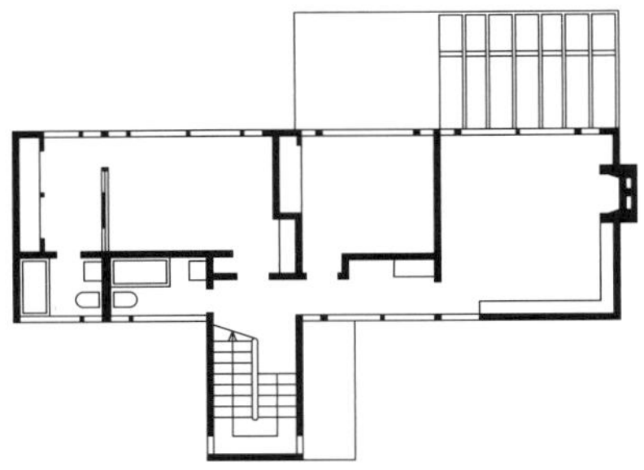

Surrounded by trees and facing a pond, the house lies on the same site as the houses for Gropius and Breuer. The modest building, which Breuer had no part in designing,[1] opens to the south overlooking the water. The building is accessed via a staircase that juts out of the north elevation, while to the south, a single-storey dining room extends forward of the main rectangular form of the building. The proportions of the floor plan adhere to the Golden Section, and the route through the house follows an S-shaped path from the entrance to the terrace. As in the neighbouring Gropius House, this path leads around a diagonally arranged glass wall that divides the living and dining areas while maintaining a visual connection between them.

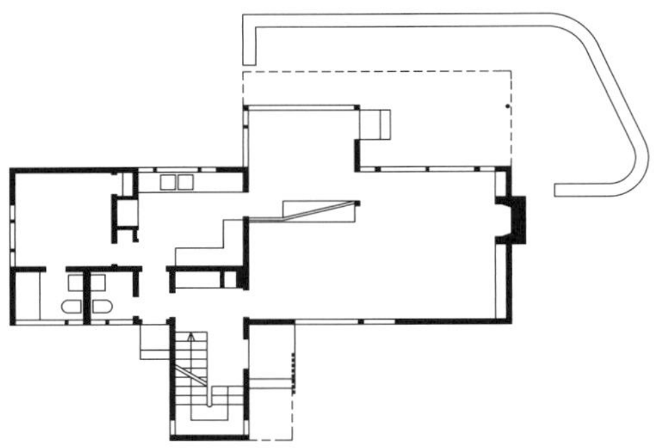

The terrace in front is contained by a curved dry stone wall. Like the Gropius and Breuer houses from this period, and in contrast to the New England vernacular, the timber cladding on the facades runs vertically. Similarly, rather than overlapping the individual timber boards, as was the convention, the vertical timber panelling is arranged flush to form a smooth wall surface that underlines the geometric abstraction of the building.

1 Cf. Winfried Nerdinger, *The Architect Walter Gropius*, Berlin 1985, p. 271, and Joachim Driller, *Breuer Houses*, London 2000, p. 102. The house, which was built in the office partnership with Marcel Breuer, was later enlarged through the addition of an extension.

Upper floor plan
Ground floor plan
View from the southwest

View from the northwest
View from the southwest

Frank House

Pittsburgh, Pennsylvania, USA
1939–40 (with Marcel Breuer)

The extremely luxurious building extends over four floors connected both by an elevator and a staircase, which is visible on the facade. The house is embedded in a slope with the entrance at the lower level, from where one sees not only the main staircase behind a curved glass wall, but also another staircase leading up to a terrace adjoining the garden that lies above a swimming pool incorporated within the building.

While the cubature of the house is strictly orthogonal, corresponding to the steel skeleton frame, the character of the main interiors is dominated by curved walls. Curved forms also feature in the cantilevered steps of the stair, covered with brown carpet, and the numerous items of furniture designed by Marcel Breuer. The same organic curves of the plywood furniture – quite atypical of Bauhaus – can be seen in the shape of the pool in the garden, a principle that extends throughout the building, lending it a consistent design language that informs everything from the detailing of the furniture to the light fittings down to the way the building is embedded in the terrain.

In keeping with the idea of a *Gesamtkunstwerk*, the house is a synthesis of the design disciplines, although not in the same way as the Bauhaus buildings from the 1920s, such as the Masters' Houses in Dessau. Here the walls are wood-panelled like ship's cabins or clad with travertine. For the wall coverings, Anni Albers designed a textile with copper threads, while the silk curtains were left a natural light beige. "Throughout the house materials are used in their natural color, without stain or painting,"[1] explained Gropius and Breuer. "The intention of the designers was to arrange the interior as a quiet background for the innumerable forms and colors of the constantly changing daily life."[2] Even though they strived to create a neutral background, the overall design still bore the hallmarks, according to a critique in *The Architectural Forum* magazine, of a "relapse into fashionable mannerisms".[3] At the same time, Gropius and Breuer found themselves accused of having betrayed their social ideals through their willingness to engage in such luxurious design.[4]

1 Walter Gropius and Marcel Breuer in a manuscript, Marcel Breuer Archive, Syracuse University, ID 04476-003.
2 Ibid., ID 04476-002.
3 "House in Pittsburgh, PA. – Walter Gropius and Marcel Breuer, Architects", in: *The Architectural Forum*, March 1941, p. 162.
4 Cf. Joachim Driller, Breuer Houses, London 2000, pp. 132–137.

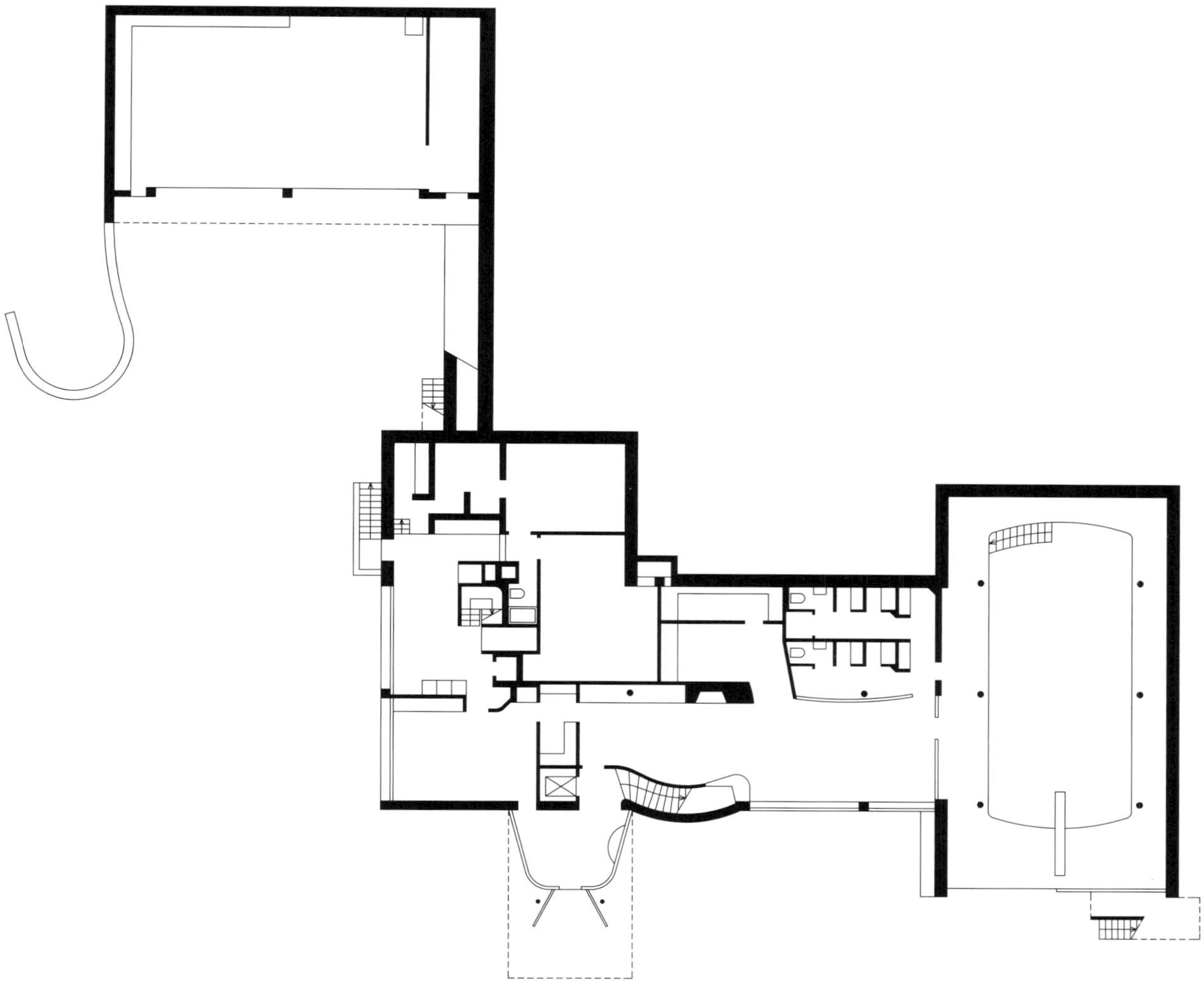

Ground floor plan with entrance
View from the garden

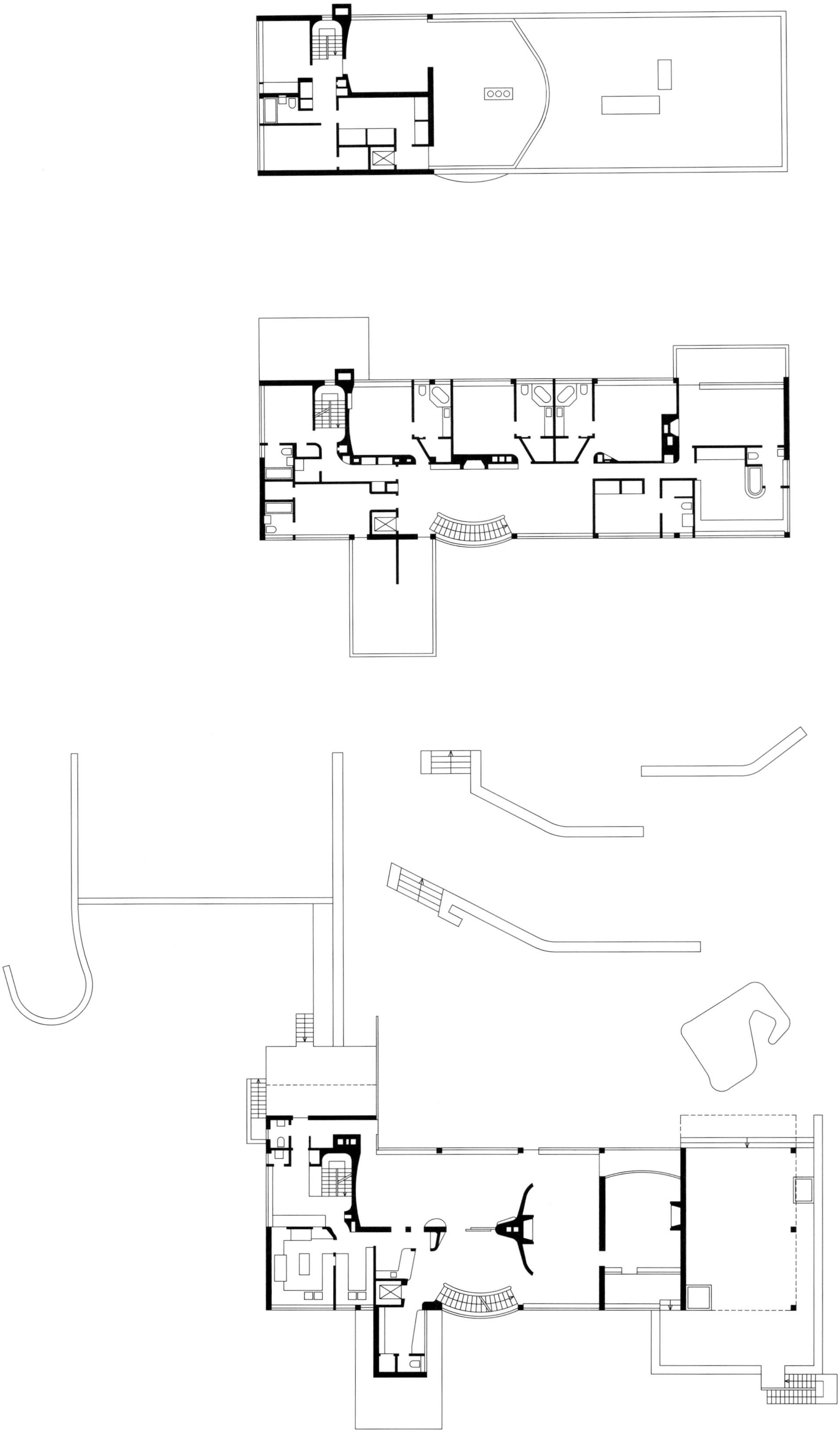

Floor plan of roof level
Upper floor plan
Ground floor plan at garden level

View from the garden
South elevation

Entrance to the house
Detail of house entrance

Chamberlain House

Wayland, Massachusetts, USA
1940–41 (with Marcel Breuer)

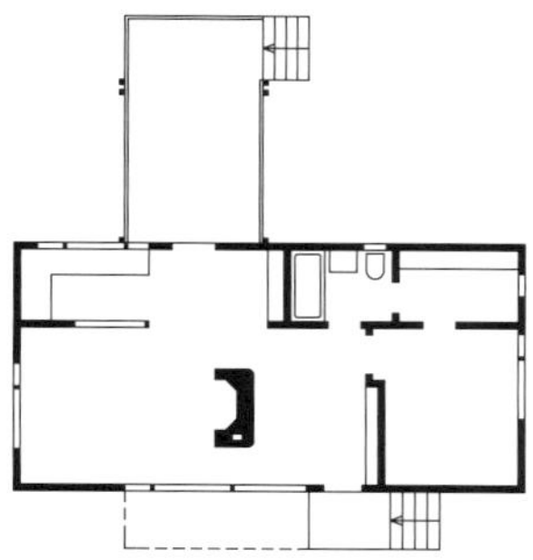

Located near a river "in the middle of the woods",[1] the building is composed of different cubic volumes. A light timber structure rests on a massive pedestal of rough stone walls that serves as a shelter for a canoe. The somewhat larger house rests on this pedestal, projecting forward by over two metres. Other elements of the building also extend outwards, including the entrance staircase and canopy as well as part of the veranda. At the heart of the house is a stone chimney which stands in the centre of the main space and separates the entrance area from the living room.

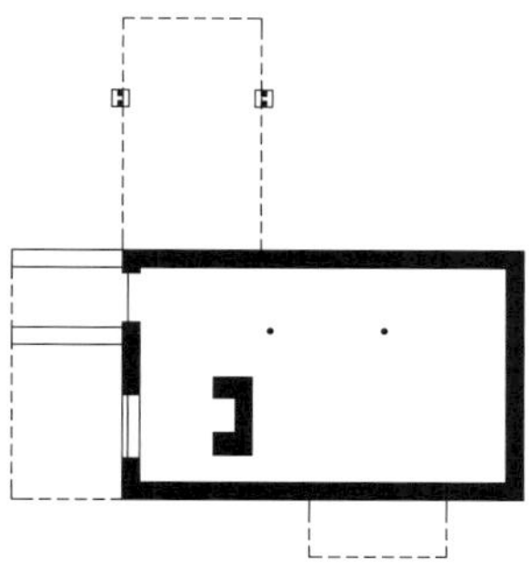

The cantilever of the timber structure was achieved by employing a layered wall construction consisting of three connected layers of timber boarding arranged vertically on the outside, horizontally on the inside and diagonally in between. "The wooden walls are considered in the construction as stiff slabs," explained Marcel Breuer, "like a reinforced concrete wall."[2]

Immediately after completion, Breuer, the building's principal designer, wrote to Gropius announcing his desire to work independently after completion of the two remaining ongoing joint projects, citing differences in their approaches.[3]

1 Marcel Breuer in a letter to Francis Reginald Stevens Yorke dated 8 March 1943, cited in: Joachim Driller, *Breuer Houses*, London 2000, p. 240.
2 Marcel Breuer in a letter to George Nelson dated 15 October 1942, Marcel Breuer Archive, Syracuse University, ID 00138-001.
3 Marcel Breuer in a letter to Walter Gropius dated 23 May 1941: "I am now convinced that our partnership is objectively and personally no longer possible. As to the reasons, we each certainly have our own ideas, which I feel it would not help to analyse." Marcel Breuer Archive, Syracuse University, ID bMS_Ger_208_folder_518_0024.

Ground floor plan
Basement floor plan
Entrance elevation

Abele House

Framingham, Massachusetts, USA
1940–41 (with Marcel Breuer)

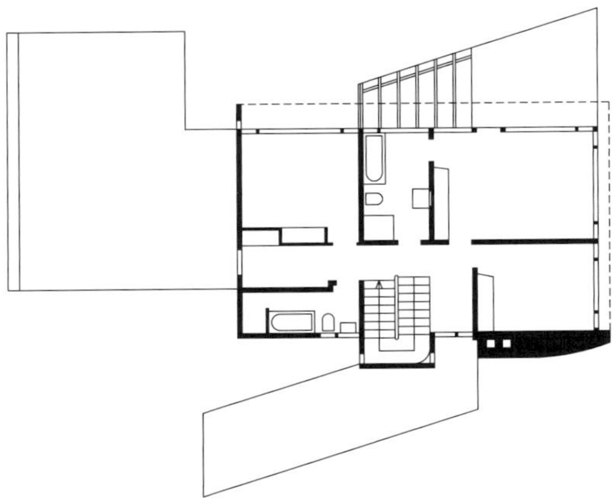

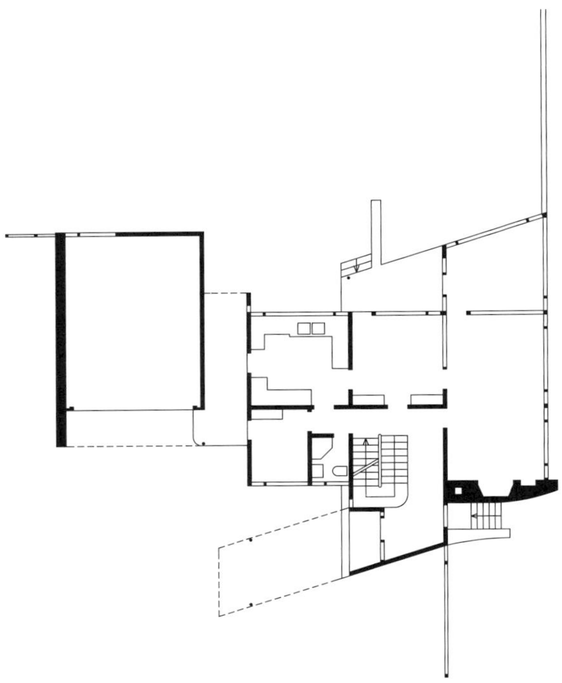

Situated on the banks of a reservoir, the entrance to the house follows the same pattern as Gropius' own house in Lincoln. Here, too, the entrance is via a porch on the north side of the building with a diagonal canopy. Although the living spaces are grouped in a compact block, the building also extends outwards into the landscape with its low walls and open fencework of vertical bars. The adjoining garage is connected to the main building at its roof and at the same time separated by an open passage passing between the two volumes.

Even though Marcel Breuer did not claim primary authorship of this house,[1] its open fireplace within the gently curving massive stone wall, and the contrast between the rough stone surface and the lacquered timber structure bears strong resemblances to Breuer's own house in Lincoln. To the south and west, the house is glazed across the entire breadth of the facade, providing panoramic views through the ribbon windows from almost all the rooms. The connection with the landscape is most dramatically evident in the fully-glazed room at the southwest corner of the building.

1 Breuer did not list this house as one of the works he was involved in designing during his office partnership with Gropius. See his letter to Gropius dated 10 September 1946, quoted in: Joachim Driller, *Breuer Houses*, London 2000, p. 102.

Upper floor plan
Ground floor plan
Entrance
View from the garden

Aluminium City Terrace

New Kensington, Pennsylvania, USA
1941–42 (with Marcel Breuer)

Designed for workers at an aluminium factory important to the war effort, the settlement blends organically into the hilly landscape. The arrangement of the rows of terraces along the contours of the topography and the predominantly south-facing orientation of the living areas creates an irregular layout that contrasts markedly with the stringent north-south alignment of the linear rows in 1920s Germany. Because the entrances were mostly on the north side, not all the house entrances face the street, some face with their private gardens to the street, which became a key criticism of the scheme and proved harder to let.[1]

The development comprises one and two-storey buildings, with one-room flats in the single-storey terraces where the living room, bedroom and kitchen combine to form a single unit. In addition to the rows of terraces, semi-detached houses were also built, some of which were elevated above the sloping terrain and are accessed via ramps.

The timber construction of the buildings is faced with yellow brick and cedar. After visiting the completed settlement, Marcel Breuer conceded that "tenants [...] object to the natural wood on the exteriors which, they think, indicates that there was not enough money for brick. It is therefore suggested that the wood should be painted."[2] The wooden shading devices above the long ribbon wincows have since been replaced by aluminium elements.

1 Cf. "Aluminum City Terrace Housing", in: *The Architectural Forum*, July 1944, pp. 65–76.
2 Marcel Breuer in: *Architectural Review*, September 1944, p. 74.

Two-storey row, garden side
Semi-detached house

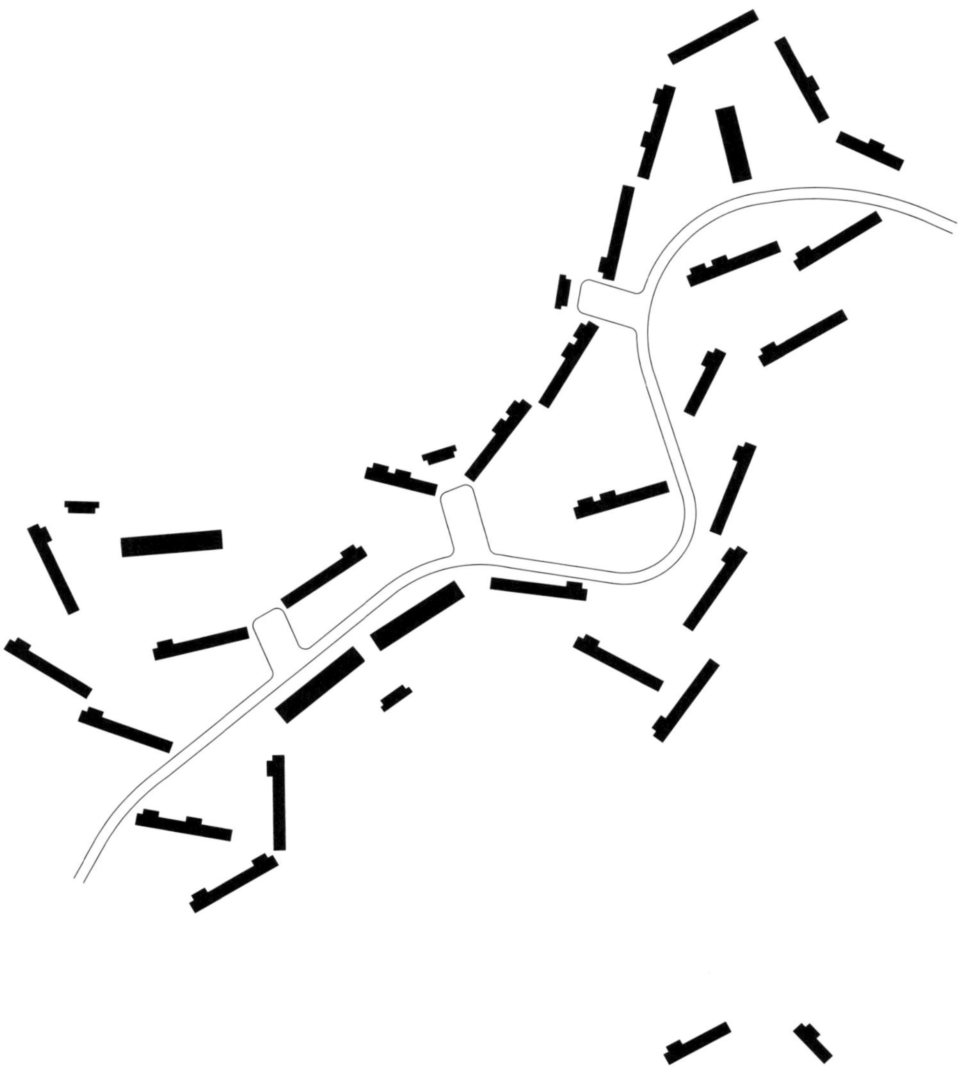

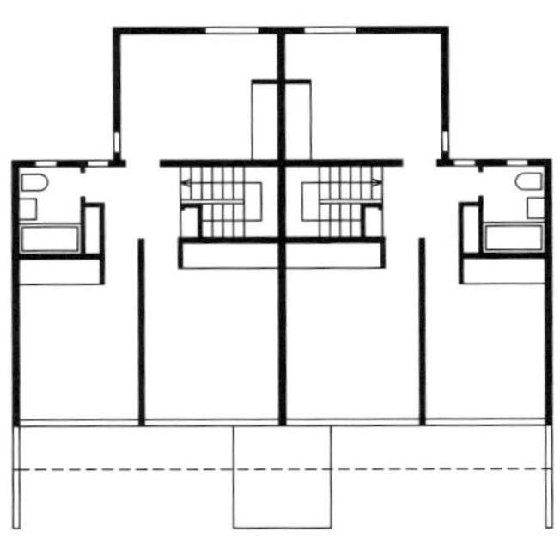

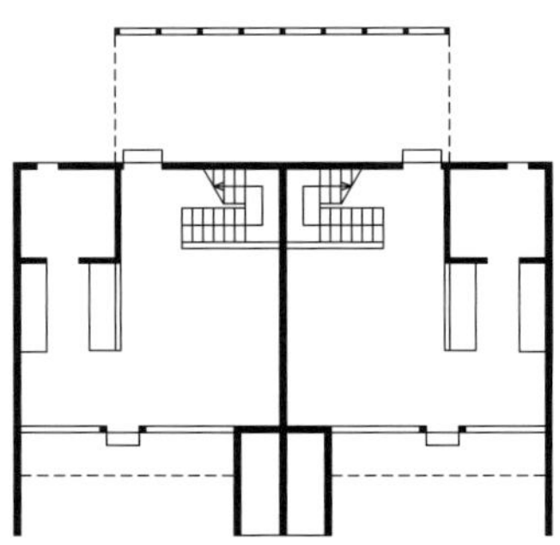

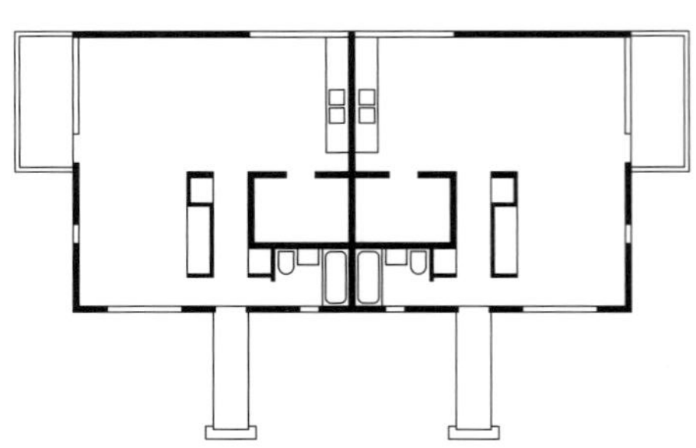

Site plan
Upper floor plan
Ground floor plan
Floor plan of semi-detached house type

Two-storey row, entrance side
Projecting section with bedrooms

Single-storey row, entrance side

Packaged House System

Burbank, California, USA
1942–52 (with Konrad Wachsmann), destroyed

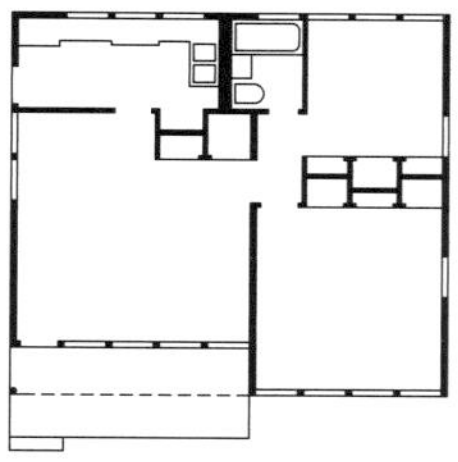

The General Panel System for prefabricated houses was designed for mass production, but relatively few houses were actually built.[1] The prefabricated, lightweight timber construction elements were delivered in a package and assembled on site in a very short space of time. For the construction, Konrad Wachsmann developed a jointing system with steel connecting pieces that made it possible to join panel modules of about one metre in size vertically and horizontally.[2] Compared with Gropius' earlier Copper Houses, this principle represented a major simplification as it enabled all connections between wall, floor and ceiling panels to be standardised.

In contrast to Richard Buckminster Fuller, who at about the same time was manufacturing identical houses and industrial projects in an aircraft factory (of which likewise only a few were actually built), Gropius and Wachsmann wanted to enable design variability. Numerous different solutions should be possible using a limited set of modular elements. One of the realised examples of their system was built as a model house next to the General Panel Corporation factory in Burbank, California. Wachsmann, who Gropius partnered with for this project, not only developed the house's construction system on his own, but also the factory's production processes.

1 According to Winfried Nerdinger, by 1952, when the General Package Corporation went bankrupt, only 150–200 houses had been built. The first prototype was presented to the public and the military on 23 February 1943 in Somerville, Massachusetts. Winfried Nerdinger, *The Architect Walter Gropius*, Berlin 1985, pp. 204–206.
2 The module is three feet and four Inches. See ibid, p. 204 and Gilbert Herbert, *The Dream of the Factory-Made House – Walter Gropius and Konrad Wachsmann*, Cambridge, MA 1984.

Floor plan of model house
The model house next to the factory

Factory for the Container Corporation of America

Greensboro, North Carolina, USA
1944–46 (with the Bellinger office)

Gropius was awarded this contract by the Container Corporation of America through his friendship with Walter Paepcke,[1] the company's director. Paepcke supported the New Bauhaus in Chicago, which was run by László Moholy-Nagy, and on Gropius' recommendation also commissioned the former Bauhaus student Herbert Bayer to undertake graphic design for the company, which produced boxes, paper and packaging. Gropius took on the role of consultant architect and designed the factory in Greensboro, but its planning and realisation was undertaken by the Bellinger architecture and engineering office.[2]

The factory building lies between a railway line and a street and is clad, like the adjoining office wing, with yellow and red brick. Its architectural expression is dominated by the strong horizontality of the ribbon windows, an impression further heightened by the dark brick base zone and the repeating delineation of the facades through the insertion of header courses at every ninth course of the otherwise regular running bond masonry.

1 Walter Paepcke was the chairman of the company's board of directors. See Reginald R. Isaacs, *Walter Gropius – Der Mensch und sein Werk*, Berlin 1987, pp. 927–928.
2 Winfried Nerdinger mentions that Gropius also advised on changes to the factory in Fernandina, Florida, of which there are numerous photographs in Gropius' legacy in the Berlin Bauhaus Archive, but no drawings. Winfried Nerdinger, *The Architect Walter Gropius*, Berlin 1985, p. 278.

Office wing seen from the road

Factory for Cartón de Colombia

Yumbo, Colombia
1945–48

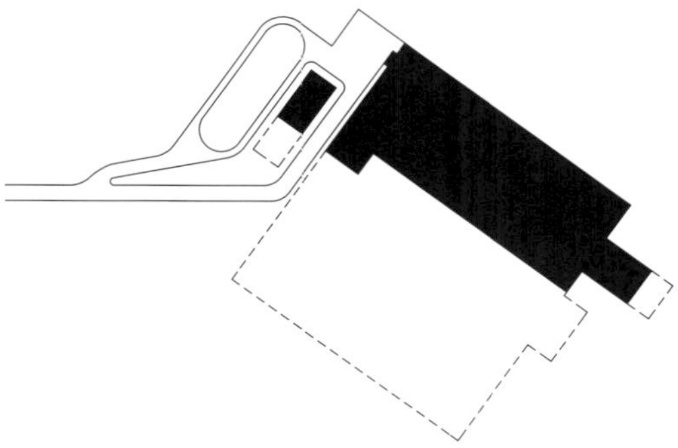

The cardboard and paper mill north of Cali on the Río Cauca was built in several stages.[1] Like the factory in Greensboro in the USA, which was built at the same time, the factory is fronted by a two-storey office building facing the road, on the roof of which the letters "Cartón de Colombia" were later mounted as envisaged by Gropius. As in Greensboro, glazing runs along the entire front of the five-section office building, interrupted only by the external columns of the skeleton frame, while the end walls are entirely unbroken. The factory building was later extended as planned to the southwest through the addition of further aisles with conventional pitched roofs and skylights. Since then the building has undergone numerous alterations and the factory no longer stands in open countryside but is now part of a densely built-up industrial district.

1 While the design plans from the Gropius Archive are held at Busch-Reisinger Museum at Harvard University, the aerial photograph shown here comes from the Bauhaus-Archiv in Berlin, where it was erroneously labelled as the "Office and Factory Building for the Container Corporation of America, Greensboro/N.C." (Inv. No. 6792/23). I would like to thank Liliana Naranjo Merino for her help in locating the building. The building is still used today as a paper mill by Smurfit Kappa Cartón de Colombia S.A.

Site plan
Phase one of the factory complex at Río Cauca

Howlett House

Belmont, Massachusetts, USA
1945–48 (with TAC)

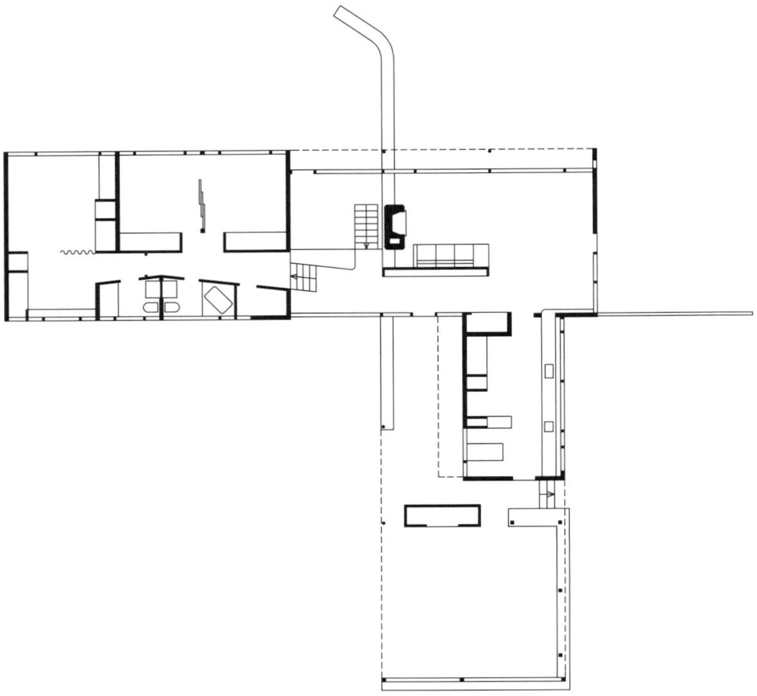

The house for Clarence and Jeannette Howlett, like Marcel Breuer's house in Lincoln, extends over three levels, with stairs leading up and down from a high living room to smaller rooms arranged on two levels above one another. It was the first building to be completed by The Architects Collaborative (TAC), which Gropius formed in 1945 together with seven younger partners.[1] All his later buildings were built in collaboration with TAC. Benjamin Thompson was the partner responsible for this house, and Gropius worked with him to completely revise an earlier preliminary design.

Access to the house is via a north-facing wing that encloses an open carport and the kitchen. The entrance to the house leads directly into an open universal space, the "living-dining and play room",[2] which is subdivided by a freestanding fireplace and a shelf and sofa element that act as room dividers. The south-facing fully-glazed room has a waxed stone floor, while the wooden structure of the building is clad with oiled cypress on the outside, with some interior walls also wood-panelled to create a sense of continuity between the interior and exterior. The commission also encompassed the choice of furniture and the design of the garden.

1 Co-founders were the partners Jean B. Fletcher, Norman C. Fletcher, John C. Harkness, Sarah P. Harkness, Louis A. McMillen, Robert S. McMillan and Benjamin Thompson.
2 Walter Gropius et al. (Ed.), *The Architects Collaborative TAC 1945–1965*, Teufen 1966, p. 54.

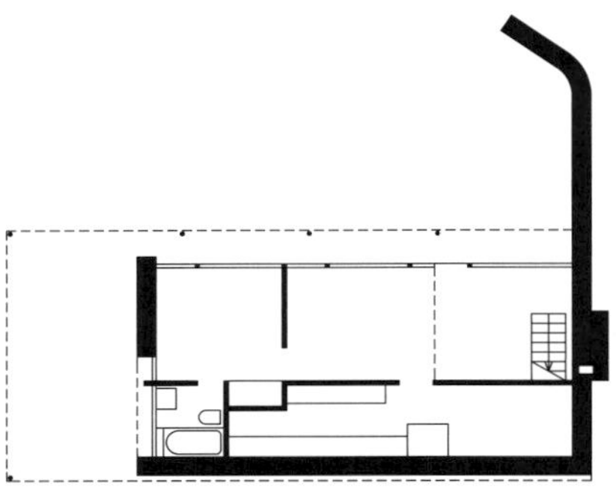

Ground floor plan
Lower floor plan
View from the garden

Michael Reese Hospital

Chicago, Illinois, USA
1945–59 (with TAC, Reginald R. Isaacs and Loebl, Schlossman & Bennett), mostly destroyed[1]

Although Gropius was not the lead architect for the project, serving only as an architectural consultant to the planning team, he still influenced the design of the complex. His input is visible in the layout of the master plan with its park-like arrangement and the architectural design of many of the buildings.[2] As with the neighbouring IIT campus for the Illinois Institute of Technology, designed by Ludwig Mies van der Rohe at the same time, the buildings here were also uniformly faced with yellow brick. In fact, the power plants of both complexes bear many architectural similarities. Unlike Mies' IIT, however, the pavilion buildings of the hospital were not arranged rigidly orthogonal to the street grid, indeed the first of the buildings that Gropius contributed to – the Singer Building, built in 1946-48 – has a Y-shaped ground plan. Gropius himself played down his contribution, remarking: "Largely, advice affecting good architectural design has not been implemented."[3] The demolition of the hospital buildings in 2009–10 was accompanied by public protests.

1 The hospital complex was demolished in 2009–10. Only the Singer Pavilion from 1946–48 was preserved.
2 Gropius advised on the architectural design of the buildings: Singer Pavilion, Laundry Building, Serum Center, Power Plant, Friend Convalescent Home, Linear Accelerator, Kaplan Pavilion and Cummings Pavilion.
3 Walter Gropius in a letter to Ferd Kramer dated 8 January 1951, cited in: Reginald R. Isaacs, *Gropius: An Illustrated Biography of the Creator of the Bauhaus*, Boston 1991, p. 266.

Power plant, designed by Reginald R. Isaacs

Peter Thacher Junior High School

Attleboro, Massachusetts, USA
1947–51 (with TAC)

Peter Thacher Junior High School comprises four different wings grouped around a central courtyard.[1] From the entrance hall, an open ramp leads to the cafeteria and on to the auditorium with theatre stage, while the south-facing classrooms are arranged in a separate wing of the building reached via glazed corridors. To the east an external gymnasium building connects to the complex. The two-storey main building houses the workshops, science rooms and school administration offices. The free disposition of the building wings is a variation of the design concept of Impington Village College from a decade earlier. That school was likewise clad with yellow brick on the outside as well as in some indoor areas.

The wing with the classrooms has since been demolished, and the remaining parts of the building have been altered almost beyond recognition. The entrance situation has also changed so that little remains of the original design concept, which Sigfried Giedion described at the time as "relaxed ground plans that spread out lightly over the landscape".[2]

1 Walter Gropius et al. (Ed.), *The Architects Collaborative TAC 1945–1965*, Teufen 1966, pp. 32–36. The responsible TAC partners were John C. Harkness and Louis A. McMillen.
2 Sigfried Giedion, *Walter Gropius – Work and Teamwork*, New York 1954, p. 59.

Entrance elevation

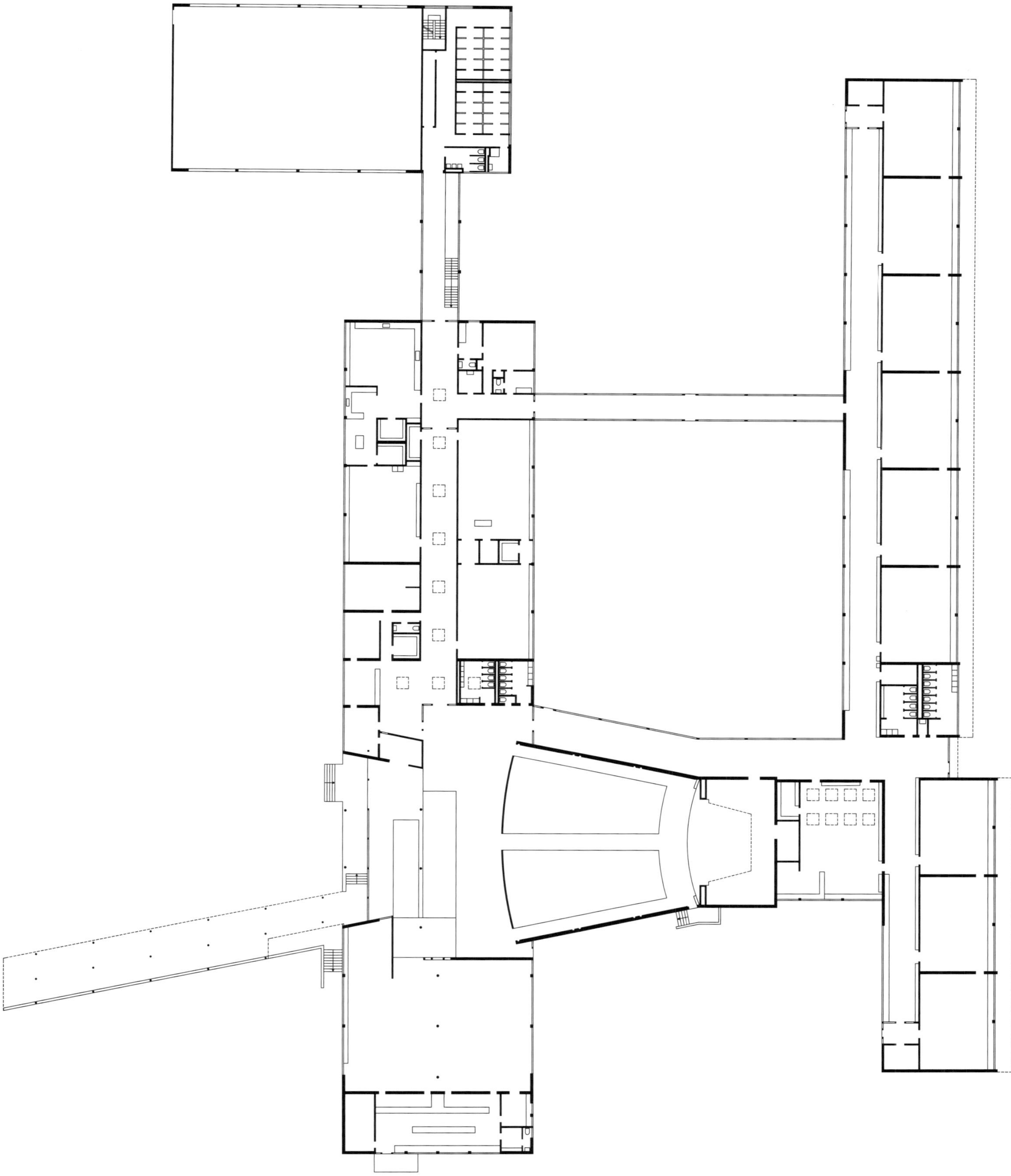

Ground floor plan

Harvard Graduate Center

Cambridge, Massachusetts, USA
1948–50 (with TAC)

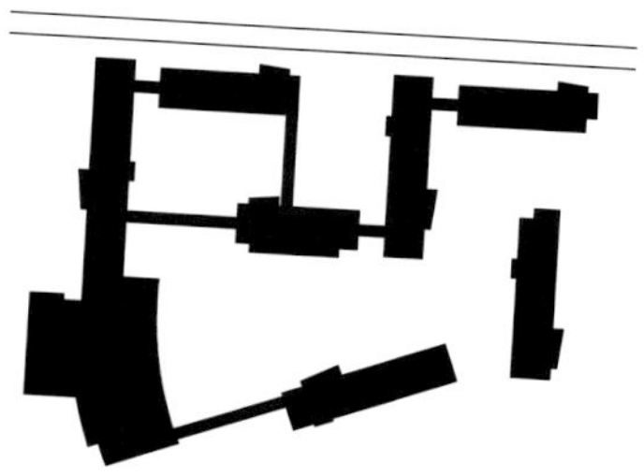

For the campus of Harvard University campus, the partners of TAC (The Architects Collaborative), led by Gropius, designed a group of residential buildings for almost 600 students with an adjacent two-storey community centre. A system of ramps connects the two floors of the central building containing common rooms and a refectory, and, on Gropius' suggestion, artworks were incorporated into the architecture, including murals by the former Bauhaus students Josef Albers and Herbert Bayer.[1]

Even though its architectural language contrasts with the surrounding buildings, Gropius saw the new building complex as maintaining the continuity of the specific architectural tradition of the Harvard campus, which in his view lay in the spatial pattern of the Harvard Yard: "A composition of quadrangles, varying in size and confined by individually different buildings, offers a sequence of arresting surprises in space".[2] With the new buildings, the aim was "to make use of repetitive standard parts, but at the same time to organize these parts in groups which vary in appearance. In the Graduate Center we strove to break the monotony which might have resulted from repetitive fenestration by changing the direction of the dormitory blocks as well as the design of their ends and links. This has resulted in a variety of different views for the onlooker."[3]

Although the colours of the buildings echoed the limestone cladding and concrete columns of the community building, the primary colours red, blue and yellow also appear on the facades. In spite of the industrial character of the very functional dormitory facades with their uniform window bands and steel profiles, visual variety was created by making the balconies reach out like drawers or by fully glazing the staircases, causing the adjoining brick and stone facades to look like independent wall planes.

1 The participating artists also included Hans Arp, Richard Lippold and Joan Miró. Cf.: Walter Gropius et al. (Ed.), *The Architects Collaborative TAC 1945–1965*, Teufen 1966, p. 71.
2 Walter Gropius, *Scope of Total Architecture*, New York 1962, p. 68. Originally published on 23 October 1949 in *New York Times Magazine*.
3 Ibid., p. 69.

Site plan

Community building

Community building, view from the southwest

Dormitory block, rear facade
Dormitory block, end elevation with stairs

Dormitory blocks, view from the rear courtyard
Facade detail
Ribbon windows with top-hung windows

Stichweh House

Hanover, Germany
1951–53 (with TAC)

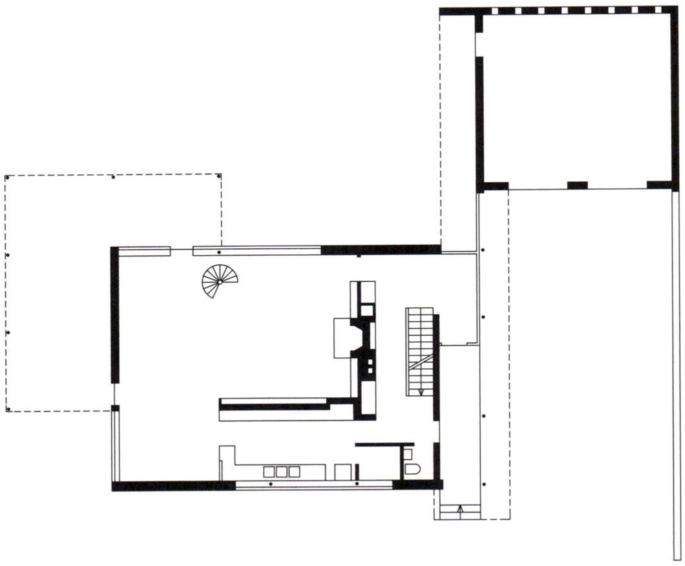

The house is a cuboid building on a rectangular floor plan of 3:4 proportions with a veranda attached on one side.[1] The spacing of the veranda's slender metal posts corresponds to their height resulting in a row of squares across the front of the elevation. Intended as a geometric abstraction of the traditional American porch, here it faces onto the garden rather than the street. At the front, a canopy leads visitors to the entrance and also connects the house with the separate volume of the garage.

The house is entered via a large glazed entrance hall offering a visual axis through the entire length of the building, while further diagonal views from the adjoining living and dining room extend outwards to create a sensation of maximum spaciousness. The door to this central L-shaped room is wood-panelled like the wall, and a spiral staircase freely placed in the room leads up to the library.

"From far away its silhouette should be simple so that it can be grasped at a glance," Gropius explained at the time. "When we come closer [...], no longer able to see the whole edifice, the eye should be attracted by a new surprise in the form of refined surface treatment."[2] In the case of the brick wall panels, which alternate with rendered and recessed surfaces in the facade, only the horizontal joints cast shadows, as the vertical joints are flush with the brick surface. The recessing of the rendered surfaces emphasised the wall-plane character of the brick surfaces. The cubature of the house was later altered by the addition of a single-storey extension.[3]

1 The owners were Wilhelm and Margret Stichweh, a businessman and a doctor. "Kleines Wohnhaus in Hannover", in: *Bauen und Wohnen*, 8/1953, pp. 450–452.
2 *Walter Gropius, Scope of Total Architecture*, New York 1962, p. 38. Originally published as "Design Topics" in: *Magazine of Art*, December 1947.
3 The 1974 extension was designed by the architects Hübotter Ledeboer Busch. Today, the building is used by the BDA Association of German Architects.

Ground floor plan
Entrance elevation

Garden elevation

Overholt Clinic

Boston, Massachusetts, USA
1953–55 (with TAC), destroyed

The heart and lung clinic attached to the New England Deaconess Hospital was connected to the hospital by a bridge.[1] The building was elevated so that cars can park beneath it and was accessed via a glazed entrance hall. On the ground floor there were also technical rooms and a staff room with another staircase leading to the upper floor. The offices, consulting rooms and laboratories on the upper floor were separated by lightweight, movable partitions,[2] creating a flexible structural framework, also achieved by dimensioning the steel skeleton frame so that the building could be extended upwards.

The building was constructed of prefabricated elements as an almost entirely dry construction. The 2.50-metre-wide facade elements, prefabricated with three different window sizes, were assembled as sandwich panels for use in the modular construction. Precast concrete elements were also used for the floors and ceilings. Only on the ground floor were some external walls clad with brick.

1 Today the hospital is part of the Beth Israel Deaconess Medical Center. See "Thoracic Clinic", in: Walter Gropius et al. (Ed.), *The Architects Collaborative TAC 1945–1965*, Teufen 1966, pp. 90–93. John C. Harkness was the responsible TAC Partner.
2 Reginald R. Isaacs, *Walter Gropius – Der Mensch und sein Werk*, Berlin 1987, p. 1032.

Entrance elevation

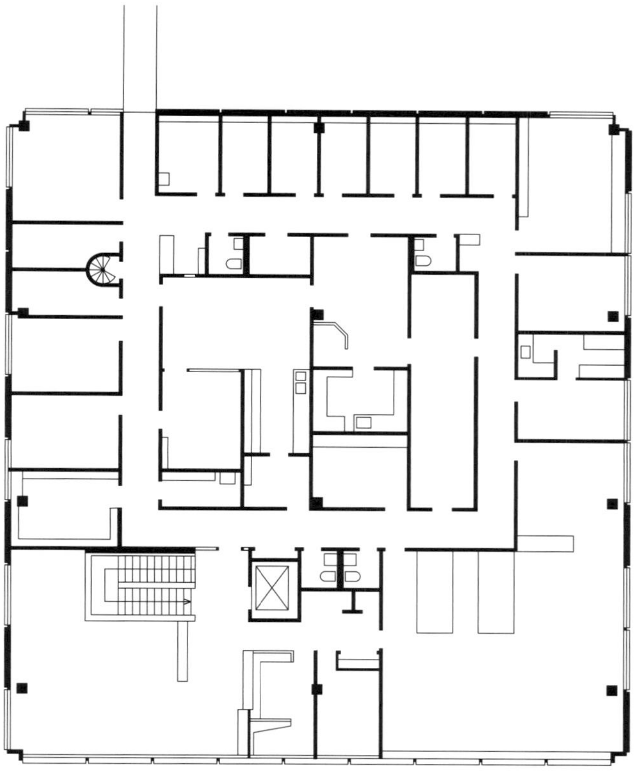

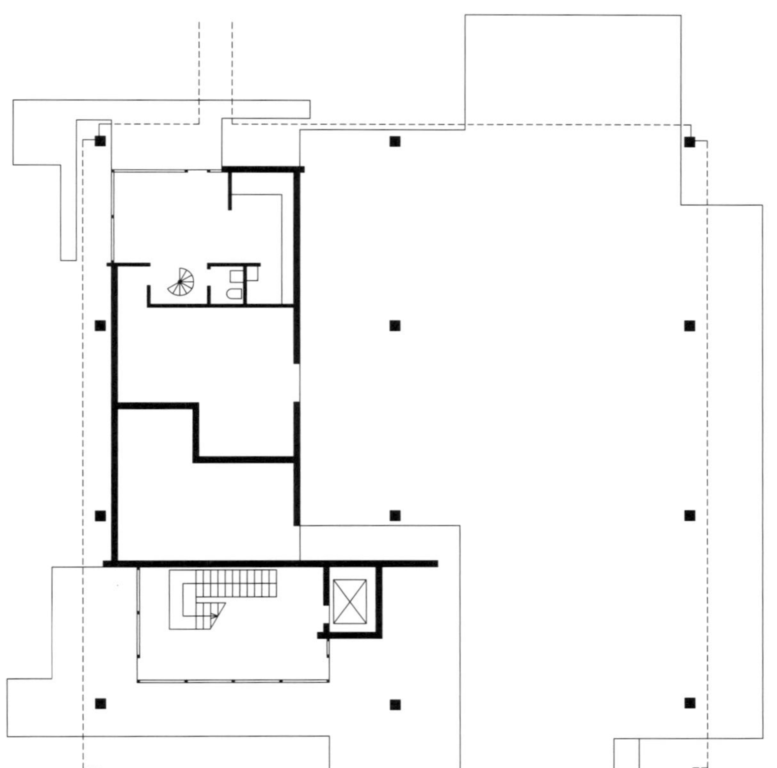

Upper floor plan
Ground floor plan

Hansaviertel Apartment Block

Berlin-Hansaviertel, Germany
1955–57 (with TAC and Wils Ebert)

For the International Building Exhibition Interbau 1957, Gropius, in collaboration with his TAC partner Norman C. Fletcher, developed a design for an apartment block with a concave facade facing south towards the Tiergarten.[1] The building directly adjoins the park and stands next to blocks by Pierre Vago and Alvar Aalto. Gropius' goal was to create an "evolution of the typical Berlin residential building"[2] and he was highly critical of the urban planning concept of individual solitaires: "The coordination is bad, more like a patternbook of architects than an organic integration".[3]

The floor plans of the apartments follow the apartment types of the Siemensstadt and Dammerstock housing estates of the 1920s, even though the skeleton construction made freer floor plans possible.[4] The apartments follow the same pattern on eight floors, except that the balconies are arranged partly in front of the living rooms and partly to the side of the living rooms, lending the facades a chessboard-like rhythm to counteract the impression of monotony. Nikolaus Pevsner, however, suggested that this was mere formalism: "The arrangement of the balconies seems at least to me more dictated by the wish for such a surface pattern than by planning considerations."[5] The top floor housed studio apartments with roof terraces and storage rooms were located on the ground floor of the building, which had no basement. As in the Siemensstadt project, the four stairwells are distinguished from one another by means of different colours. The surface treatment of the facade is also varied using blue paint for the undersides of the balconies as well as different rendering textures. The rough and smooth surfaces lend the structure of the facade a sense of tectonic articulation.

1 Walter Gropius et al. (Ed.), *The Architects Collaborative TAC 1945–1965*, Teufen 1966, pp. 94–97. Architect Wils Ebert was involved as the Berlin contact.
2 Reginald R. Isaacs, *Walter Gropius – Der Mensch und sein Werk*, Berlin 1984, p. 1073.
3 Walter Gropius in a letter to Ise Gropius dated 23 September1955, in: ibid., p. 1068.
4 The apartment floor plans are particularly conventional in comparison to the Alvar Aalto Apartments.
5 Nikolaus Pevsner, "Berlin: City of Tomorrow", in: *The Listener*, 8 August 1957, pp. 197–199.

Concave south facade facing the park

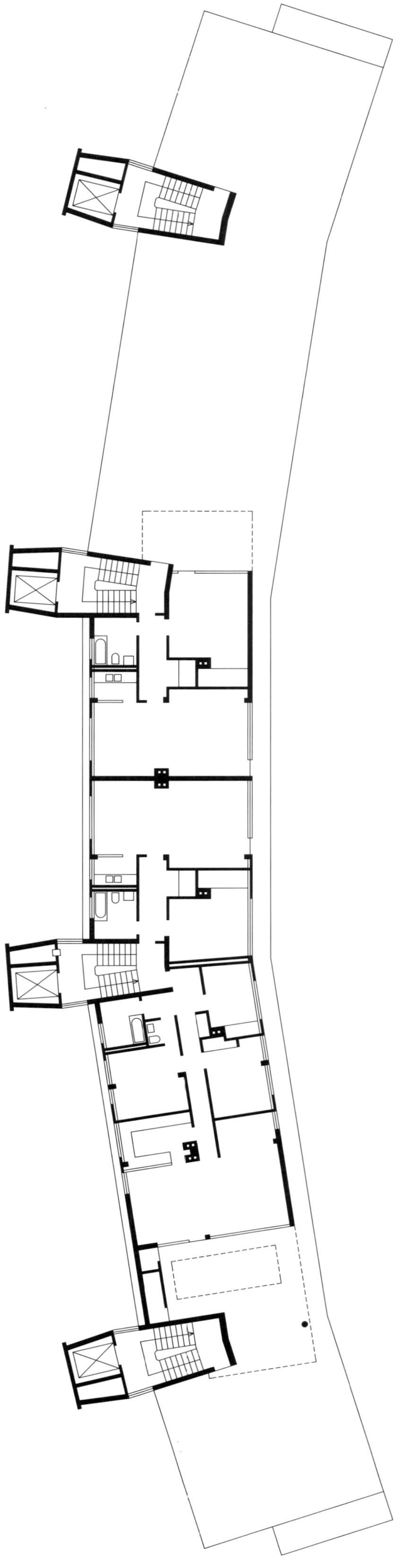

Floor plan of roof level
Ground floor plan

View from the southeast
View from the northwest

Corner with roof terrace
Base zone

US Embassy Athens

Athens, Greece
1956–61 (with TAC and Perikles Sakellarios)

The building interprets the architecture of the nearby Acropolis. Raised on a platform, the architecture is defined by a ring of clearly proportioned columns made of marble, a material used here, however, as facing for the reinforced concrete construction.[1] As with the classical temple, the front and back are the same, and here too it is possible to pass through the rows of columns. "One is, as it were, drawn into the inner courtyard,"[2] Sigfried Giedion remarked. "The architectural structure is identical on all sides of the building, inside and outside."[3]

Gropius had already studied classical Greek architecture while working in Peter Behrens' studio. "He introduced me [...] to the geometric rules of Greek architecture," said Gropius about Behrens, "I learned from his systematic design principles, from his mastery of the technique of spatial relationships and his theory of proportions."[4] After visiting the Acropolis, Gropius declared in 1957, "The Parthenon keeps its eternal promise."[5]

In the embassy building, the monumental pillars form a frame construction from which the membrane-like glass facade of the offices and a marble cornice are suspended on cantilevered beams. The overhang supports a sunshade set slightly forward of the building that shields the interior from the sun on all sides and creates openings in the roof for ventilation.[6] Despite the high-security requirements of such a building, the architecture sought to create an inviting gesture through its open structure. Its modular design, like that of a megastructure, was planned to incorporate the possibility of change. Since then, rooms have been added on the ground floor with the result that the building is no longer as open as it once was.

1 The embassy is clad in the same Pentelic marble that was used to build the Parthenon. Cf. Walter Gropius et al. (Ed.), *The Architects Collaborative TAC 1945–1965*, Teufen 1966, p. 105.
2 Sigfried Giedion, *Raum, Zeit, Architektur – Die Entstehung einer neuen Tradition*, Basel, Berlin, Boston 2015, pp. 325–326.
3 Ibid., p. 325.
4 Walter Gropius in: *Peter Behrens*, exhibition catalogue, Pfalzgalerie Kaiserslautern 1966, p. 5.
5 Walter Gropius in a postcard to Reginald R. Isaacs dated 14 June 1957, in: Reginald R. Isaacs, *Walter Gropius – Der Mensch und sein Werk*, Berlin 1987, p. 1032.
6 "Amerikanische Botschaft in Athen", in: *Bauen + Wohnen*, Vol. 12, 1959, p. 412.

View from the road

Stairs leading up to the building
Inner courtyard

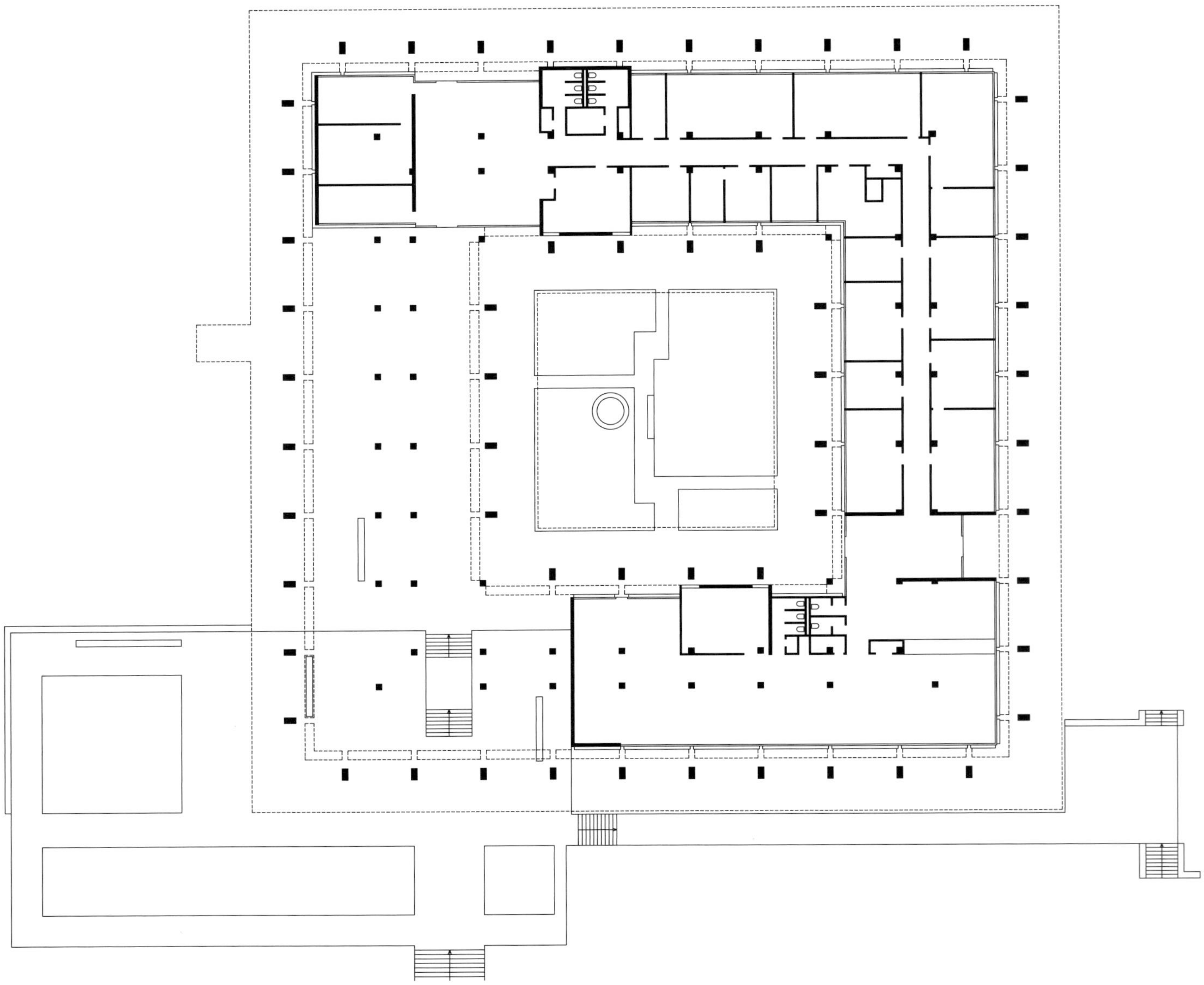

Ground floor plan

Oheb Shalom Synagogue

Baltimore, Maryland, USA
1957–60 (with TAC and Leavitt Associates)

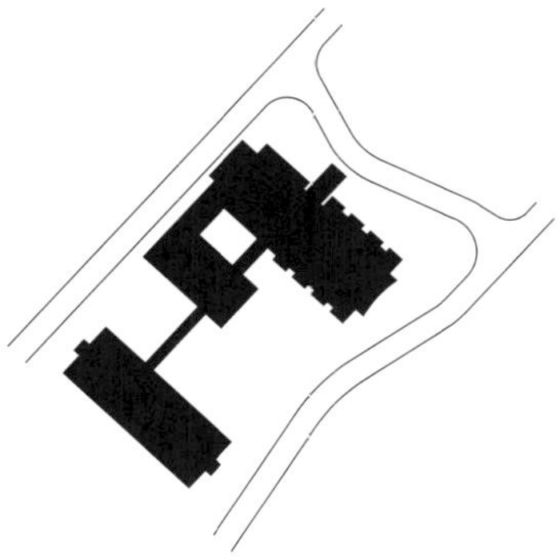

Attached to the synagogue are a community centre and a school, the different parts are linked together by a central access corridor. The main synagogue hall to the left of the entrance and a community hall to the right can be joined together with the entrance hall to form a large space for special events for up to 2,000 people.[1] The main synagogue hall is articulated on the facades by four twelve-metre-high barrel vaults arranged crosswise. Skylights on the north side of the vaults, together with coloured glass windows, illuminate the hall.[2]

The building, clad in limestone and red brick, was later altered both inside and out. While the two long sides of the synagogue with their rhythmic arched facades were originally identical, only the facade next to the main entrance now remains after the addition of further extensions. The interior of the synagogue was also completely redesigned: while the room was originally entered from the north and sloped to the south, today it is oriented in the opposite direction.

1 The narrow sides of the two halls could be opened with the help of large folding doors. Cf.: Walter Gropius et al. (Ed.), *The Architects Collaborative TAC 1945–1965*, Teufen 1966, pp. 106–109.
2 The glass windows were designed by György Kepes who also designed the central Ark of the Covenant.

Site plan
View from the north
Interior of the synagogue

University of Baghdad

Baghdad, Iraq
1957–83 (with TAC and Kisham A. Munir)

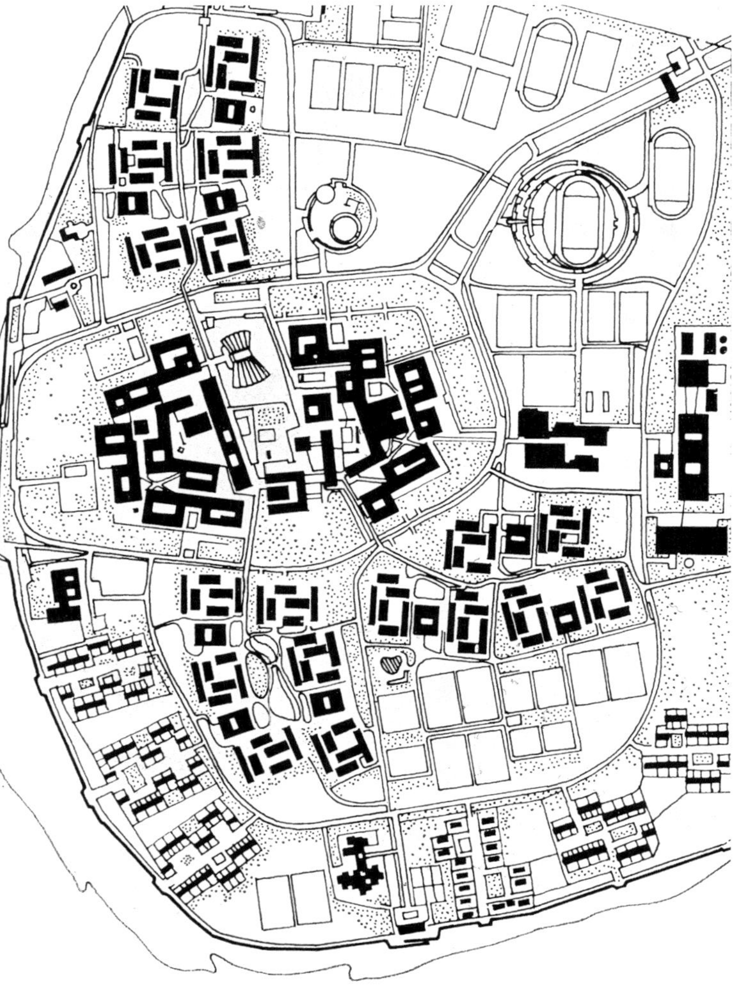

Gropius was invited to build a university with 273 buildings on the banks of the Tigris that was "to be a small town",[1] a commission brokered by a former student whose father became prime minister of Iraq in 1957.[2] To undertake the project, The Architects Collaborative opened another office in Rome with at one point 150 employees,[3] but due to political upheavals in Iraq in the following years, execution was delayed and only part of the design was ever realised.

A monumental entrance gateway was built first as a symbolic gesture and, at the client's request, a high-rise building that was not part of the architects' original master plan. The team of architects, who also drew up the extensive programme of spaces for the institution, had envisaged a low-rise, dense development, like those of a traditional Arabian settlement: "The basic concept has been the idea of the balance of unity and diversity, of integration and differentiation," Gropius wrote.[4]

Arranged around the central campus, enclosed within a ring road, were clusters of student dormitories as well as a mosque designed as a round dome. "All buildings are placed round patios of various sizes, which are filled with plants, water basins, and fountains," Gropius explained, "The interrelationship of the individual buildings and the landscaped open spaces with their water fountains between them, as well as the shadow effects from the strong sunlight obtained by cantilevers and undercuts will cause a significant rhythm."[5]

The layout of the student dormitories is based on a system of eight interconnected buildings grouped around a central courtyard that enclose further courtyards with stairwells arranged between the buildings. Communal kitchens were located in separate buildings, so that the rooms had no cooking facilities. Although the arrangement of the buildings varies, the same building type is repeated.[6]

1 Walter Gropius et al. (Ed.), *The Architects Collaborative TAC 1945–1965*, Teufen 1966, p. 124.
2 Nizar Ali Jawdat and his wife Ellen, who also studied with Gropius, met him in Baghdad in 1954 and introduced him to leading figures in the country. Cf.: Regina Göckede, *Spätkoloniale Moderne – Le Corbusier, Ernst May, Frank Lloyd Wright, The Architects Collaborative und die Globalisierung der Architekturmoderne*, Basel, Boston, Berlin 2016, p. 352.
3 As described in: Winfried Nerdinger, *The Architect Walter Gropius*, Berlin 1985, p. 288.
4 Walter Gropius, "Universität in Bagdad", in: *Bauen + Wohnen*, Vol. 11, 1959, p. 392.
5 Ibid.
6 In each of the three housing clusters the building scheme shown in the TAC publication of 1966 (see note 1) is repeated four times, partly in a mirrored arrangement, while the northern cluster to the south is repeated again in a mirrored arrangement. In terms of its urban planning, however, the housing follows only the original master plan.

Master plan from 1960, realised differently
Entrance pavilion

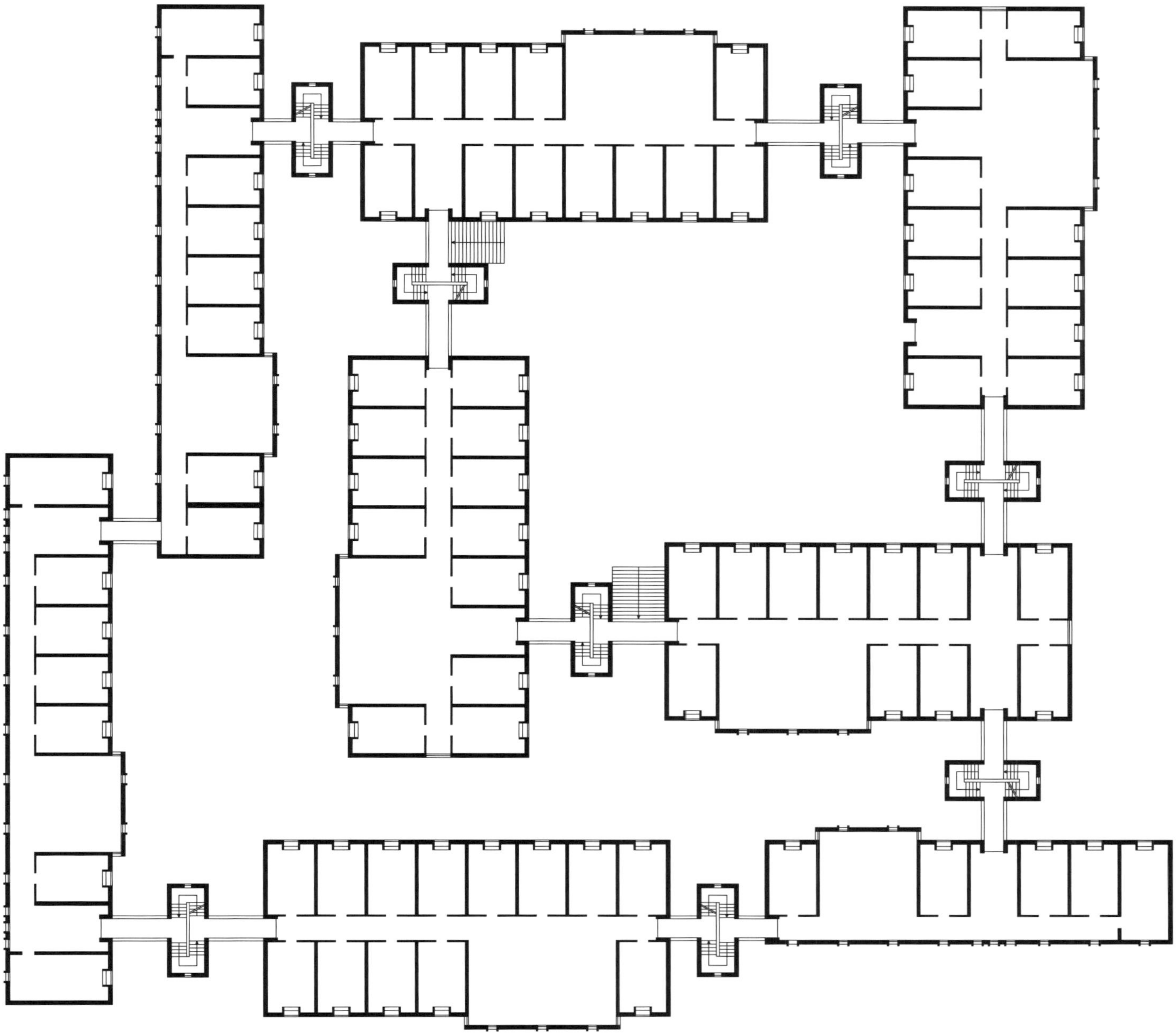

Floor plan of the dormitories, upper floor
Dormitory

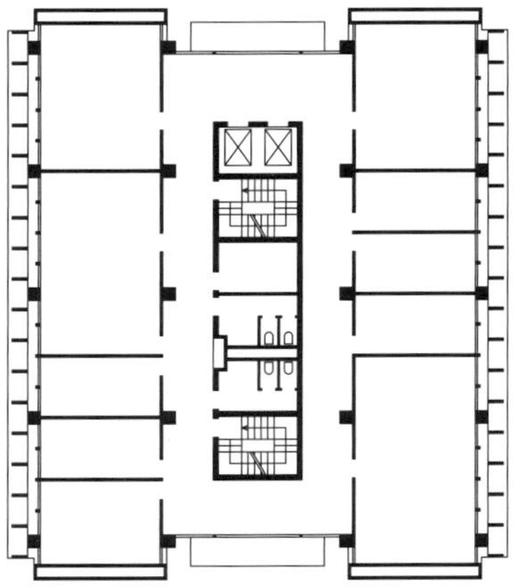

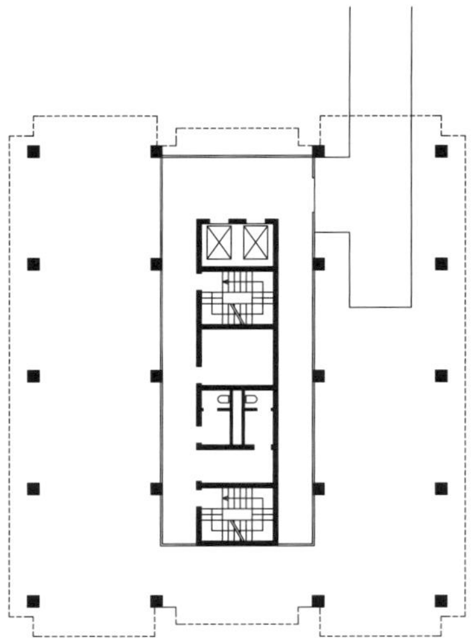

Typical floor plan of the high-rise tower
First floor plan of the high-rise tower
High-rise tower

Pan Am Building

New York, USA
1958–63 (with TAC, Emery Roth & Sons and Pietro Belluschi)

The building is the only skyscraper in New York to stand above the intersection of two streets. Although a tower was erected on Park Avenue in 1929 above the underground railway lines of Grand Central Station, the Pan Am Building is also situated on the axis of a road crossing. Gropius and Pietro Belluschi were brought in by the architects Emery Roth & Sons as consultants for the design and were responsible for the outer form of the building, the compressed octagonal plan and the detailing of the facade. Reportedly "Gropius' most controversial commission",[1] the project was subject to immense criticism, though more due to the building's magnitude and scale on the site than its design.[2]

Gropius and The Architects Collaborative argued that the development was necessary to increase the density of the city: "Concentration of high building masses placed close together – so undesirable for residential districts – has proved to simplify business interchange by replacing horizontal vehicular traffic by vertical traffic communication (in the Pan Am Building by 64 elevators and 18 escalators)."[3] The location of the elevators in the centre of the tower was the reason for its prismatic shape. The tower crowns a lower, nine-storey block of buildings and is directly connected to the subterranean metro station, while the roof has a helipad providing a direct connection to New York's airports.

Like the tower, the base building is clad with a facade of precast concrete elements. White quartz in the concrete mix gives it the character of stone, an impression heightened at the base by the traditional tectonic articulation of the facade. At the corners, in particular, the impression is of heavy blocks stacked on top of each other, in contrast to the precast curtain-wall like concrete elements attached to the facade of the tower.

1 Reginald R. Isaacs, *Gropius: An Illustrated Biography of the Creator of the Bauhaus*, Boston 1991, p. 283.
2 Philip Johnson proposed a park for this site, and Frank Lloyd Wright is said to have forbidden taxi drivers from driving down Park Avenue so that he would not have to see the building. The building for Pan American Airlines was even declared a symbol of the failure of modern architecture. For more on the controversial history of the building's reception. See Meredith L. Clausen, *The Pan Am Building and the Shattering of the Modernist Dream*, Cambridge, MA 2004.
3 Walter Gropius et al. (Ed.), *The Architects Collaborative TAC 1945–1965*, Teufen 1966, pp. 152–160.

View from the north of Park Avenue

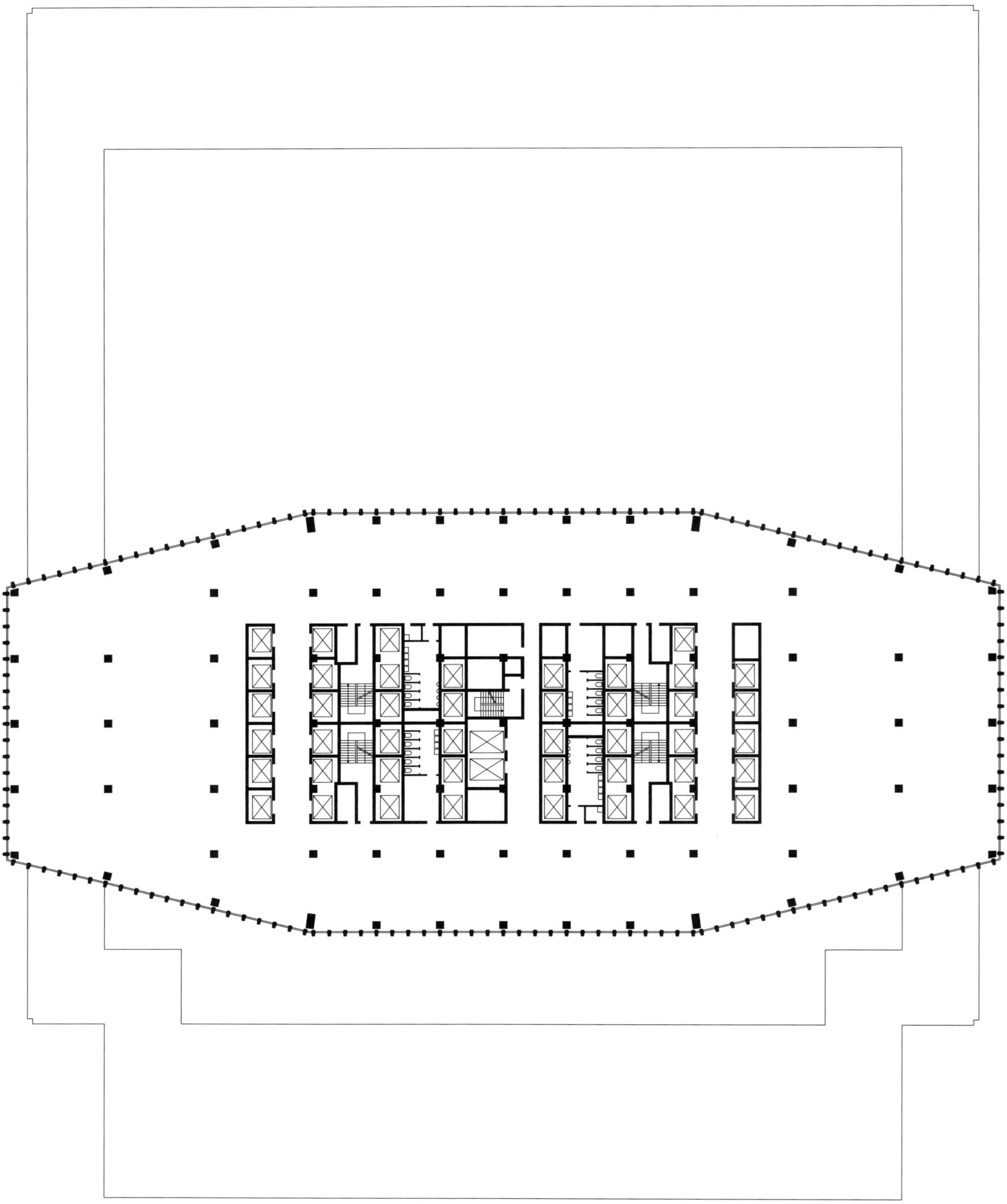

Floor plan of the tower

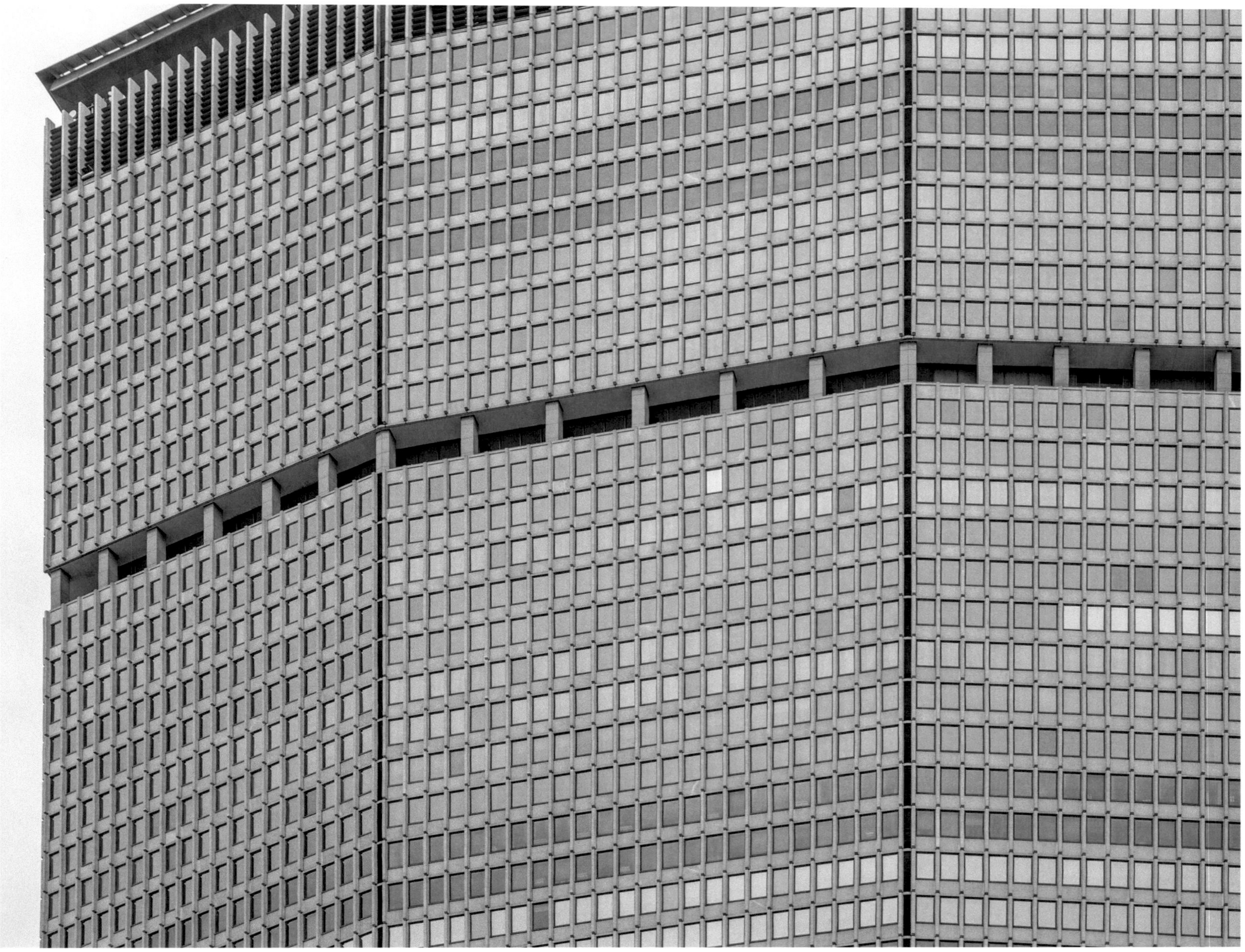

Facade of the tower
Junction between the base building and the tower
Corner of the base building and the tower

Gropiusstadt

Berlin-Gropiusstadt, Germany
1959–72 (with TAC and Wils Ebert)

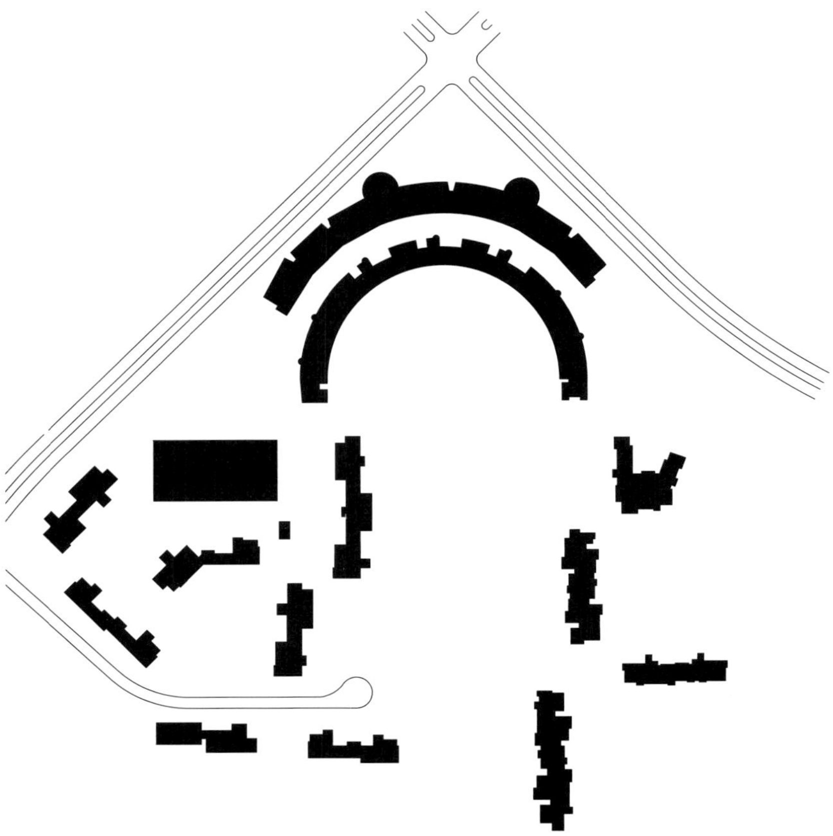

Gropius' office was commissioned to design a completely new district on the outskirts of Berlin for almost 50,000 people. The large Britz-Buckow-Rudow housing development was to separate the paths of pedestrians and cars. The master plan drawn up in 1960 extended the principle of Bruno Taut's neighbouring Hufeisensiedlung (Horseshoe Estate), arranging loose rows of buildings grouped around ring-shaped buildings with green courtyards. However, the design, as well as a subsequent revised plan in the following year, was rejected by the housing association and the West Berlin Senate. Just after the project was presented, the Berlin Wall was erected, and since West Berlin could no longer expand into the surrounding area, a denser arrangement of buildings was necessary. Gropius' contact architect in Berlin, Wils Ebert, was commissioned with the revision, but as the lead architect he now developed his own design, incorporating higher buildings.

In his speech at the laying of the foundation stone of the settlement, Gropius did explain that "according to the latest research, a greater density of the building mass can where necessary be desirable",[1] but his original role as the overall coordinator was waning. In a letter to the Berlin Senate he complained that Ebert "has ignored the basic concept of my development plan," and was instead pursuing an urban ideology of strictly north-south oriented housing blocks developed in the 1920s that was, however, "now obsolete".[2] Even though Gropius was later commissioned to design a group of programmatic buildings for part of the settlement, he concluded: "I must confess that this undertaking is the most disappointing I have ever had to deal with."[3]

Of the numerous ring-shaped buildings that he planned for the settlement, only one was realised, and that with a radius about half as large as originally planned. In addition, Gropius and The Architects Collaborative designed a building layout for use in different variations as well as a high-rise tower, even though he declared at the time: "I find myself in a strange position. In the 1930s, I propagated the residential tower in Berlin and was ridiculed by the press and the Stadtbaurat Martin Wagner. Today I tend to resist excessive density where I can."[4] Gropius did not live to see the completion of the building ensemble in 1972, nor the naming of the entire district after him in the same year.

1 Walter Gropius, speech on the occasion of the laying of the foundation stone on 12 November 1962, in: Hans Bandel and Dittmar Machule, *Die Gropiusstadt – Der städtebauliche Planungs- und Entscheidungsvorgang,* Berlin 1974, p. 76.
2 Walter Gropius in a letter to Rolf Schwedler dated 21 June 1966, in: ibid., p. 114.
3 Walter Gropius in a letter to Rolf Schwedler dated 19 April 1966, in: ibid., p. 112.
4 Walter Gropius in a letter to Hans Bandel dated 25 October 1966, in: ibid., p. 111.

Site plan

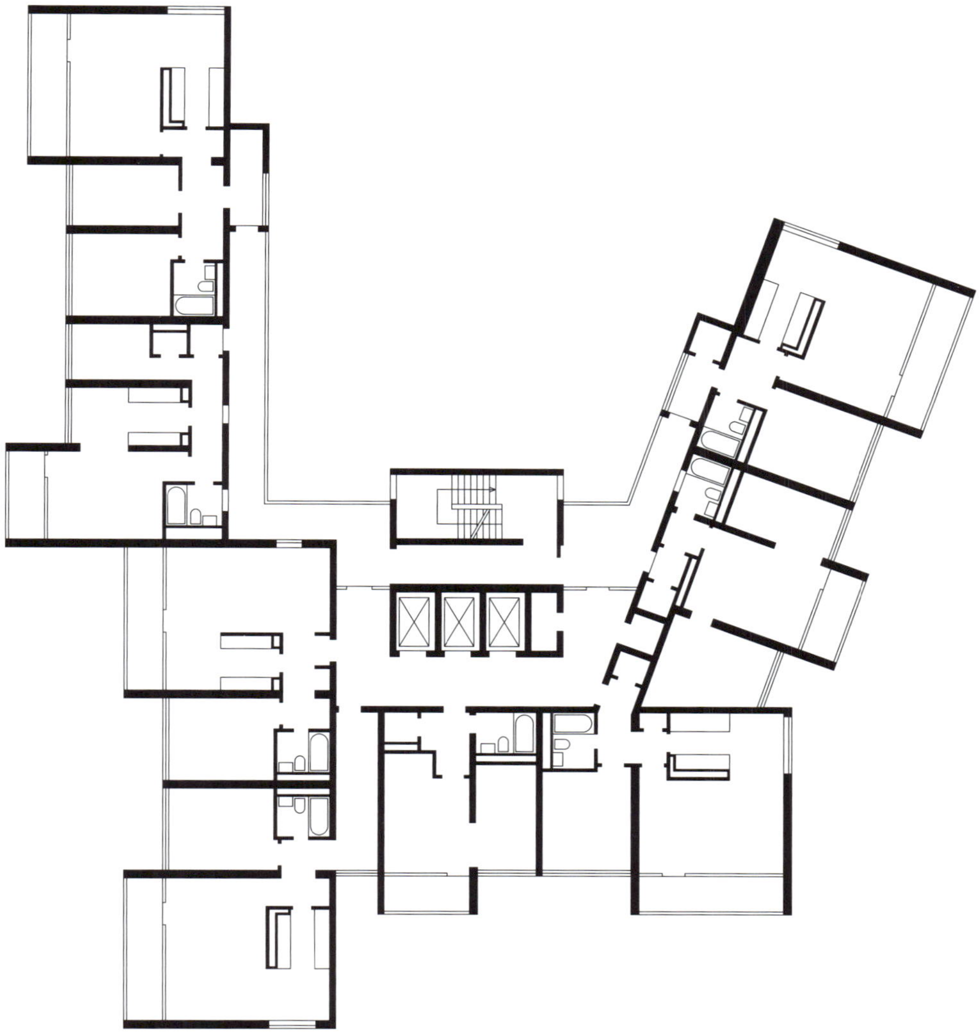

Floor plan of the high-rise tower
High-rise tower
Facade with cantilevering elements

Ring-shaped building, south elevation
North elevation

John F. Kennedy Federal Building

Boston, Massachusetts, USA
1961–66 (with TAC and Samuel Glaser Associates)

The building complex is situated opposite the new Boston Town Hall, built at the same time, with a paved plaza between the buildings. Built as an administrative complex, it comprises a high-rise tower and a four-storey building and stands on a platform reached via various flights of steps. As with Mies van der Rohe's buildings, the podium and the crowning structure form an architectural unit. The formal principle draws on an idea used for the Dreischeibenhaus in Düsseldorf and subdivides the high-rise into staggered planes to give the building a slender appearance,[1] an impression further heightened by siting the glazed stairwells in the gap between them. In the low building, meanwhile, a long section cantilevers forward underlining the building's horizontality. The facing of the facade is hung from the skeleton frame and is made of uniform precast concrete sections, while the base of the building is clad with slabs of dark granite. The rounded corners of the buildings make the facade look like an enclosing skin.

1 The TAC partner responsible for the project, Norman C. Fletcher, explained that the design idea came directly from the Düsseldorf building completed in 1960. Norman C. Fletcher, "The John F. Kennedy Federal Office Building in Boston", in: National Gallery of Art (Ed.), *Symposium Papers XXX: Federal Buildings in Context*, New Haven 1995, p. 41.

View from the plaza

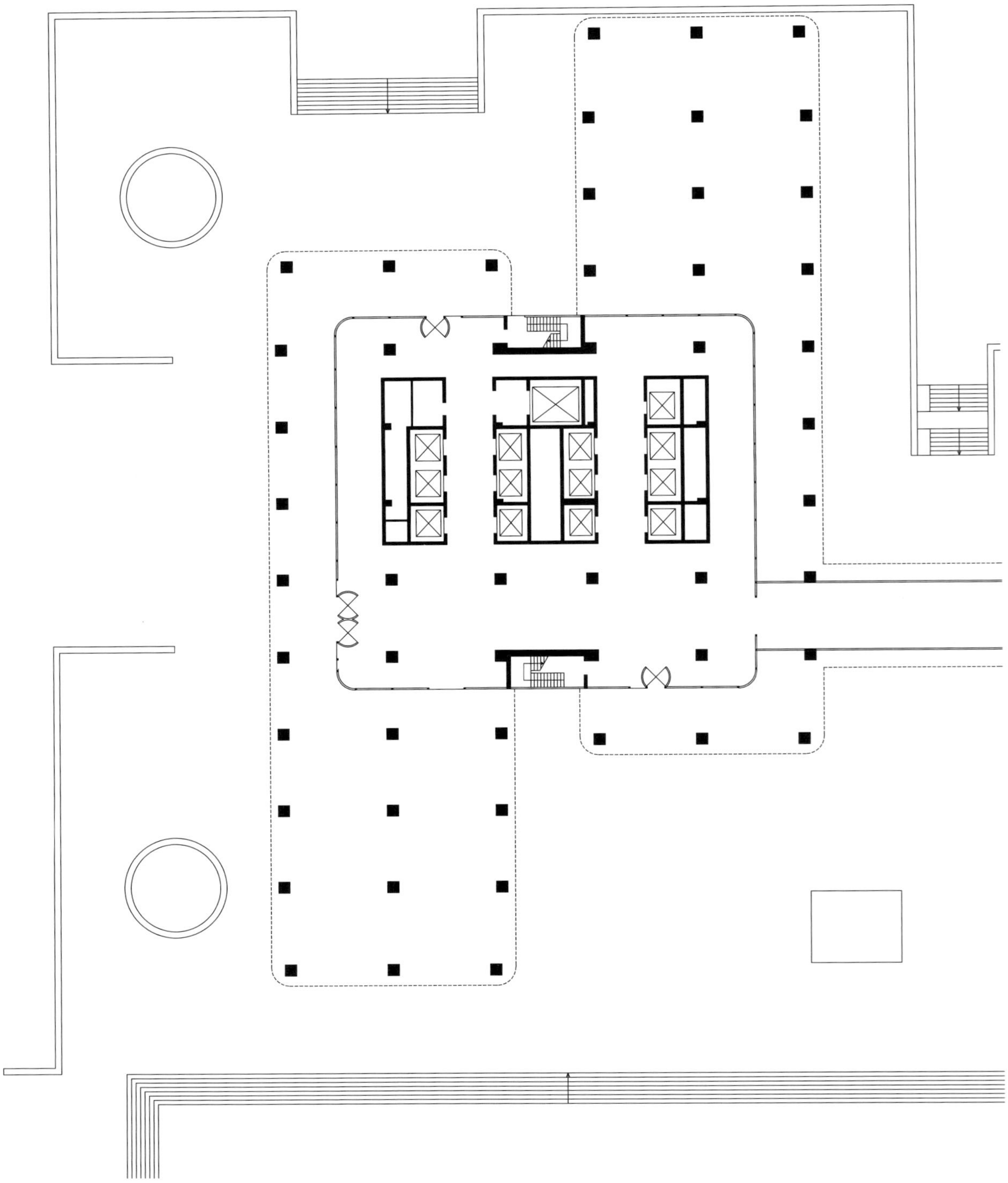

Ground floor plan of the tower

Corner of the building at ground level
Zone beneath the tower

Elevation of the two high-rise towers and glazed stairwell

Modulatec surface of the concrete facade

School and Kindergarten, Gropiusstadt

Berlin-Gropiusstadt, Germany
1962–68 (with TAC and Wils Ebert)

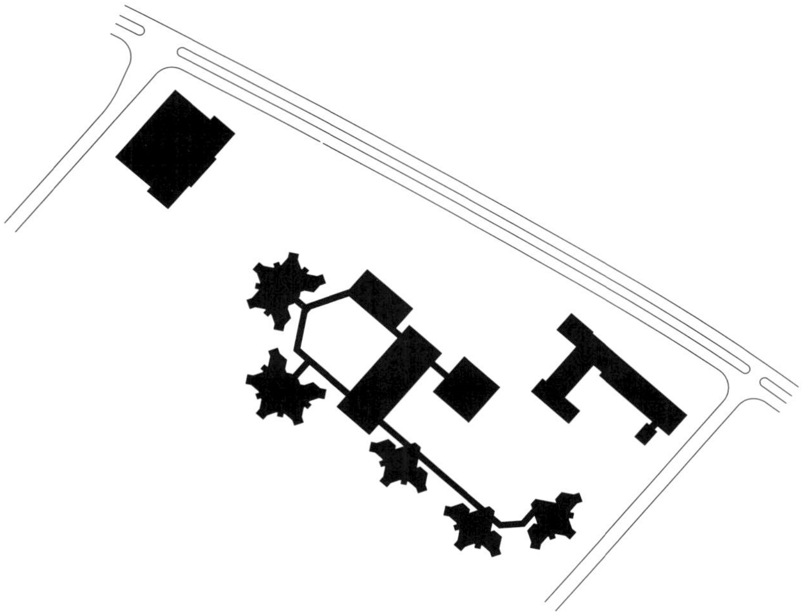

The school consists of a series of pavilion-like buildings connected by a glazed corridor. In each pavilion, the classrooms are grouped as hexagonal modular units around a central common room. Accessed from the multifunctional common room as well as via external staircases, the classrooms and common core echo the principles of structuralist architecture. While the concrete surfaces have in parts been given a ribbed texture, the interiors were painted according to a colour scheme by the Bauhaus designer Lou Scheper-Berkenkamp.

Gropius described the building as an "experimental school"[1] and also proposed a new school plan.[2] It was the first comprehensive school in the Federal Republic of Germany and also had an adjoining kindergarten and nursery school. Alexander Cvijanovic played a central role in the design of the project and went on to become the design architect in the TAC office for Gropius' later buildings in Germany.[3]

1 Walter Gropius et al. (Ed.), *The Architects Collaborative TAC 1945–1965*, Teufen 1966, p. 197.
2 Bauhaus-Archiv Berlin (Ed.), *Walter Gropius – Bauten und Projekte 1906–1969*, Berlin 1980, p. 24.
3 Alexander Cvijanovic, a native of Yugoslavia, spoke German and became a partner of the office. Wils Ebert acted as the contact architect in Berlin for this building.

Site plan
Pavilion type 2

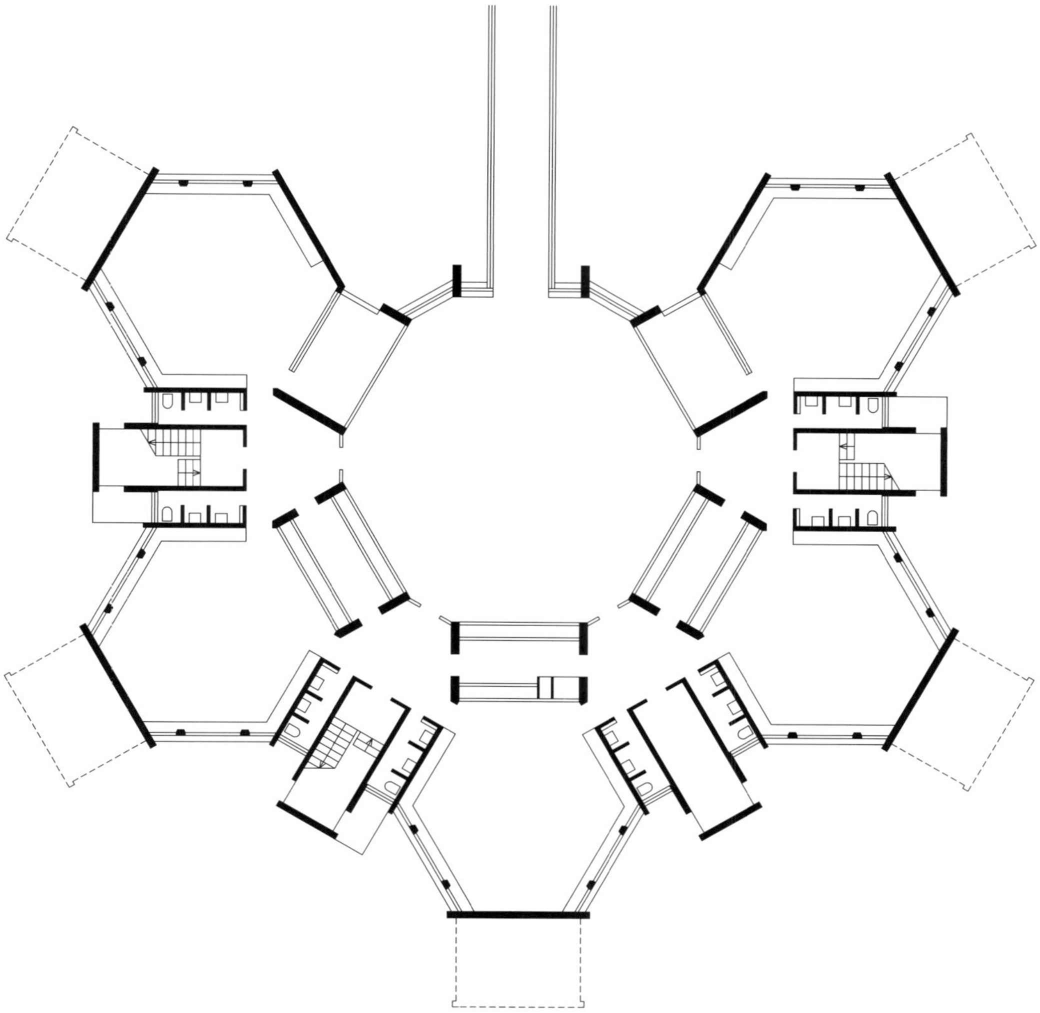

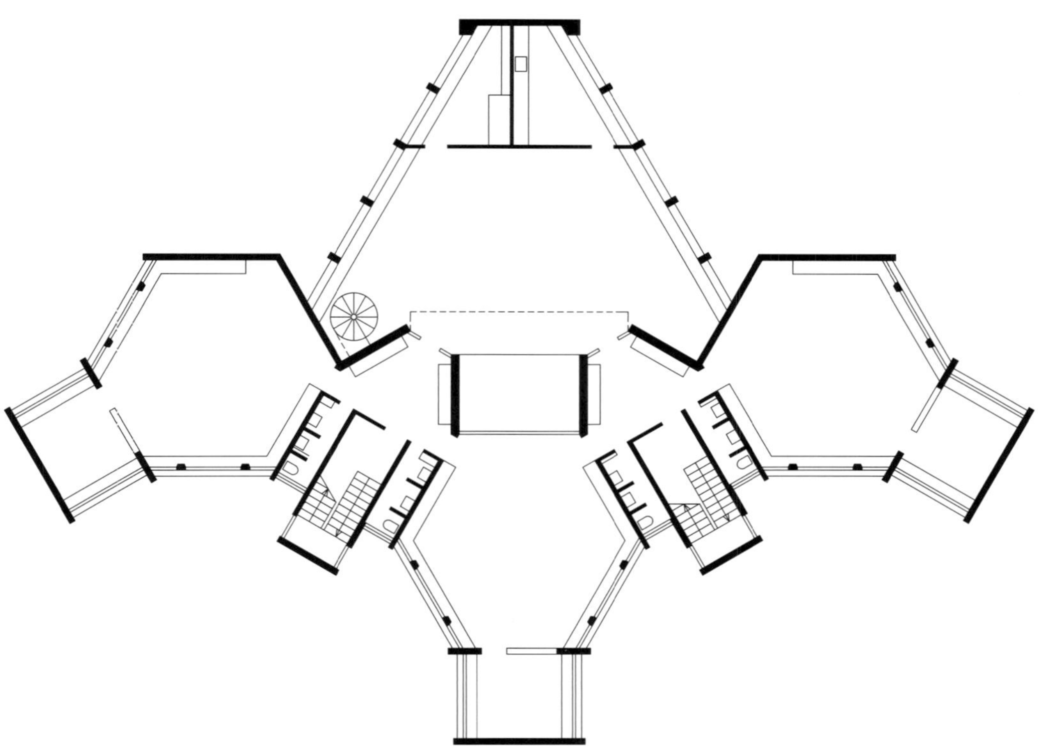

Floor plan of type 1 pavilion
Floor plan of type 2 pavilion

Glazed corridor
Entrance to the sports hall

Tower East

Shaker Heights, Ohio, USA
1964–68 (with TAC)

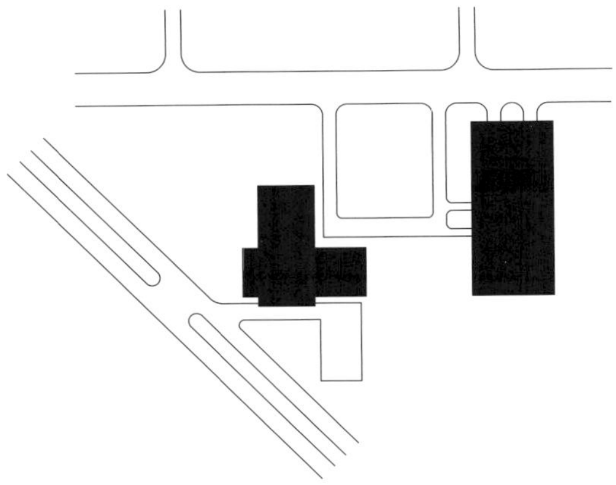

The two parts of this office building intersect as if one volume were pushed under the other. The building volumes are articulated to look as if they are separate, the flat surface of the low building passing between and behind the pillars of the tower without appearing to touch them.[1] The tower, built alongside a separate multi-storey car park, is the sole prominent landmark in this otherwise low-rise suburban area around Cleveland.

The building is clad with a vigorously modulated concrete facade, its deep relief casting strong shadows that accentuate its delineation. This three-dimensionality is a product of the recessed dark-tinted glazing, inclined sun breakers and the pillarless cantilevered corners of the building. The smooth concrete surface was achieved using formwork made of fibreglass and concrete with a quartz additive that gives it a light colour.[2] At the base of the tower, by contrast, the surfaces of the columns and the horizontal ceiling slabs are rough, as the concrete has been sandblasted. As in classical architecture, the base was given a more rusticated treatment than the upper part of the building, and the exposed concrete wall surfaces in the entrance lobby further reinforce the building's Brutalist character.

1 Bauhaus-Archiv Berlin (Ed.), *Walter Gropius – Bauten und Projekte 1906–1969*, Berlin 1980, pp. 26–27.
2 "A Suburban Office Building by TAC – Designed as Focal Point and Landmark", in: *Architectural Record*, March 1969, pp. 129–134.

Site plan
View from the east

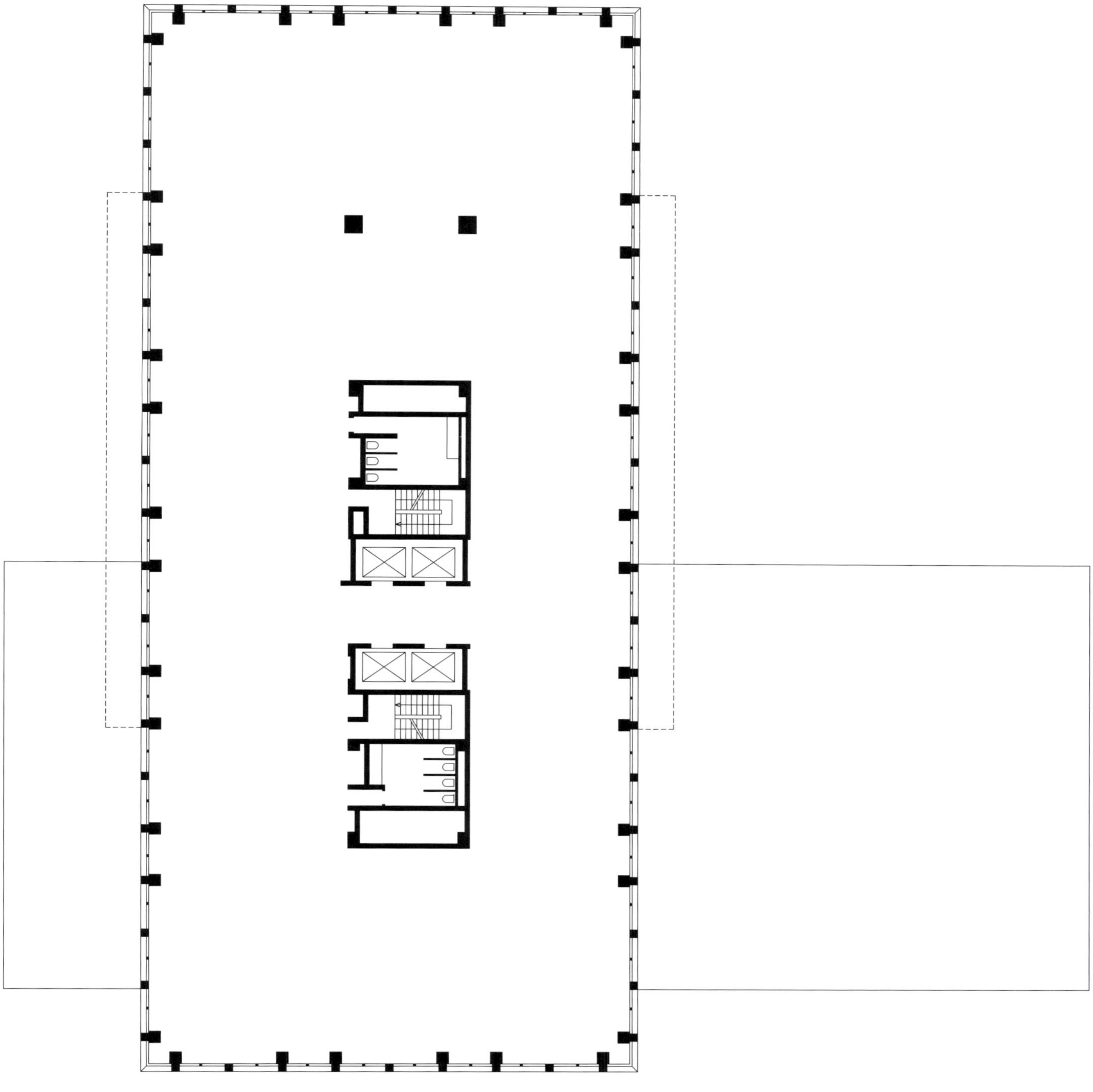

Floor plan of the tower

Bauhaus Archive

Berlin-Tiergarten, Germany
1964–79 (with TAC and Hans Bandel)

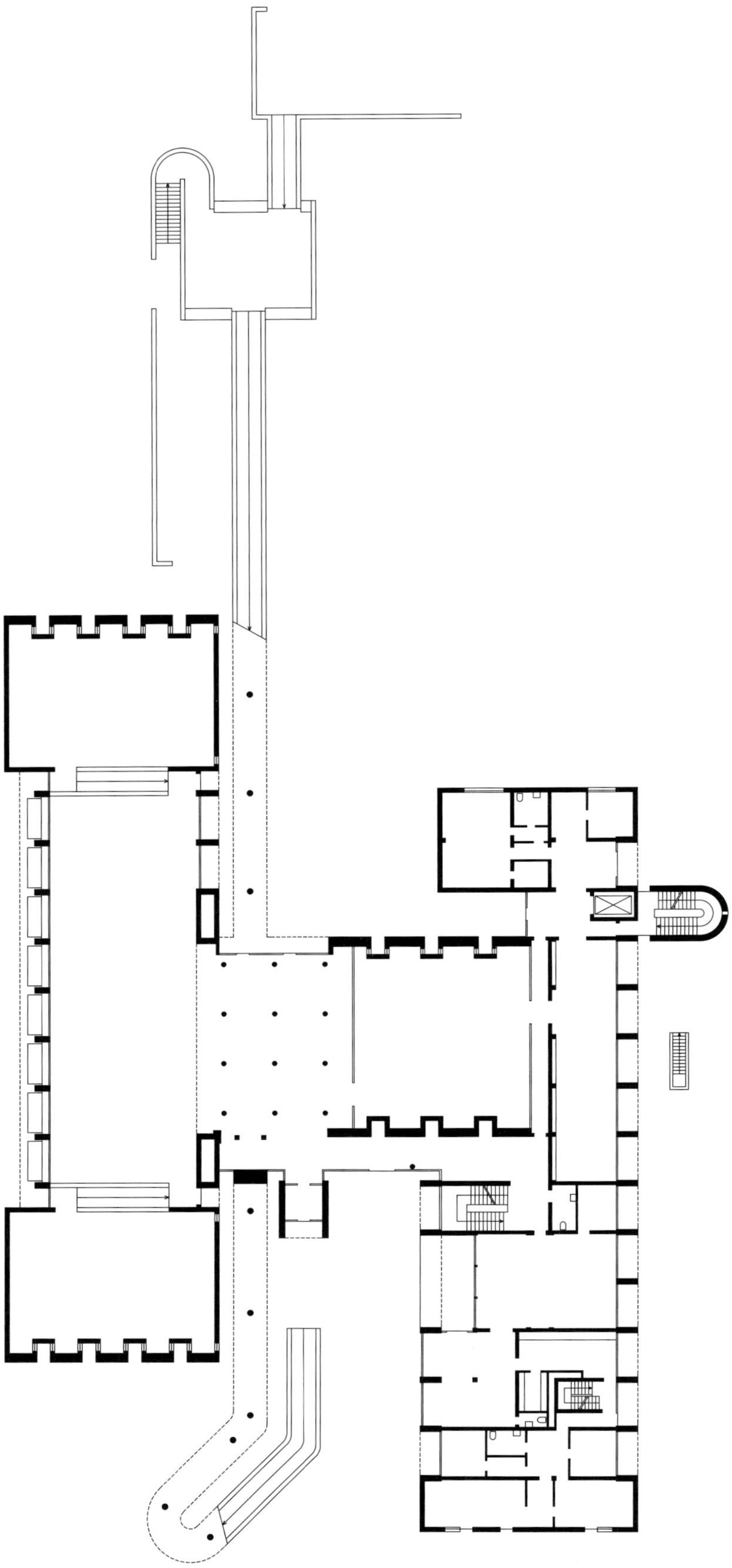

The building was designed by the architect Alexander Cvijanovic.[1] Although Cvijanovic and Gropius had designed a building for the Bauhaus Archive for a site in Darmstadt in 1964, it was decided after Gropius' death to relocate the project to a site in Berlin next to the Landwehr Canal. In 1976, Cvijanovic extensively redesigned the project for The Architects Collaborative but retained the basic structure and central elements of the design, such as the rounded shed roofs, although these now faced in the opposite direction. The orientation of the entire complex was turned by 180 degrees for the new location, so that the extensive glazing of the central exhibition space no longer opens to the north but to the south facing the canal. This was less optimal for the museum exhibits, and they remain covered most of the time. Cvijanovic also planned a ramp passing through the complex that was not part of the original design. Similarly, the decision to use prefabricated concrete elements resulted in very distinct joint lines in the facade that were not in the original design. A hall for temporary exhibitions in the centre of the building was, however, retained.

1 The construction planning was carried out by the office's contact architect in Berlin Hans Bandel. Cf.: Bauhaus-Archiv Berlin (Ed.), *Walter Gropius – Bauten und Projekte 1906–1969*, Berlin 1980, pp. 24–25, and Reginald R. Isaacs, *Gropius: An Illustrated Biography of the Creator of the Bauhaus*, Boston 1991, p. 291.

Ground floor plan

View from the southwest
View from the east

View from the Landwehr canal
Ramp through the complex

Rosenthal Porcelain Factory

Selb, Germany
1965–67 (with TAC)

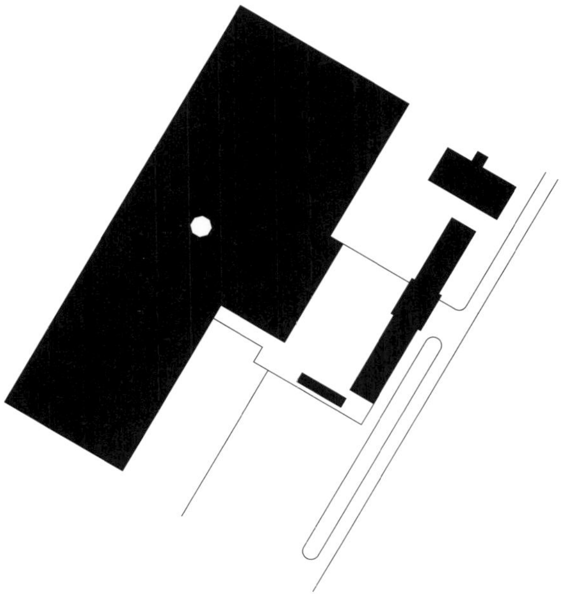

The factory consists of several buildings grouped around a central courtyard.[1] While two building wings with garages and offices flank the factory entrance, the remainder of the courtyard is bounded by a silo structure and a building for communal activities. Gropius and his client Philip Rosenthal shared a common goal "to make the workplace a more humane environment with the help of workplace psychology and sociology".[2] The factory space had large windows with views of the landscape and a tropical greenhouse that housed flamingos.

The structural framework of the factory building is based on a system of T-shaped concrete columns custom-developed for the building. The hammer-like heads of the columns, arranged at ten-metre intervals, bore modular trusses, likewise prefabricated as precast concrete elements. This differentiation between the load-bearing structural elements and the non-load-bearing wall infill is also reflected in the design of the building facades by giving them different surface treatments.

Gropius' work for the company went beyond the construction of the factory: he also designed a tableware series and an urban development plan for the town of Selb.

1 The architect responsible for the design in the TAC office was Alexander Cvijanovic. Hartmut Probst and Christian Schädlich, *Walter Gropius – Band 1: Der Architekt und Theoretiker*, Berlin 1985, pp. 288–289.
2 Walter Gropius cited in: Reginald R. Isaacs, *Walter Gropius – Der Mensch und sein Werk*, Berlin 1987, p. 1101.

Site plan
Greenhouse

Storage building
Factory entrance
Silo

"After-work building", view from the road
Entrance from the yard

Huntington Galleries

Huntington, West Virginia, USA
1967–70 (with TAC)

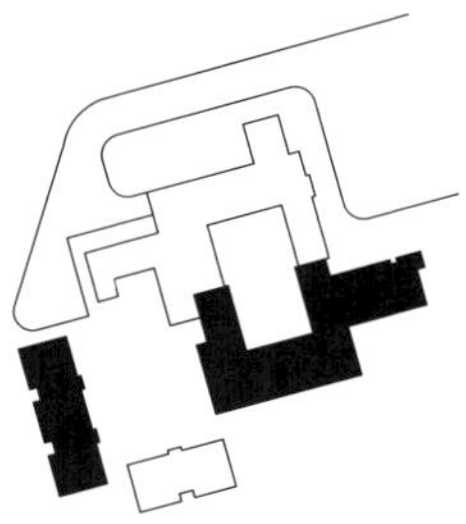

Gropius created an extension for an existing museum along with associated ateliers.[1] A lecture hall was placed on the east side of the building with wall planes arranged diagonally for acoustic reasons. In addition to an exhibition area, the commission also encompassed a library. The new building adjoins the existing building in a U-shape creating a central inner courtyard overlooked by the floor-to-ceiling glazing of the building. A staircase leads from the courtyard under the building to a sculpture garden, connecting the internal and external spaces.

Gropius explained that he preferred natural lighting for a museum over artificial light, as the latter is unchanging. To avoid a monotonous spatial experience, a series of varied visual impressions must be created with dynamic rather than static lighting.[2] Since the building is located on a hill outside the city amidst a wooded landscape, further large openings were created with views of the natural surroundings. And the exhibition hall was additionally illuminated by a strip-like skylight placed within a half-barrel vault, much like the system used for the Bauhaus Archive. The resulting lighting situation was uneven, a configuration that is considered undesirable for modern museums. The concrete honeycomb ceiling houses additional spotlights.

The textile covering of the walls of the exhibition hall is beige-tinted to match the parquet flooring, while the external walls harmonise with the existing building by adopting the colour and surface of its bricks.

Of the five adjacent ateliers, only three were realised according to the plans by The Architects Collaborative. The southern building was later built in a modified form. The ateliers are likewise illuminated with the same half-barrel vaults as the museum. For Gropius, these rooms for use as adult education spaces and by children were a key part of the overall concept, as it is here, as he explained in his speech at the laying of the foundation stone, that future generations learn to look at the world.[3]

1 Gropius collaborated with Malcom Ticknor on the design in the TAC office. The museum's original building from 1950–52 was designed by the architects Small, Smith & Reeb. See the chapter "Walter Gropius and the Huntington Galleries", in: John Coolidge, *Patrons and Architects – Designing Art Museums in the Twentieth Century*, Fort Worth 1989, pp. 59–68.
2 Ibid., p. 61.
3 Ibid., p. 62.

Site plan
Inner courtyard
Exibition area skylight

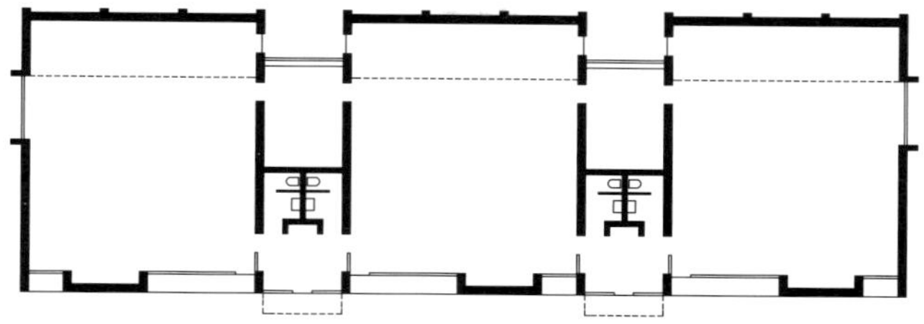

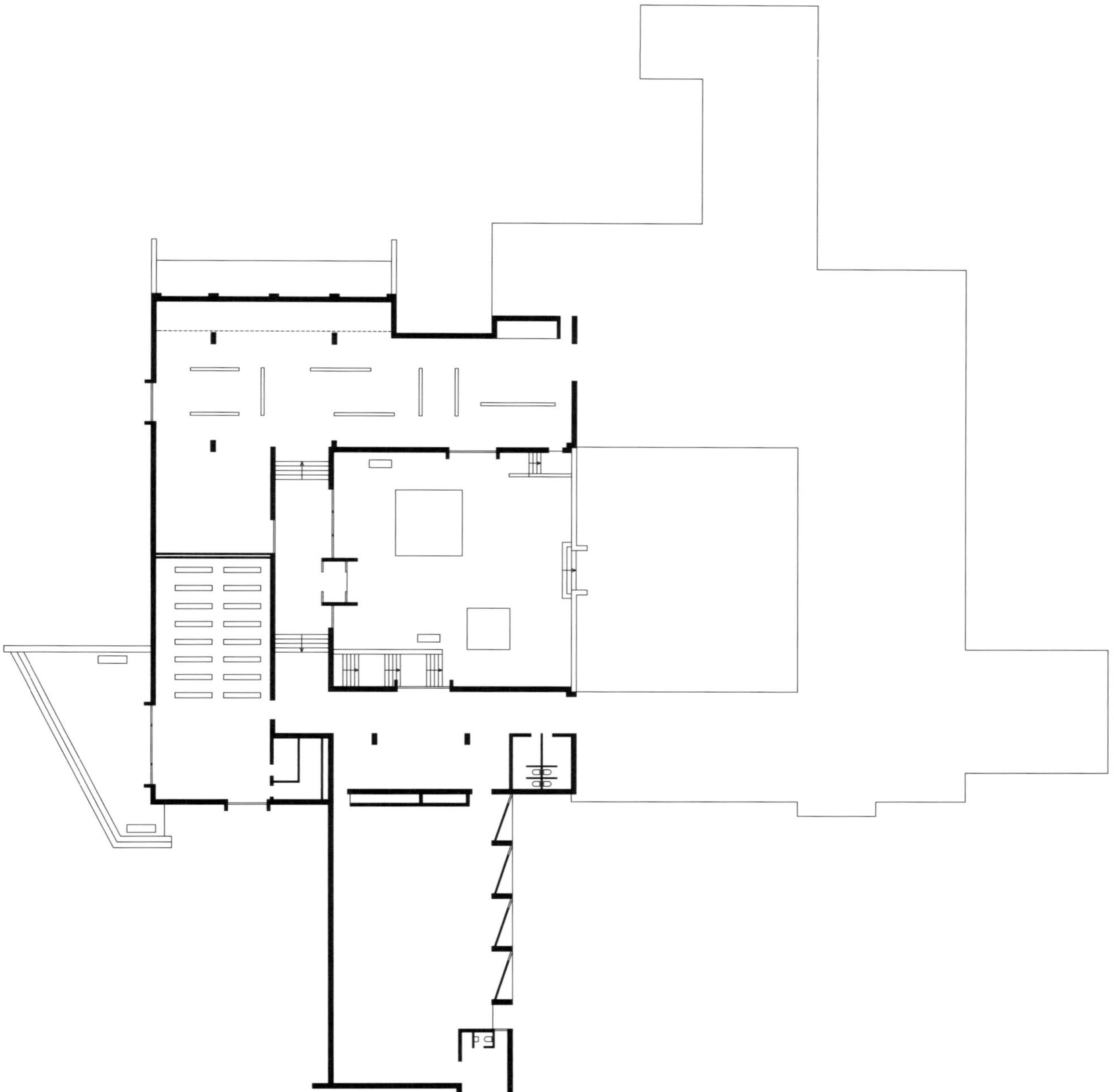

Ground floor plan

Amberg Glass Factory

Amberg, Germany
1967–70 (with TAC)

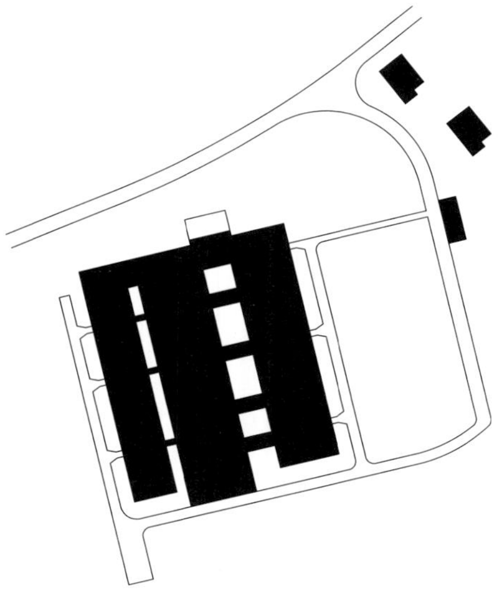

After the construction of the porcelain factory in Selb, Gropius was commissioned by the same client to build another factory.[1] The primary task for the glassworks was to find an architectural solution to the extreme heat generated in the factory works. The hall contained not only melting furnaces but also workplaces for hundreds of glassblowers who originally blew the glass products manually. The shape and construction of the roof was designed to facilitate natural ventilation without air conditioning by allowing hot air to exit via the ridge of the roof and fresh air to be drawn into the lower part of the building.[2] Glazed walls on the ground floor provide views onto the greened courtyards. The vast monumental concrete structure had the spatial dimensions of a cathedral. The Architects Collaborative also designed workers' housing for the complex, which still produces glass today.

1 Philip Rosenthal commissioned Gropius to build the factory for a subsidiary of Rosenthal, the Thomas Glas- und Porzellan AG. Gropius again worked with Alexander Cvijanovic on the project design. Bauhaus-Archiv Berlin (Ed.), *Walter Gropius – Bauten und Projekte 1906–1969*, Berlin 1980, p. 26, and: Hartmut Probst and Christian Schädlich, *Walter Gropius – Band 1: Der Architekt und Theoretiker*, Berlin 1985, pp. 290–291.
2 The system of permanent air circulation is no longer ideal for modern-day production machinery.

Site plan
View from the northwest

View from the northeast
View from the northwest

Inner courtyard
Interior

Bibliography

Walter Gropius, *Idee und Aufbau des Staatlichen Bauhauses Weimar*, Munich 1923
Walter Gropius (Ed.), *Walter Gropius mit Adolf Meyer – Weimar Bauten*, Berlin 1923
Walter Gropius (Ed.), *Internationale Architektur*, Munich 1925
Walter Gropius, *Bauhausbauten Dessau*, Munich 1930
Sigfried Giedion, *Walter Gropius*, Paris 1930
Walter Gropius, *The New Architecture and the Bauhaus*, London 1935
Herbert Bayer, Walter Gropius and Ise Gropius (Ed.), *Bauhaus 1919–1928*, New York 1938
Walter Gropius, *Rebuilding our Communities*, Chicago 1945
Giulio Carlo Argan, *Walter Gropius e la Bauhaus*, Turin 1951
Ruth V. Cook, *Walter Gropius – A Bibliography 1919 to 1950*, Chicago 1951
Walter Gropius, *Ein Weg zur Einheit künstlerischer Gestaltung*, Frankfurt am Main 1952
Sigfried Giedion, *Walter Gropius – Work and Teamwork*, New York 1954
Walter Gropius, *Scope of Total Architecture*, New York 1955
Gilbert Herbert, *The Synthetic Vision of Walter Gropius*, Johannesburg 1959
Helmut Weber, *Walter Gropius und das Faguswerk*, Munich 1961
James Marston Fitch, *Walter Gropius*, New York 1962
Walter Gropius et al. (Ed.), *The Architects Collaborative TAC 1945–1965*, Teufen 1966
Walter Gropius, *Apollo in the Democracy – The Cultural Obligation of the Architect*, New York 1968 (*Apollo in der Architektur*, Mainz 1967)
Marcel Franciscono, *Walter Gropius and the Creation of the Bauhaus in Weimar – The Ideals and Artistic Theories of its Founding Years*, Urbana 1971
Ise Gropius, *Walter Gropius – Buildings, Plans, Projects 1906–1969*, Cambridge, MA 1972 (*Bauten und Projekte 1906 bis 1969*, Zurich 1971)
Alberto Busignani, *Walter Gropius*, Lucerne 1972
Hans Bandel and Dittmar Machule, *Die Gropiusstadt – Der städtebauliche Planungs- und Entscheidungsvorgang*, Berlin 1974
Bauhaus-Archiv Berlin (Ed.), *Ein Museum für das Bauhaus? Zur Eröffnung des nach Plänen von Walter Gropius errichteten Museumsgebäudes am 1. Dezember 1979*, Berlin 1979
Gábor Preisich, *Walter Gropius*, Berlin 1982
Walter Gropius 1907/1934, Rassegna 15, 1983
Paolo Berdini, *Walter Gropius – Works and Projects / Obras y projectos*, Barcelona 1994 (*Walter Gropius*, Bologna 1983)
Bauhaus-Archiv Berlin (Ed.), *100 Jahre Walter Gropius – Schließung des Bauhauses 1933*, Berlin 1983
Karin Wilhelm, *Walter Gropius Industriearchitekt*, Braunschweig, Wiesbaden 1983
Reginald R. Isaacs, *Gropius in Harvard / Gropius at Harvard*, Berlin 1983
Reginald R. Isaacs, *Gropius: An Illustrated Biography of the Creator of the Bauhaus*, Boston 1991 (*Walter Gropius – Der Mensch und sein Werk,* 2 volumes, Berlin 1983 and 1984)
Gilbert Herbert, *The Dream of the Factory-Made House – Walter Gropius and Konrad Wachsmann*, Cambridge, MA 1984
Stefan Woll, *Das Totaltheater – Ein Projekt von Walter Gropius und Erwin Piscator*, Berlin 1984
Winfried Nerdinger, *The Architect Walter Gropius / Der Architekt Walter Gropius*, Berlin 1985
Hartmut Probst and Christian Schädlich, *Walter Gropius – Band 1: Der Architekt und Theoretiker*, Berlin 1985
Hartmut Probst and Christian Schädlich, *Walter Gropius – Band 2: Der Architekt und Pädagoge*, Berlin 1986
Horst Claussen, *Walter Gropius – Grundzüge seines Denkens*, Hildesheim 1986
Hartmut Probst and Christian Schädlich, *Walter Gropius – Band 3: Ausgewählte Schriften*, Berlin 1987
Wolfgang E. Tonne, *Chancen und Grenzen beim Entwerfen langfristig brauchbarer Wohngebäude, untersucht am Beispiel eines Architekten und einer ökonomischen Methode: Walter Gropius und die Investitionsrechnung*, dissertation Universität Stuttgart 1987
Winfried Nerdinger, *The Walter Gropius Archive*, 3 volumes, New York 1990
John C. Harkness (Ed.), *The Walter Gropius Archive – The Work of The Architects Collaborative*, New York 1991
Dennis Sharp, *Bauhaus, Dessau – Walter Gropius*, London 1993
Brigitte Franzen, *Die Siedlung Dammerstock in Karlsruhe – Zur Vermittlung des Neuen Bauens*, Marburg 1993
Yukio Futagawa (Ed.), *Walter Gropius – Bauhaus, Dessau, Germany, Fagus Factory, Alfeld-an-der-Leine, Germany, 1911–25 (with Adolf Meyer)*, Tokyo 1994
Annemarie Jaeggi, *Adolf Meyer – Der zweite Mann – Ein Architekt im Schatten von Walter Gropius*, Berlin 1994
Sabine Kraft, *Gropius baut privat – Seine Wohnhäuser in Dessau (1925/26) und Lincoln/Massachusetts (1938),* Marburg 1997
Badisches Landesmuseum (Ed.), *Neues Bauen der 20er Jahre – Gropius, Haesler, Schwitters und die Dammerstocksiedlung in Karlsruhe 1929*, Karlsruhe 1997
Annemarie Jaeggi, *Fagus – Industrial Culture from Werkbund to Bauhaus*, New York 2000 (*Fagus – Industriekultur zwischen Werkbund und Bauhaus*, Berlin 1998)
Bernd Fritz, *Das Teegeschirr TAC 1 von Walter Gropius*, Frankfurt am Main 1998
Margret Kentgens-Craig, *The Dessau Bauhaus Building 1926–1999*, Basel, Boston, Berlin 1998
Thilo Hilpert, *Walter Gropius – Das Bauhaus in Dessau – Von der Idee zur Gestalt*, Frankfurt am Main 1999
Klaus-Jürgen Winkler and Gerhard Oschmann, *Das Gropius-Zimmer – Geschichte und Rekonstruktion des Direktorenraumes am Staatlichen Bauhaus in Weimar 1923/24*, Weimar 1999
Norbert Michels (Ed.), *Architektur und Kunst – Das Meisterhaus Kandinsky-Klee in Dessau*, Leipzig 2000
Joachim Driller, *Breuer Houses*, London 2000
Wolfgang Paul, *"... Das Treppenhaus ist meine ganze Freude ..." – Meisterhäuser in Dessau – Das Feiningerhaus*, Frankfurt am Main 2001
Barbara Geiser, *Vom individualistischen Künstlerhaus zum Modell*

für die Serie: Die Meisterhäuser von Walter Gropius in Dessau, dissertation Universität Bochum 2002
Barbara Happe and Martin S. Fischer, *The Auerbach House by Walter Gropius with Adolf Meyer*, Berlin 2018 (*Haus Auerbach von Walter Gropius mit Adolf Meyer*, Tübingen 2003)
Klaus-Jürgen Winkler, *Baulehre und Entwerfen am Bauhaus 1919–1933*, Weimar 2003
August Gebeßler (Ed.), *Gropius – Meisterhaus Muche/Schlemmer – Die Geschichte einer Instandsetzung*, Stuttgart 2003
Klaus-Jürgen Winkler and Herman van Bergeijk, *Das Märzgefallenen-Denkmal in Weimar*, Weimar 2004
Ulrich Müller, *Raum, Bewegung und Zeit im Werk von Walter Gropius und Ludwig Mies van der Rohe*, Berlin 2004
Gilbert Lupfer and Paul Siegel, *Walter Gropius 1883–1969 – The Promotor of a New Form*, Cologne London 2004
Robin Rehm, *Das Bauhausgebäude in Dessau – Die ästhetischen Kategorien Zweck, Form, Inhalt*, Berlin 2005
Meredith L. Clausen, *The Pan Am Building and the Shattering of the Modernist Dream*, Cambridge, MA 2005
Ulrich Müller, *Walter Gropius – Das Jenaer Theater*, Cologne 2006
Walter Prigge (Ed.), *Icon of Modernism – The Bauhaus Building Dessau / Ikone der Moderne – Das Bauhausgebäude in Dessau*, Berlin 2006
Jill Pearlman, *Inventing American Modernism: Joseph Hudnut, Walter Gropius, and the Bauhaus Legacy at Harvard*, Charlottesville 2007
Britta Merten, *Der Architekt Hannes Meyer und sein Beitrag zum Bauhaus – Ein Vergleich mit Walter Gropius und Ludwig Mies van der Rohe*, Saarbrücken 2008
Gerda Breuer and Annemarie Jaeggi (Ed.), *Walter Gropius – American Journey 1928 / Amerikareise 1928*, Berlin 2009
Thomas Oppermann and Friederike Schmidt-Möbius, *Fagus Benscheidt Gropius – Wege in die ästhetische und soziale Moderne*, Göttingen 2011
Christine Fuhrmann, *Eine Stadtkrone für Halle, Saale – Walter Gropius im Wettbewerb*, Halle 2011
Reinhard Matz and Andreas Schwarting, *Das Verschwinden der Revolution in der Renovierung – Die Geschichte der Gropius-Siedlung Dessau-Törten*, Berlin 2011
Karsten Thieme, *Kupferhäuser in Berlin und Brandenburg und der Einfluss von Walter Gropius auf ihre Entwicklung*, dissertation Technische Universität Berlin 2012
Andreas Schwarting, *Die Siedlung Dessau-Törten 1926 bis 1931*, Leipzig 2012
Britta Bommert, *Studien zum Raumverständnis bei Ludwig Mies van der Rohe und Walter Gropius: dargelegt an den Räumen der Werkbundausstellungen Stuttgart 1927 und Paris 1930*, Cologne 2013
Christin Irrgang and Ingolf Kern, *Das Bauhausgebäude in Dessau*, Leipzig 2014
Monika Markgraf and Wolfgang Thöner, *Die Meisterhäuser in Dessau*, Leipzig 2014
Ira Mazzoni, *Walter Gropius – Glaswerk Amberg*, Amberg 2015
Monika Markgraf, *Die Dessauer Bauhausbauten*, Leipzig 2016
Regina Göckede, *Spätkoloniale Moderne – Le Corbusier, Ernst May, Frank Lloyd Wright, The Architects Collaborative und die Globalisierung der Architekturmoderne*, Basel, Boston, Berlin 2016
Ursula Muscheler, *Mutter, Muse und Frau Bauhaus – Die Frauen um Walter Gropius*, Berlin 2018
Joaquín Medina Warmburg (Ed.), *Walter Gropius proclamas de modernidad – Escritos y conferencias, 1908–1934*, Barcelona 2018
Arnold Körte, *Begegnungen mit Walter Gropius in "The Architects Collaborative" TAC*, Berlin 2019
Fiona McCarthy, *Walter Gropius – Visionary Founder of the Bauhaus*, London 2019
Bernd Polster, *Walter Gropius – Der Architekt seines Ruhms*, Munich 2019

Subject Index

Illustration Credits

All colour photographs and redrawn plans were taken or drawn by Carsten Krohn.

Architect's Journal, Aug. 1937: 121 top
Architectural Review, Dec. 1939: 127 top
Giulio Carlo Argan, *Walter Gropius e la Bauhaus*, Turin 1951: 115 left
James Marston Fitch, *Walter Gropius*, New York 1960: 18 bottom, 19 top
Walter Gropius, et al (Ed.), *The Architects Collaborative TAC 1945–1965*, Teufen 1966: 19 top, 152, 172
Walter Gropius, *Apollo in der Demokratie*, Mainz 1967: 13 bottom
Walter Gropius 1907/1934, Rassegna 15, 1983: 51
John C. Harkness (Ed.), *The Walter Gropius Archive – The Work of the Architects Collaborative*, New York 1991: 193, 194, 198 bottom
Hartmut Probst and Christian Schädlich, *Walter Gropius – Band 1: Der Architekt und Theoretiker*, Berlin 1985: 11 bottom
Martin Wagner, *Das wachsende Haus – ein Beitrag zur Lösung der städtischen Wohnungsfrage*, Berlin 1932: 115 right
Wikimedia Commons: 198 top
Hans Maria Wingler, *Walter Gropius – Das Spätwerk*, Darmstadt 1970: 19 bottom

All other figures and photographs are from the Bauhaus-Archiv Berlin. Selected photographs can be attributed to the following photographers/sources:
I. L. Allwork: 124
Atelier Helene Hüttich – Susanne Oemler: 33 top
Baubüro Gropius: 86
Bayer & Schmölz: 40–43
Annelise Bousset: 101 left
British Council: 127 bottom
Daderot: 198 top
Paul Davis: 133, 134
Herrmann Eckner: 54, 55
Gottscho-Schleisner: 145
Walter Gropius: 56, 58
Haskell: 136
Louis Held: 100 left
Keystone View Company: 66
Edmund Lill: 28
Dr. Lossen & Co: 93
Meriman Photo Art: 149
Lucia Moholy: 79, 85 right, 101 right
Joseph W. Molitor: 171 right, 175
Sidney W. Newbery: 120 top
Louis Reens: 169, 171 left, 198 bottom
Carl Rogge: 47 top, 102
Stefan Rosenbauer: 108, 109 top
Rosenthal GmbH: 195
Ezra Stoller: 139, 152, 154, 190
Fred Stone: 157
Adolf K. Fr. Supper: 105 top
Emil Theis: 95
Otto Wedekind: 85 right

About the Author

Carsten Krohn was born in Hamburg and studied architecture, urban planning and art history at the University of Fine Arts Hamburg, the University of Hamburg and at Columbia University in New York. He obtained a PhD in art history with a study on the reception of Buckminster Fuller in architecture. Carsten Krohn worked in the Berlin offices of Daniel Libeskind and Norman Foster and has taught at Karlsruhe Institute of Technology, the Technical University of Berlin, Humboldt University of Berlin and as professor at Anáhuac University and at the Tecnológico de Monterrey in Mexico. He is the author of books on the work of Peter Behrens, Mies van der Rohe and Hans Scharoun, curated the exhibition *Unbuilt Berlin* and worked with Knut Klaßen on video projects. His photographs have been shown in various exhibitions.